Kings of
Georgian Britain

For the rakish Colonial, brewer of teas.

Kings of Georgian Britain

Catherine Curzon

PEN & SWORD
HISTORY

First published in Great Britain in 2017 by
Pen & Sword History
an imprint of
Pen & Sword Books Ltd
47 Church Street
Barnsley
South Yorkshire
S70 2AS

ISBN 978 1 47387 122 9

A CIP catalogue record for this book is available from the British Library

Typeset in Ehrhardt by
Macstyle Ltd, Bridlington, East Yorkshire
Printed and bound in Malta by Gutenberg Press Ltd

Pen & Sword Books Ltd incorporates the Imprints of Aviation, Atlas,
Family History, Fiction, Maritime, Military, Discovery, Politics, History,
Archaeology, Select, Wharncliffe Local History, Wharncliffe True Crime,
Military Classics, Wharncliffe Transport, Leo Cooper, The Praetorian Press,
Remember When, Seaforth Publishing and Frontline Publishing.

For a complete list of Pen & Sword titles please contact
PEN & SWORD BOOKS LIMITED
47 Church Street, Barnsley, South Yorkshire, S70 2AS, England
E-mail: enquiries@pen-and-sword.co.uk
Website: www.pen-and-sword.co.uk

Contents

Acknowledgements

My warmest thanks go to all the team at Pen and Sword Books, especially the inestimable Heather, who has more than earned her chocolates, to Lucy, for her good humour and sharp editing nib, and of course, to Kate.

A huge thank you is due to all at T&Cake and Bex's in West Yorkshire for keeping me well-fed, full of tea and never at a loss for cake. Endless gratitude also goes out across the world to the wonderful folk who stop by my blog once in a while. You have cajoled, encouraged and kept me on the Georgian royal road!

A special merci must go to Adrian and Caroline for letting me be a small part of Jane Austen's world. To the marvellous musicians and performers who bring the eighteenth century to life, never, ever stop.

To friends near and far, to those who list and those who listen, I salute you from here to eternity.

Mayhem and magic to you, Willow Winsham, keep on keeping on.

To Pippa, Nel and Custard, you bring the snuggles. Don't ever stop.

And Rick, this one is for you. Are you brewing?

List of Illustrations

Cover illustrations:
King George IV. Robert Bowyer, after John Bromley, 1827. (*Courtesy Wellcome Library, London, under Creative Commons Attribution only licence CC BY 4.0 http://creativecommons.org/licenses/by/4.0/*)

His Majesty King George III returning to Town from Windsor with an Escort of tenth Prince of Wales' Own Light Dragoons. Charles Turner, after Richard Barrett Davis, 1806. (*Courtesy of The Yale Center for British Art. Public domain*)

13. The Pavilion & Steyne at Brighton. James Mitan, after Charles Cracklow, 1806.
14. King George III. Thomas Frye.
15. George III and his family visit Dorchester jail. Charles Howard Hodges, 1793.
16. Carlton House. Anonymous, 1800.
17. Carlton House, North Front. Richard Gilson Reeve, after William Westall. 1819.
18. George III, King of Great Britain, France and Ireland etc. Anonymous.
19. George III. Anonymous, 1789.
20. George the III, King of Great Britain. Anonymous.
21. The Coronation Procession of His Majesty King George the IV, July 19th 1821. George Johann Scharf, 1821.
22. King George III analyzing the residue from a large glass retort containing a small figure satirizing the English view of Napoleon. T West, 1803.
23. The gouty Prince Regent being helped onto his horse by means of an elaborate contraption outside an oriental pavilion in Kew Gardens. Anonymous, 1816.
24. George IV's Public Entry into the City of Dublin on August 17th 1821. Robert Havell, 1823.
25. His Royal Highness George Prince of Wales. Anonymous, 1794.
26. Coronation Procession of H. M. George IV, 19 July 1821. William Heath.
27. George the Fourth When Prince of Wales. Anonymous.
28. Windsor Castle from the Thames. William Daniell, 1825.
29. Peter, the Wild Boy. Anonymous.
30. Windsor Castle View – King George IV Gate and the Round Tower, 28 July 1832, 11.30 am. Dr. William Crotch, 1832.
31. Dr Francis Willis, holding a book in his right hand. R Page, 1830.
32. Liberty Triumphant, or The downfall of oppression. Anonymous, 1775.

Introduction

They weren't Englishmen, these kings of the Georgian era ...

They were German, of course. Fat, mad, wig-wearing Germans who refused to learn the language and hardly ever set foot in the country they were supposed to rule, let alone did anything to make their mark on the realm they inherited.

Four kings of Great Britain who spoke German, spent more time on the continent than in England, wore corsets, lived at Windsor and were greedy, crazed and *terrible* at holding onto the colonies.

And that's that, or so you might think. In fact, there was a *lot* more to the Georgian kings than their ancestral lands, their weight and their mental disorders. Whether losing America, building a Royal Pavilion or nursing a dying wife with a taste for chocolate, the four Georges of Great Britain lived lives as dramatic as *any* work of fiction.

Just for now though, forget Great Britain, forget the colonies and forget all that you *think* you know about the King Georges. That might seem like an unusual request for the opening lines of a book devoted to those very men and that very land, but humour me, because the man who lent his name to the Georgian era did not draw his first breath on English soil or anywhere near it. Not that history will ever let him forget it.

The world inhabited by eighteenth century royalty was light years away from anything we might see in the programmes, magazines and newspapers of today. Far from the media-managed, publicity friendly machine that is modern celebrity, where spin doctors and PR gurus ensure that the crowned heads of Europe are never less than squeaky clean; more than two centuries ago, there was really no such thing as *too much* or *too far*.

In this world, kings and emperors wielded power that would be unthinkable in modern Europe. Houses rose and heads rolled, legends were created in the strangest places and elsewhere, unhappy obscurity beckoned. Some of the men and women whose bottoms rested on the most famed thrones of Europe have gone on to become icons, saints, sinners or martyrs. Others are remembered only for the manner of their passing, their defeat or, perhaps their rip-roaring scandals.

Though the twenty-first century House of Windsor enjoys a *mostly* easy public relationship, even they have faced fierce critics and loud catcalls, so for a king parachuted in from the continent to take on a brand new realm, life was never going to be easy. The Georgian era which started with George I saw the royal family lurch from popularity to parody with alarming speed and regularity. Assailed by political opponents and battered by the winds of change, the Georges witnessed some of the most momentous times known to history.

So as we delve into the lives of the kings who presided over the people of England, Scotland, Ireland and Wales, our journey must start in Hanover. It will end in a lonely bedroom deep within Windsor Castle over a century later, but that's a long way off for now. In the glittering palaces and ancient castles of Europe, the world is still run on old rules, a little more *war* than *jaw*, to borrow an expression from Winston Churchill. Ferocious conflicts leave lands in ruin, royal houses rise and fall and for those who rule, neither a long reign nor a happy life can be taken for granted.

In this world of high stakes and rich rewards, life was pure soap opera. Within these pages, husbands throttle wives, actresses and heirs galavant about without care and hearts are broken overnight. Far from the poised, dignified figures immortalized on canvas and in marble, the four Georges of the long eighteenth century lived lives that were sometimes passionate, sometimes shocking, but never, ever dull.

As a Prince Regent flings borrowed money around with wild abandon, his father submits to horrific treatment intended to cure the madness of a king. A forgotten wife fades away in a gilded prison and some very famous sons and their fathers simply *cannot* get along.

Within these four biographical chapters you will not find maps and battle plans, speeches and state papers, though these weighty matters are covered elsewhere in innumerable and excellent volumes on the Georgian era. These are the tales of the men behind the title. These four Georges might have been of impeccable lineage and literally born to rule, but they were as human as the subjects who occasionally found them so utterly loathsome. Within these pages, you will follow the kings of Great Britain from cradle to occasionally premature grave and learn what shaped them into the characterful men they became.

In *Kings of Georgian Britain*, you will meet their parents and friends, their wives, mistresses and children and learn how reputations were made and lost.

Perhaps one of these kings will catch your imagination, or maybe somebody or something in these stories will fire your inner historian to delve deeper into these fascinating, complex men; I certainly hope so.

So settle in your seat and prepare to journey back to the green and pleasant land of the long eighteenth century, but watch out for those radicals, and beware the disgruntled wives – you never know what they're planning!

George I, King of Great Britain and Ireland

(Osnabrück, Hanover, 28 May 1660 – Osnabrück, Hanover, 11 June 1727)

History can sometimes seem to be a series of momentous yet disparate events; of battles and treaties, emperors and queens. It can be baffling, intriguing and deal in numbers and concepts so immense that they might seem impenetrable. Still, at the basis of every story, every legend and every empire and kingdom is one simple thing: the people.

Even those who know very little and care even less about the reign of George I are usually sure of one thing: George I was German. He *spoke* German, loved the land and rarely even bothered to visit England. Of these three widely accepted facts only the first two are true and for all his trips home, the majority of George's near thirteen year reign was spent in Great Britain. Of course, since George was born, bred and left his metaphorical heart in Hanover, it's hardly surprising that he was devoted to the land of his birth. This unswerving devotion has led to him being remembered as the *German* king.

And so we meet our first Georgian monarch, the man who begins our romp through the court of eighteenth century Great Britain. Born George Louis, he is better known as George I, King of Great Britain and Ireland. This is the story of the man who founded an era.

The Making of a Monarch

In 1660, the birth of a baby boy in the far away land of Hanover changed the course of British history forever. Though nobody suspected it at the time, the first child and heir of Ernest Augustus, Duke of Brunswick-Lüneburg, and his wife, Sophia of Hanover, would become the head of a dynasty that would rule the British realm for over one hundred years. Three Georges would follow him to the throne and an era would bear their name.

Of course, when that unsuspecting newborn babe gave his first plaintive cries he did not stand in line to the throne of Great Britain, nor was it even a distant dream. If this sounds like the start of a fairytale, a story of a life that went from rags to riches or from humble beginnings to undreamt of luxury, don't be fooled. People born in castles are rarely the heroes of rags to riches romances and little George Louis's prospects were bright from the off. As he slumbered innocent and uncaring in his cradle, he could rest easy in the assurance that bar some sort of catastrophe, he would one day rule substantial lands of his own. Of course, catastrophes weren't uncommon thanks to the perilous state of seventeenth century politics, but George Louis had a long life ahead of him.

When George was born, the Hanoverian territories that would one day pass into his care were under the rule of his father and three paternal uncles. As the fourth son of the late Duke of Brunswick-Lüneburg, there was very little chance that little George's father would ever wield sole power yet he had his own part of the world to administer. As we shall soon learn, fate, dukedoms and unexpected electorates can be *full* of surprises.

Ernest Augustus might be a long way down the waiting list thanks to all those annoyingly robust brothers, but he had one thing none of his siblings did: a male heir. So long as this status quo didn't change, when all of those troublesome uncles finally went to meet their maker, little George Louis could look forward to inheriting all of the territory that was currently split four ways.

When George Louis was little more than a year old, the family welcomed another son, Frederick Augustus, and the two adored boys were known affectionately as *Görgen* and *Gustchen*. Although Sophia was a caring mother, in the early years of George and Frederick's lives she was laid low by an illness that robbed them of her presence. Leaving Görgen and Gustchen at home, their parents travelled to Italy so that Sophia might convalesce peacefully away from the cares and responsibilities of the seat of power whilst her husband pursued his political interests.

Absent in body but not in mind, Sophia kept in constant written contact with the governesses entrusted with the care of her children, including her

Mistress of the Robes, Katharine von Harling, who would later also care for the young George II. Frau von Harling was as devoted to the children as their own mother and through her Sophia was able to follow their progress. She bitterly missed the boys, perhaps more than she had anticipated she would and news that both had been afflicted by smallpox rocked her to the core. That proved the final straw for the worried mother and in 1665 Sophia came home to the boys she adored.

Whilst Frederick hardly wanted for affection, it was little George who was the apple of his mother's eye thanks to his sensible countenance yet others found him cold, aloof and unknowable. In fact, as the years passed, this appears to be exactly what he became and if any trace of the child so lauded by his mother remained, by the time he occupied the British throne it had long since been erased.

Ernest Augustus had faced an uphill battle against his own brothers to gain what power and territories he *did* control and it had instilled in him an ambition and dedication to furthering the fortunes of his line that could not be underestimated. Looking to his eldest son he knew that this boy might one day face similar challenges both from inside Hanover and those rattling sabres elsewhere, and he determined to prepare George for what might be to come. George's tender age was hardly of any concern to Ernest Augustus, who knew that life could be nasty, brutish and short, with surprises conceivably around every corner. Whether his son was a boy or man, Ernest Augustus was all too aware that there was no guarantee of a long life and should he die early, then young George must be ready to seize the reins without hesitation.

Accordingly, little George was given the very best education money could buy and though he was a conscientious student to some degree, his passion was not for studying. Like his father, his true love was for outdoor pursuits and all matters military. This came as a great relief to Ernest Augustus, who no doubt took great pleasure in seeing a son who so reflected his own interests. Not only that, but he could now rest assured that his heir was more than willing to take to the field of conflict to protect his lands should that moment ever come.

Imagine then, Sophia and Ernest Augustus's consternation when their beloved George's promised territories quite unexpectedly began to dwindle. The three heirless uncles suddenly experienced a change in fortune one way or the other, with death claiming one and brides claiming the others. Should either of these brides produce heirs, then George's inheritance could be massively reduced and this, his parents thought, would never do.

The Trouble With Uncles

George's eventual inheritance, whatever it might be, depended entirely on the romantic and childbearing fortunes of his father's brothers, with whom the family's territory was split. Many years before his birth though, the decision by one of these uncles to tie the knot had repercussions that echoed right through George's life.

The uncle in question was George William, who just happened to have been the original husband-to-be of none other than Sophia, George's mother. It was an arrangement that the intended groom had absolutely no intention of sticking to. However, if he was to be released from this obligation, then sacrifices must be made and a deal was hashed out between the brothers before young George was even born.

Under the terms of the agreement, George William promised to award Ernest Augustus one of his territories, Lüneburg, as well as giving his solemn word that he would never marry. This ensured that he could produce no heir that might threaten the succession of Ernest Augustus's line. In fact, Ernest Augustus didn't only take his brother's lands, he also ended up marrying Sophia himself, a typically seventeenth century state of royal affairs.

The bride was not delighted with this new twist of fate or the fact that she was being handed around like sweets in a playground. Sophia had rather liked George William and he cruelly rejected her, palming her off on his little brother for whom she felt no dislike, but no love either. Still, Sophia was a realist and a woman of enormous ambition, not one to let a broken heart cloud her judgment. She recognized that this new role brought with it the influence and power she so craved and accepted it, submitting to the marriage and perhaps, in time, coming to love the man she called husband. She was a powerful and influential woman, a force to be reckoned with and one who fiercely defended and controlled her son. As we shall see when we learn more of George I's marriage, Sophia's influence reached even as far as that former fiancé who had abandoned her, to catastrophic effect.

Despite his best intentions and the terms of the deal, in 1665 George William was proven to be anything but a man of his word. That year, he went back on the bargain he had made with Ernest Augustus and gave in not to ambition, but romance. Despite having promised never to marry, he tied the knot with his adored mistress, Éléonore Desmier d'Olbreuse. Although he might not have won Ernest Augustus's respect, let us take a moment to recognize that this was that rarest of noble marriages, one of love. However, the morganatic marriage wasn't *quite* legitimate just yet, not that either party really cared. The year after they became husband and wife, the newlyweds welcomed their newborn daughter, Sophia Dorothea. That young lady would later become the ill-fated wife of George I.

For now marriage was a long, long way off, but that didn't mean that it wasn't time to start giving it some thought. Although an early scheme to marry him off to England's Princess Anne came to nothing, with new aunties suddenly popping up in the family tree, the chance of a legitimate heir being born to George's remaining uncles had become worryingly prescient.

So, what's a teenager to do when his whole life has been spent preparing to rule territories that, quite unexpectedly thanks to those self-same aunties, might suddenly never be his? The unpalatable answer is, of course, to look for an alternative career and that's just what George did. His natural path led straight into the military. At just 15-years-old, George joined his father on the battlefields of the Franco-Dutch War. Here he more than proved his mettle, to the pride of his family and nation, yet fate had another part to play in the life of young George Louis. Death. And lots of it.

The uncles suddenly started dropping like flies, leaving no male issue behind. With no sons forthcoming from the remaining candidate it finally seemed that George's inheritance was secure. Yet Ernest Augustus had no intention of letting history repeat itself and embarked on a controversial scheme.

Sons Divided

The history of the House of Hanover is filled with feuding fathers and their sons and we will meet several of the most illustrious personalities in this volume. Ernest Augustus knew all about feuds and family disputes, of course, and a decision he took in 1682 caused a little bad blood itself.

Mindful of the wheeling and dealing he had to do over the years with his own brothers and the fact that a word is only good so long as it is kept, Ernest Augustus determined that his sons would not be required to rule over carved up territory as he had been. Not only that, but he had *other* lofty ambitions for his land and dreamt of Hanover one day becoming an Electorate of the Holy Roman Empire. To make this dream a reality, Hanover had to be in the strongest possible political position and half a dozen sons jockeying for power would not help.

When he first mooted the idea of adopting primogeniture in 1682, Ernest Augustus was likely unsurprised to find that five out of his six sons were not at all fond of the scheme. George, of course, was not averse to the plan. After all, it meant that nothing would stand in his way. As eldest son, he alone would inherit and unite the duchies of Brunswick-Lüneburg. As we will learn, the marriage of George was central to the success of the primogeniture plans, and it would be disastrous.

Still, despite the opposition of the other sons to the scheme, the family agreed to adopt the principle of primogeniture in 1684. At first, it must have seemed to Ernest Augustus that his younger sons had given in yet two had not. Frederick Augustus, the second son who had lost so much by the decision to adopt primogeniture, refused to accept that the matter was concluded. He sought allies at home in his struggle against the drastic changes yet found few who were willing to help him. Although his mother did all she could to keep relations between the menfolk cordial it was a losing battle and when Frederick Augustus died on the field of St Georgen in 1690, he and his father were bitterly at odds.

As third son, Maximilian William had been far enough along the line of succession to not feel too disenfranchised but on the death of Frederick Augustus, things changed. Now Maximilian William was the second son and the inheritance he had been denied was suddenly and tantalizingly within his grasp.

With the support of one of his surviving brothers, Maximilian William declared that he would not accept the principle of primogeniture and wished to receive the lands and titles that were rightly his. With his protests met by a wall of resistance, Maximilian William swung into action with plan B, conspiring with associates to claim his inheritance.

Unsurprisingly, the plot ended in disaster when Maximilian William's sister, Sophia Charlotte, revealed the existence of the conspiracy to Ernest Augustus. One of the conspirators was executed whilst others, such as Maximilian William, were exiled.[1]

For George, things were a little easier. Thanks to his father's keen eye for politics and iron grip on the business of government, the future looked bright. Lands were secure, George was a competent military force and though the family might not be happy, at least nobody was locked in a tower or buried under flagstones ... that was to come later.

The year 1682 was pivotal for George and, with his inheritance under discussion, there was one more thorny matter on the horizon for the future king ... marriage. Not romance, of course, this was a different matter altogether.

Mothers, Marriages and Miniatures

George William, the uncle who just couldn't keep his word, might not have an heir, but he did have a daughter and on top of that, he had a nephew without a bride. At 16, Sophia Dorothea, daughter of George William and his mistress, Éléonore Desmier d'Olbreuse, was not, on paper the perfect candidate. The points in her favour were not inconsiderable. She had money and territory to spare, a marriage within the House of Hanover would keep Hanoverian lands in the family and such close ties hopefully also meant that no surprise challenges might lurk on the horizon. However, the points against her were not inconsiderable either and she was not quite what George's mother, the protective and ambitious future Electress of Hanover, wanted for her son.

The year before the birth of Sophia Dorothea, her parents had contrived a morganatic marriage that raised George William's adored Éléonore above the status of mistress. However, it also ensured that neither Éléonore nor any children of the union would ever be able to inherit the titles or privileges that would otherwise be forthcoming to the wife and offspring of one so noble as George William.

---

1. Maximilian William established himself in Austria, where he converted to Catholicism and served the Holy Roman Empire. He died in Vienna in 1726.

For a time this was the status quo but despite his promise never to marry, George William and Éléonore eventually tied the knot not once, but twice. Whilst the first was morganatic and questionable in its legitimacy, the second legitimized their loving union. It also elevated young Sophia Dorothea's status to legitimate, but that was only half of the battle. Legitimate she *may* be but as far as Sophia of Hanover was concerned, this was all a little bit academic because Éléonore, a Huguenot, was of noble birth but was nowhere near a royal. Yet when George William made the suggestion that she might make a perfect wife for his nephew, George Louis, the wheels of diplomacy began to turn. Ever the watchful mother, Sophia debated with herself, her advisors and her husband on the possibility of the marriage between her son and his cousin.

There was, of course, the matter of the bride to be's questionable early legitimacy and the not-quite-good-enough rank of her mother. However, there were also a few unquestionable benefits, chiefly a dowry big enough to sink a battleship and the chance to finally, once and for all, tie up any possible territorial disputes that might arise should the young woman marry an ambitious noble from outside the family. Those Hanoverian lands would be a tempting prize indeed to someone looking to build their own empire, and with relations between brothers Ernest Augustus and George William frosty at best, this was the worst case scenario.

Given that George William had already broken his promise not to marry, it was not difficult to imagine a future in which Sophia Dorothea's marriage could lead to territorial problems in which her father might prove unwilling to intervene. With no love lost between the two brothers, any husband of Sophia Dorothea must be carefully chosen. After all, the very future of the House of Hanover lay in the balance, not to mention that far-off day when it might become an electorate.

In fact, history came close to being a very different place thanks to Sophia Dorothea's prospective husbands. As an only child, she stood to inherit the sort of power, wealth and territory that any ambitious young man would find immensely attractive and while she was merely a child, any number of eligible and enthusiastic nobles beat a path to the door of her parents. Indeed, it seemed as though her fate had been decided by the age of nine, when it was announced that Sophia Dorothea would in fact marry Augustus Frederick of Wolfenbüttel, heir to the powerful dukedom of Brunswick-Wolfenbüttel and nearly a decade his fiancée's senior. Although he would not inherit the duchy of Celle, which would go to his bride, she would bring with her an enormous dowry.

Happily for the ambitions of Sophia, though unhappily for the young groom-to-be, life in the seventeenth century was anything but certain and Augustus Frederick was not destined to become a husband to anybody. In fact, he met a violent end in 1676, when he suffered fatal head injuries at the Siege of Philippsburg, leaving the marriage plans in tatters. Ever the pragmatist, his father offered to provide another son to take his place at the altar and though Éléonore was amenable to the plan, her husband was decidedly less so.

As others jockeyed for position in Sophia Dorothea's favours, Sophia of Hanover turned to her husband and put her case for marrying the young lady to their eldest son, George. The shrewdly political lady knew exactly how to play her hand, and focused not on romance or even money, but on ambition. She reminded Ernest Augustus of his dreams that Hanover would one day become an Electorate of the Holy Roman Empire and pointed out that uniting Celle and Hanover by marriage would bring the electorate one step closer. Crucially, it would put an end to any risk of a marriage between Celle and the already powerful families who sought advancement of their own.

Upon hearing that the Duke of Brunswick-Wolfenbüttel was set to travel for Celle to discuss marriage plans, Sophia journeyed through the night to be sure to arrive ahead of him. Once there, she set to work on the brother-in-law who had once been her fiancé, convincing him that it would be in everyone's best interests if Celle and Hanover were united by marriage. She got her way, of course.

Though the marriage of Sophia Dorothea of Celle's parents might not have begun respectably, it was founded entirely on love. For the newly betrothed young couple, however, this was not the case. When the bride-to-be was informed of the identity of her groom she became distraught and, smashing George's miniature against the wall, exclaimed, 'I will not marry the pig snout!'.[2] The groom, on the other hand, might not have been in love but he knew that he must accept the marriage for the sake of Hanover.

As we will discover, the wishes of bride and groom are all too often a secondary concern in matters of royal marriage. The wedding was set for 1682 even though, on her first meeting with her future husband, the dismayed Sophia Dorothea supposedly fell to the ground in a dead faint! She might have been better had she never woken up at all …

The Birth of an Electorate

Before we dive into the choppy, dark waters of the marriage of George and Sophia Dorothea, let us take a political diversion. The ambitious Ernest Augustus had long since set about making his house and its forces invaluable to the Holy Roman Empire, determined to get his feet firmly under the diplomatic table.

At every turn, Ernest Augustus was there, whether it was in the debating chamber or the battlefield. His forces fought for the Holy Roman Emperor, Leopold I, proving time and again what an invaluable ally Hanover could be. The final piece in the jigsaw fell into place in 1688 courtesy of the Nine Years' War, in which the emperor joined a coalition against Louis XIV. Hopelessly mismatched, the forecast for Leopold I was not good until Ernest Augustus made him an offer he could not refuse. Should Hanover be made the ninth electorate of the empire, then Ernest Augustus would commit the full weight of his military might to the campaign. Should the condition be refused, Hanoverian troops would stay away.

So what's an emperor to do?

It was an audacious gamble and one that paid off royally when, much to the delight of Ernest Augustus, Leopold agreed to the terms and Hanover was finally created an electorate of the Holy Roman Empire. In fact, the course of history was almost changed forever when George come close to losing his life in 1693 during fierce fighting at Neerwinden. It was a powerful reminder of his own mortality and he survived thanks only to the

---

2. Morand, Paul (1972). *The Captive Princess: Sophia Dorothea of Celle*. Florida: American Heritage Press, p.23.

quick action of General Alexander von Hammerstein, who was later richly rewarded for his actions.

Things could really not have been better for Ernest Augustus with his longest and most dearly held ambition finally in the process of becoming a reality. However, if everything was going politically well for the duchy that George would inherit, at home things were far less rosy. The marriage that neither bride nor groom had particularly longed for was about to hit a very rocky patch. So let us return to the altar and find out exactly how the supposedly happy couple became the bitterest of enemies.

The Elephant and the Maypole

The marriage between George Louis and Sophia Dorothea of Celle took place at Celle Castle on 22 November 1682 and was, without a doubt, a marriage of duty on both sides. The year after their marriage the newlywed cousins welcomed their first child, George Augustus, and in 1687, a daughter, named Sophia Dorothea (just to add to the confusion over names) joined the family. Both were destined for great things, with the youngsters eventually rising to the dizzy heights of George II and Queen of Prussia respectively. In fact, the little girl would one day have a family of her own and you might have heard of one of her many children; a certain chap named Frederick the Great.

Still, regardless of children and the facade of an amicable marriage, the Electoral Prince and Princess of Hanover's union was nothing more than their duty required of them. The heir had been born, the court was satisfied and George's affections could now be lavished elsewhere, and lavished they *certainly* were. Throughout his life, two particular women commanded George's attentions above all others, and these ladies were destined to become known to the people of Britain by the less than flattering nicknames of the Elephant and the Maypole.

Of the two, the Elephant was perhaps the more scandalous thanks to a rather worrying rumour that was doing the rounds in Hanover. She was Sophia von Kielmansegg, daughter of Clara Elisabeth von Meysenburg, Countess of Platen and Hallermund. So far, not so scandalous, but Clara, Sophia's mother, just happened to be the long-time mistress of George's own father as well as the sister of one of the young man's early mistresses, and rumours had long since existed that Sophia was Ernest Augustus's daughter courtesy of his affair with Clara. Were that the case, it would mean that George and his whispered lover were half-siblings, which was a step too far even by royal court standards.

The rumours of an affair gained such traction that George's mother was forced to deny that his relationship with the Elephant went any further than intimate friendship, hoping to lay the perceived scandal to rest forever. Of course, court intrigues weren't so easily silenced and the rumour that George was bedding his own half-sister was too delicious not to spread. After all, the gossips mused, perhaps the family connection was precisely why George and the Elephant got on so very well!

Regardless of the truth, the friendship between the couple was intense and abiding. The pair remained fiercely loyal to one another throughout their lives and Sophia even moved to England to join George when he began his reign as king. So close were they that courtiers simply assumed they were lovers, though no evidence exists to suggest that they actually were.[3]

The Maypole, however, was a very different matter. She was Melusine von der Schulenberg, Maid of Honour to George's mother and a close confidante of Clara, mother of the Elephant. Whether Countess von Platen was active in planting Melusine we can never know for sure, but this most adored of mistresses would come to wield enormous influence over her besotted lover until his dying day. Together the couple had three children, born in 1692, 1693 and 1701, and their affair was widely acknowledged, which no doubt left the already unhappy Sophia Dorothea not only hurt but humiliated too.

Royal mistresses should have been an accepted fact of life and the duty of the official wife was to paint on a smile and say nothing. Instead, Sophia Dorothea found her patience stretched to its limit. With the arrival of their son, George considered his duty as a husband finished and he certainly exhibited no desire to produce the spare to that heir, even as he was busily making babies with Melusine!

Rumours of a secret wedding would follow Melusine and George for the rest of their lives, though they were never proven either way. It cannot have

---

3. Sophia, *the Elephant*, died in London in 1725; Melusine, *the Maypole*, lived until 1743.

been any comfort to Sophia Dorothea though and little by little the unhappy woman found herself sidelined in favour of the Maypole, her husband increasingly absent from her life and her place at court usurped. When she could stand no more, Sophia Dorothea challenged George angrily on the matter of infidelity and he literally went berserk, physically attacking his wife on more than one occasion.

Alienated, humiliated, brutalized and increasingly isolated, one can hardly imagine how utterly alone Sophia Dorothea must have felt. As George galavanted with his mistress, it was only a matter of time before the wife he had set aside sought comfort elsewhere and when she did, the consequences would be devastating.

The Disappearing Nobleman

The seeds of tragedy arrived in Hanover in 1688 in the shape of a suave, handsome and wealthy Swedish soldier and adventurer named Count Philip Christoph von Königsmarck. Having distinguished himself in military service, he had a reputation as a cultured, charming chap who was no stranger to the bedchambers of some very noble women indeed. When you learn that one of the ladies who took a shine to him was none other than Clara, Countess von Platen, it won't surprise you to discover that things did not end happily for our soon-to-be star-crossed lovers.

Königsmarck and Sophia Dorothea had met in childhood and now the count was a boy no longer, but the sort of chap who lonely noblewomen were just praying to encounter. Indeed, Königsmarck must have seemed impossibly experienced and exciting to the young woman and when the couple danced together at a masked ball, their friendship was more than rekindled. Sophia Dorothea was costumed as Flora, Goddess of Spring, he as a flamboyant Rosenkavalier, as her biographer terms him, and no one could deny that the couple made the most handsome pair at the party. There was an undeniable chemistry between them from that first dance and the night no doubt crackled with electricity, yet Sophia Dorothea was a realist and she was all too aware of the violence of her husband's temper. At first, she resisted the mutual attraction between her and the soldier, holding true to her marriage vows. Of course, when Clara saw that Königsmarck had failed to win the younger woman's affections, the opportunity was just too good for her to miss.

The experienced and manipulative noblewoman seduced the more than willing Königsmarck to her bed with ease, though one so worldly wise as she could not have failed to see the attraction between her new lover and the princess. No doubt, Königsmarck soon realized his mistake as the ambitious Clara became his unwanted shadow, watching jealously lest he be tempted by another woman, let alone the true object of his affections. When the opportunity to join an expedition that would take him away from Hanover arose, Königsmarck grabbed it with both hands, happy to escape his cloying mistress even if it meant saying goodbye to Sophia Dorothea.

It was during this absence that the young couple realized that their feelings ran far deeper than friendship. The adventurer who had never been short of lovers no longer cared for other women and pined for Sophia Dorothea whilst she, unloved by her husband, thought of him and him alone. The letters between the two grew increasingly heated, passionate and incriminating until, on his return, they succumbed to their desires. If ever the nature of the affair was in doubt, one need only read the following lines, penned by Königsmarck to Sophia Dorothea, to know that they had progressed far beyond good friends.

'Oh God, if I ever saw you kiss anyone with as much passion as you have kissed me, and ride astride with the same desire, I never want to see God if it would not drive me mad.'[4]

The passionate letters between the couple cannot be verified and perhaps they were forgeries, intended to either drive a permanent wedge between Sophia Dorothea and her husband. Maybe they were a cynical attempt to justify the fate that later befell Sophia Dorothea but taken at face value, they clearly point to a sexual affair.

Little that happened at court escaped the attention of Clara and, seeing herself so thoroughly usurped by the young woman, she was overcome

---

4. Morand, Paul (1972). *The Captive Princess: Sophia Dorothea of Celle*. Florida: American Heritage Press, p.85.

by jealous fury. She wasted no time in ensuring that Sophia Dorothea's influential, domineering mother-in-law was well aware of the affair and Sophia of Hanover was as furious as her informant when she realized just how far things had gone. With Königsmarck and George both away on military matters, Sophia Dorothea's letters were full of anguish at the danger her lover faced yet contained subtle clues that, at home in Hanover, skullduggery was afoot.

Suddenly, it seemed, her mother-in-law wanted to talk about nothing but Königsmarck and his many and varied virtues. It is ridiculous to assume that this was because Sophia had been dazzled by his famous looks and charm. She was far too worldly and wily for that, so perhaps her motives were more sinister.

'She praises you so highly and with such pleasure that if she were younger I could not help being jealous, for really I think she is fond of you. She could not give me more evidence of it than she does. It even makes me uncomfortable.'[5]

Of course, the thought of the cunning Sophia being smitten by Königsmarck simply does not seem plausible. Instead, one wonders, was she attempting to draw her daughter-in-law's rumoured indiscretions out into the open? Perhaps she thought that by singing the praises of Königsmarck so loudly, Sophia Dorothea might share her own adoring opinion of him, thus uncovering their infidelities once and for all. The besotted young woman was not so easily fooled though, and she said nothing that might incriminate herself. Still, her circumspection was short-lived as when Königsmarck returned to Hanover, they resumed their passionate affair, as the court went into a gossip-induced meltdown.

The couple communicated through letters delivered via intermediaries and a complex language of secret signals. Yet if Sophia Dorothea and Königsmarck thought they were invisible, they were to be sorely and fatally mistaken. When the Count's own friends and family warned Königsmarck that the relationship with Sophia Dorothea had gone too far and become

5. Ibid., p.119.

too obvious, the couple continued their liaisons unabashed. For George and his wife, however, things had reached breaking point. A public argument between husband and wife turned violent and George attempted to throttle Sophia Dorothea, providing the final straw for the unhappy princess. With the bruises on her throat not yet faded, she knew that the time had come to flee Hanover forever, with her lover by her side.

Over a series of secret meetings Sophia Dorothea and Count von Königsmarck plotted their flight to freedom and, they hoped, their happy ever after. After sharing one final goodnight with Sophia Dorothea in July 1694 Königsmarck simply disappeared from the face of the earth, never to be seen again.

The fate of the adventuring count remains a mystery despite rumours, whispers and all manner of fanciful stories. One thing that is in no doubt is that Königsmarck's sudden disappearance left his lover bereft and her husband certain that rumours of their attachment must be true. Some whispered that George or his family had seen to it that the man was murdered, or that loyal and helpful courtiers had been the culprits, yet no likely suspects came forward.

Still more looked to the manipulative and powerful Clara, seeing in the disappearance the bitter revenge of an ambitious woman scorned. Jealous, rejected and filled with fury, did Clara really conspire to commit murder or was she simply another victim of the royal court's gossip-hungry excitement? It is a mystery that remains unsolved yet for Sophia Dorothea, it marked the end of her days as a royal consort.

In his *Memoirs of the Life and Administration of Robert Walpole*, the political colossus who bestrode the reigns of the first two Georges, William Coxe suggests that George I actually sought reconciliation with his wife and that she refused him. Whether or not this happened we cannot be sure, but the words he attributes to Sophia Dorothea are worth reporting.

'If what I am accused of is true, I am unworthy of his bed; and if my accusation is false, he is unworthy of me; I will not accept his offers.'[6]

---

6 Coxe, William (1816). *Memoirs of the Life and Administration of Robert Walpole*. London: Longman, Hurst, Rees, Orme & Brown, p.261.

Still grieving for the man she loved and the escape she had been denied, the young woman was imprisoned in her chambers. Her fate was placed in the hands of her father, husband and father-in-law and their decision was swiftly made and mercilessly executed.

In December 1694 the marriage of George and Sophia Dorothea was dissolved on the grounds that Sophia Dorothea had abandoned her husband. She was then spirited away to captivity at Ahlden House in Celle. Not yet 30, it was the last home she would ever know.

In Ahlden House, Sophia Dorothea was kept as a genteel prisoner to the end of her lonely days more than thirty years later,[7] kept apart from her children and, George hoped, forgotten by history. Discussion of the marriage was forbidden at court and George expressly forbade his children from speaking about their mother, a decision that was doubtlessly a major factor in the collapse of his relationship with his son. Although Sophia Dorothea was visited by her mother, whose heart was broken by her daughter's lonely fate, her father never saw her again. When his health failed he expressed a forlorn hope that he might perhaps meet her one last time to set right their estrangement, but that day never came.

Her son, too, missed the woman who was hidden away and written out of court history. Apocryphal stories exist of young George desperately swimming the moat at Ahlden to see her and Coxe shares another version of that story:

'George the Second, who doted on his mother, was fully convinced of her innocence. He once made an attempt to see her, and even crossed the Aller on horseback opposite to the Castle, but was prevented from having an interview [...] Her memory was so dear to him that he secretly kept her portrait in his possession: and the morning after the news of the death of George the First had reached London, Mrs. Howard observed (in the antechamber of the king's apartment) a picture of a woman in the electoral robes, which proved to be that of Sophia.'[8]

---

7 Sophia Dorothea died on 13 November 1726, aged 60.

8. Coxe, William (1816). *Memoirs of the Life and Administration of Robert Walpole*. London: Longman, Hurst, Rees, Orme & Brown, p. 262.

The little boy whose mother was torn from him at just 11, later famed as George II, would never forgive his father for keeping him from the woman he adored. It was yet another building block in the unhappy history of the men of Hanover.

A Future King?

As romantic intrigue and rumours of murder rocked the court of Hanover, one of its strongest pillars began to wobble. At 68, the health of Ernest Augustus, Elector of Hanover, was in swift decline. As he grew frailer the once robust, ambitious man handed over the reins of government to the well-prepared George, who immediately set about the business of ruling. It was to be a wise decision because, on 23 January 1698, Ernest Augustus died.

Thanks to the adoption of primogeniture, George inherited his father's territories, titles and privileges, filling the court with music, philosophy and learning. Alone in her tower, all discussion of the ill-fated Sophia Dorothea remained forbidden, though her spectre loomed large at the court that had once been her marital home. Of course, whilst he may now be Elector of Hanover, George still did not stand to inherit the throne of Great Britain; for that, yet another twist of fate was needed ...

George's future was decided by the Act of Settlement in 1701. This act changed the course of history and ruled that if no heir was born to the current incumbent, William III, or his sister-in-law, the future Queen Anne, then the throne would pass to the closest living Protestant branch of the family tree. This just happened to be Sophia, mother of George. The ambitious Dowager Electress was ecstatic, seeing great things in the future for the son she had always adored. For his part, George was a canny politician and he threw himself into research for his forthcoming role, determined that he would be ready to make a splash when the moment came.

At the same time, George ably steered Hanover through the War of the Spanish Succession as an active and engaged front line commander. He remained on active duty until 1709, rising to the rank of Imperial Field Marshal. As the years wore on, his reputation as a politician and soldier grew and flourished among his fellow rulers on the continent but in England, things were not nearly so rosy.

In 1703, the Scottish Estates declared in no uncertain terms that they did not want a Hanoverian for their ruler once the queen passed away. Instead, they decided, they would choose a Protestant successor of their own to rule Scotland and it would *not* be George or anyone from Hanover. The result was the Act of Security in 1704, which determined that the country would choose its own monarch from the legitimate descendants of earlier Scottish kings.

When negotiations with the English Parliament failed to reach an agreement, England responded with sweeping legislation of its own and in 1705 passed the Alien Act, placing strict embargoes on Scottish trade and ruling that all Scottish nationals in England would be considered as foreign nationals. Of course, this was not a happy state of affairs for the people of Scotland and discussions swiftly began again. Eventually the 1707 Acts of Union joined the two countries together, a status that remains a hot topic of debate to this very day. The act also guaranteed that either the Dowager Electress or her heir would be keeping the throne of England and Scotland warm one day in the future. It was no longer a matter of if for George, but when. For the elector, however, the more important achievement in the first years of the new century was just a little closer to home.

In 1708, after years of discussion and negotiations that had started all the way back in 1688, Hanover was finally and formally named as the ninth electorate of the Holy Roman Empire. It had been a long and sometimes bloody road from the agreement made by Ernest Augustus on the eve of the Nine Years' War to this historic moment and it sealed George's reputation as a man of both business and battle, equally at home in the debating chamber as he was on the field of war. It was undoubtedly quite a coup for a king-in-waiting.

Mother Makes Trouble

With George's interests fully occupied at home and England tussling with the Scottish problem, trouble came for the elector in 1705 courtesy of his devoted and opinionated mother. Always rather enamoured with England from her home in Hanover, the Dowager Electress Sophia had developed a fanciful notion that she would be most happy in the land that might one day be hers. In fact, she had become rather preoccupied with the idea of moving her household there, regardless of whether Queen Anne was alive or not!

Hearing this, the English Parliament began to hustle. The Tories, sniffing an opportunity to shake things up at home, issued an invitation to Sophia to turn her dream into reality and take up residence in England with their full support. Perhaps, Lord Haversham ventured, the queen might like to issue an official invitation to her successor-in-waiting to relocate to the country her family stood to inherit. One might almost suspect that Haversham was being a little mischievous and attempting to stir up trouble for the Whigs. After all, they could not agree with the motion without antagonizing Anne, nor disagree with the idea without antagonizing the Hanoverians. Either way, he kicked off a hell of a stink.

For Queen Anne, the idea of a rival court appearing wholesale in London was unthinkable and she was determined to block the plan at all costs. She was not some innocent idealist after all, and was sure that some who supported the measure had devilish motives and, 'did it with a design to depose her'.[9]

Unsurprisingly, the Whigs eventually spoke out against the Tory plan, mindful that nothing must disrupt the carefully laid plans for the succession. For her part, the queen now faced something of a diplomatic problem. Should she object too loudly to Sophia's desire to move to England, she might seem less than keen to support the Protestant succession. However, were she to encourage the dowager electress in her scheme, then the risk of setting the stage for her opponents to rally support around the Hanoverian incomer might be dramatically and disastrously increased.

Although in public Anne maintained a cool head, in private she was incensed. This was not, she thought, the simple fancy of an elderly woman, but a concerted political effort to create some sort of drama. It must be stopped, she told one of her most senior advisors, the Duke of Marlborough, and she placed her trust in him to do so.

'The disagreeable proposal of bringing some of the house of Hanover into England, which I have been afraid of so long, is now very near being brought into both houses of parliament, which gives me a great deal of uneasiness, for I am always of a temper to fear the worse. [...]

---

9. Gregg, Edward (2014). *Queen Anne*. New York: Yale University Press, p.211.

I shall depend upon your kindness to set things right, in notions of things here, and if they will be quiet I may be so too; or else I must expect to meet with a great many mortifications.'[10]

Anne's solution was a masterstroke of diplomacy and she decided to award George Augustus the Order of the Garter and the title of Duke of Cambridge as a mark of the high esteem in which she held the Hanoverians. In the case of the latter honour, Anne was less certain. After all, might George Augustus use this title as an excuse to make the journey to England and set up the rival court she so feared, under the innocent cover of simply taking his seat in the House of Lords?

For counsel she turned to her advisors, the Duke of Marlborough and Lord Halifax, who was entrusted with taking word of the ennoblement to Hanover. The pair assured the queen that she need not fear, business on the continent was keeping the elector more than occupied and he had no intention of establishing a court in England to challenge her own. Suitably placated, the queen agreed to the plan, satisfied that it served the dual purpose of honouring the elector's family without bringing any of his kin onto English shores.

Families, however, can sometimes be nothing but trouble and Sophia's love of the English life was about to cause all sorts of problems at home.

As the decision was being taken to ennoble the electoral prince, a troubling pamphlet appeared. Apparently endorsed by Sophia, the pamphlet was highly critical of the Whigs for opposing her wish to move to England and it was proving to be a hugely popular and controversial read in that very land. The pamphlet was authored by philosopher, Gottfried von Leibniz, whom the late elector had commissioned to write a history of Brunswick, and contained a transcription of a letter written by Sir Rowland Gwynne, an Englishman at the Hanoverian court who had known his fair share of scandal in the past.

George was utterly furious to hear of the existence of the pamphlet, coming as it did just as Halifax's visit to Hanover to ennoble his son was

---

10. Coxe, William (1818). *Memoirs of John, Duke of Marlborough, Vol I*. London: Longman, Hurst, Reese, Orme and Brown, p.501.

imminent. When Sophia simply shrugged her shoulders and declared herself unable to see why he was so very upset, his annoyance only grew. The English Parliament was incandescent with rage at the scathing content of the paper and made heavy weather of censuring it, all of which did nothing to improve the elector's ill-humour. Sophia, however, serenely commented that she couldn't understand what all the fuss was about. After all, the Whigs had vetoed the Tory invitation, so why shouldn't her supporters make their disappointment felt?

George decided to give Sophia the benefit of the doubt, deciding that his mother was nothing but an unwitting, trusting dupe. In his version of events, the Tories had hoped to manipulate the trusting Sophia into opposition to the queen. No doubt Anne's relatively relaxed reception to the pamphlet was helped by the decisive action George took in Hanover, when he dismissed Gwynne from the court and censured Leibniz, who had always been a favourite of his mother. Disaster was averted and, as proof that she held no grudge against the elector, Queen Anne duly kept her word and dispatched Lord Halifax to Hanover to present his son with the Order of the Garter.

What, though, of Marlborough's mission to smooth over the cracks Haversham's mischief had created in the Hanoverian court? As it turns out, Anne had no reason to fear for '[George] did not want many arguments to convince that his and the queen's interest were the same. He has commanded me to assure her majesty that he will never have any thoughts but what may be agreeable to her's.'[11]

Up until this point, George had been happy to let his politically astute, usually clearheaded mother deal with the question of relations with the English but now all of that changed. Mindful of the possible embarrassment or worse that she might have caused him and the damage her schemes and favourites could have wrought, George curtailed Sophia's authority over the England-Hanover relationship. For what was left of the life of the dowager electress, business in England was conducted in concert with her son and *nobody* moved overseas.

---

11. Ibid., p.501.

The Death of a Queen

Following the narrowly averted invitation crisis, Sophia did not indulge in any further plans to move abroad but instead settled into an influential old age in Hanover. The dowager electress wasn't getting any younger though and in 1714, at the age of 83, she died. With Sophia's death George lost an influential if troublesome force and was finally, unquestionably, the sole ruler in Hanover. No longer would his mother be there to advise him, to cajole and make the odd bad call. Whatever decisions were made, whether for better or worse, they were entirely *his*.

Just two months later, Queen Anne followed the dowager electress to the grave. Her death left the British throne unoccupied in the physical sense, but not in the spiritual or legal. Now, more than a decade after it was first agreed, the Act of Settlement finally came into play and the Georgian era dawned across Great Britain.

With the death of Anne, George prepared to travel from The Hague to England but until he arrived, there was a tension from the north. In his diaries, Ralph Thoresby, a historian, captures the nervous excitement in the city of London as news of Anne's death spread and was rescinded before being shared again. The tension at the proximity of the Pretender in Europe, just waiting for his chance to snatch the crown, is palpable.

'[…] was sadly surprised with the lamentable news of the Queen's death, who was seized with an apoplectic fit in the night, and was speechless three hours, and thought to be dead but was by Dr Mead's cupping &c. brought to her speech. She continued very weak and was frequently reported to be dead, to the great terror of all good men of whatever denomination, as expecting nothing but confusion, and the effusion of much Christian blood before the matter can be brought into the former state, by reason of the absence of the Elector of Brunswick, and the dreaded invasion of the Pretender with an army of French and Irish. I was deeply concerned at this matter and so were most persons, as was evident by their very countenances. The Lords of the Council sent to the Lord Mayor, &c. to take special care of the City; the trained bands were immediately raised and a triple guard sent to the Tower.'[12]

---

12. Thoresby, Ralph (1830). *The Diary of Ralph Thoresby, Vol II*. London: Henry Colburn and Richard Bentley, p.245.

George was very keen to travel to his new realm immediately and relieve the regency council that ruled in his absence, but he found the weather against him. The voyage was an onerous, dangerous one yet he would not hear of any delay or postponement, he had waited long enough.

Accompanying him were almost a hundred courtiers, advisors and staff members and his son, George Augustus, who would become the new Prince of Wales. With the men never having reconciled after the imprisonment of Sophia Dorothea, it was a far from happy party and the two Georges hardly helped to lighten the dark mood that descended during the troublesome journey.

In England, the people awaited the arrival of their new king with apprehension and, if Thoresby is typical, excitement. They mourned their late queen but this was a new chapter and a new start that the nation looked forward to with anticipation.

'Walked […] to see the solemnity of the proclamation of the new King; it was mightily to the satisfaction of all people that there was not only the chief ministers of State (Lord Chancellor, Treasurer, &c.) and Lord Mayor, Alderman, and Sheriffs of London, but the greatest concourse of the nobility in their coaches that was ever known, with the Bishop of London, &c. of the clergy. Blessed be God for so promising a token of good to this nation!'[13]

Of course, all of the new king's time and energy must, for the time being at least, be dedicated to getting to know this new land, its characters and foibles. That meant that a caretaker was needed in his beloved Hanover and in the absence of a more trusted figure, that vital role was entrusted to a regency council. Ceremonial occasions were a different matter, of course, and the new king decided that they would be the responsibility of his seven-year-old grandson and newly appointed official figurehead, Frederick. As George's relationship with his beloved Frederick grew and flourished, the boy's bond with his own father, the future George II, became more and more unhappy. Once again, another building block was placed in the fractious and

---

13. Ibid., p.247.

unhappy family history of the gentlemen of Hanover, but that is a sorry tale for another chapter ...

The new king finally arrived in England on 18 September 1714, accompanied by that aforementioned gang who would form the foundations of his new British court. As the evening drew in, he stepped from the ship that had survived all manner of storms onto Greenwich soil, taking a moment to gather himself in these new surroundings. He did not tarry there for long and the king was soon on the road to the Queen's House, where he spent his first night in England. The next day was filled with a grand and glittering reception and then he was off once more, met with curiosity everywhere he went.

George processed to London with his party, arriving at St James's Palace on the evening of 20 September having spent the previous two days in an eventful blur of welcome and celebration. It must all have been rather overwhelming even for the elector but he maintained that same cool exterior that some found so very difficult to read.

As far as the people were concerned, all was going splendidly. Everyone involved knew their place and played their role to perfection and best of all, there had been no unexpected surprises. Now though, George must face Parliament and that was a many-headed beast!

The Coronation Riots

When one pictures a royal Coronation, what instantly springs to mind? Finery, pomp and circumstance, perhaps? Ermine, velvet and silk? Certainly there will be jewels, priceless gemstones, diamonds and gold, not to mention the ceremonial anointing in prestigious surroundings, steeped in history and ancient tradition. The scent would, perhaps be incense, a suitably holy and reverent fragrance with which to mark the accession of a monarch, and the halls would echo with words of solemn ceremony, innumerable choral voices rising in praise and adoration.

All of the above and more seem just right for a Coronation. The reign of George I, however, started with a little less rejoicing and a little more rioting.

On the eve of his Coronation, George appointed his first ministry and, mindful of the long-standing loyalty of the Whigs who had supported the

Hanoverian succession and headed off the possible embarrassment of the invitation crisis, it was they who would dominate. He did at least attempt to balance the political scales by sprinkling the administration with a few hand-picked Tories, but if he thought that would head off criticism, he was to be sorely mistaken. Not all of the Tories who were offered a post accepted and George learned his first lesson about the bitter oppositions that existed within English politics; this Parliament was not about to bow quietly to its new monarch, after all.

If sections of Parliament had their own issues with the new king, it was to become swiftly apparent that they weren't alone. Indeed, dissent seemed to be brewing all over the kingdom and rather than celebration and rejoicing, it was among scenes of rioting and civil unrest that George was finally crowned at Westminster Abbey on 20 October 1714.

Riots broke out across the south of England and were led by supporters of the High Church and the slighted Tories, many of whom noisily declined to attend the Coronation. The Act of Settlement had ended forever the chance for James Francis Edward Stuart, known as the Old Pretender, Catholic half-brother of the late Queen Anne and second cousin of George I, from ascending the throne. Whilst he flatly ruled out the possibility of converting to Protestantism for the chance to pursue the crown, the Pretender did *not* rule out the possibility of ever ruling. This was a fine line but a crucial one and for decades, the war of words and weapons raged on.

For now, his case was made by the Jacobite sympathizers who risked charges of treason to raise their voices in support of the unrest. Alongside them were those subjects who simply did not want a king from Hanover who barely spoke their language. They wanted a British monarch, not this foreign intruder!

Coronation celebrations across the south and west of England came under attack from the rioters, who chose their targets to create the maximum public upheaval. People were assaulted, property was destroyed and the night rang with bellows of dissent and treason. It was a shocking and very public challenge to the new authority and the king and Parliament who sat at its heart. It would not go unpunished.

Rather than reports of the glittering Coronation and public rejoicing, the newspapers reflected on riots and unrest. Within weeks, the following passage appeared in the pages of the press, hardly the first move of a happy new king:

'[…] whereas by an Act of Parliament made in the thirteenth year of the reign of King Henry the Fourth, It is Ordained and Established, That if any Riot, Assembly, or Rout of People against the Law be made in Parts of the Realm that the justices of the Peace, Three or Two of them at the least, and the Sheriff or Under-Sheriff of the County where such Riot, Assembly or Rout shall be made shall come with the Power of the County, if need be, to Arrest them […]'[14]

In the cold light of day, Parliament and Crown struck back with force and vigour. The Riot Act was invoked, arrests were made and peers were impeached, though in fact, the efforts to deal out swift, harsh justice were to be frustrated. In the event, few charges were actually brought against the rioters and those impeached peers were eventually freed to resume their business. One of these, Robert Harley, Earl of Oxford, left the Tower of London with an abiding hatred of the king, and for George, this loathing was more than mutual. Indeed, when the Indemnity Act 1717 freed and pardoned Jacobite prisoners including those awaiting execution, Oxford was specifically excluded. It made little difference since the peer was already enjoying his freedom, but the message was one that nobody could fail to understand.

As George faced opposition to his reign in Scotland from both political opponents and a Jacobite rebellion led by the Old Pretender, at home his opposition came from a much more intimate source: George Augustus, now Prince of Wales.

The resentment between father and son that began with the imprisonment of Sophia Dorothea had festered into adulthood and now it was set to explode. The king was keeping Frederick from George Augustus just as he had kept George Augustus from Sophia Dorothea, and no amount of pleading would convince him to change his mind. George Augustus had not wanted to leave

---

14. *London Gazette* (London, England), November 2, 1714 – November 6, 1714; issue 5274, p.1.

Hanover, let alone Frederick. He had not asked to come to England and be Prince of Wales, and now he was here, he was damned if he was going to make life easy for his father.

A Very Social Court

George I and George Augustus were in myriad ways utterly different and in others, sadly and tragically similar. When their minds were made up, it took a superhuman effort to change them. Each was as stubborn as the other and given, unhappily, to drama.

As we will learn when we meet George II, the smouldering embers between father and son burst into flames thanks to a domestic dispute over the name and godparents of George Augustus's newborn son. This spark erupted into an all-out war that resulted in George Augustus being banished from the king's presence and establishing his opposing court at Leicester House. His children, however, were kept in St James's Palace in the custody of the monarch, who was by now establishing something of a routine for keeping parents and children apart.

The Prince and Princess of Wales quite understandably missed the youngsters dreadfully, especially after the earlier wrench of being forced to leave their seven-year-old son at home to serve as the figurehead of the House of Hanover. Forbidden permission to travel home to visit him and with the king's influence over the boy becoming ever more pronounced, it appeared that George was now moving to exert the same power over their other offspring too. Although the desperate pleas of the Princess of Wales eventually resulted in a partial thaw that allowed the couple some limited access to their children, it was another blow from which the relationship between father and son would never fully recover. Sadly for all concerned, no lessons were learned and this same miserable relationship would be echoed once more in that of the Prince of Wales and his own son in years to come.

The gatherings at Leicester House did, however, have an unexpected impact on the court of George I. Never the most sociable of chaps, the king watched as his son became a beacon of conviviality and, with far more serious implications, a rallying point for opposition forces. The welcoming atmosphere to be found at the home of the Prince and Princess of Wales was quite different from the court life of the king. He preferred his own company and that of his trusted advisors, quite happy to pass quiet evenings not at parties and salons, but with his adored mistress, Melusine. However, he was not a fool nor was he naive and as the fun continued at Leicester House, George recognized the need to promote a more convivial image of his own, even if it went against every scrap of reserve in his personality.

Quite out of nowhere, then, time had come for George I to be sociable.

Although visitors had never been banned from George's company, they were now positively encouraged. Each day, some were allowed to watch the king and his guests dining, which would no doubt be quite unthinkable to today's royalty. Social engagements became order of the day and the king's diary was soon full as he made himself more available than ever before, visiting nobles and doing all he could to spread the perhaps dubious pleasure of his company far and wide.

Of course, George had never been a recluse and though he was not a party animal on the scale of George IV, he certainly knew how to throw a bash. He also knew that partygoers expected something more than a round of whist and last year's favourite tunes, so he turned to George Frideric Handel, former *Kapellmeister* at the Hanoverian court, to commission a composition to accompany one particularly ambitious gathering. After all, if one is providing entertainment, one must provide the very best.

George's vision was of a party for the great and good with a difference. This summer celebration would take place on a river barge during a leisurely cruise along the Thames, eventually docking at Chelsea for a grand gathering. Travelling in the early evening, the tide would propel the barge upstream at a leisurely pace, allowing the partygoers to enjoy the view as well as the illustrious company. A second barge would travel alongside and this would carry fifty musicians, performing the music that Handel had been commissioned to compose.

It would be a magnificent event, one to remember for a lifetime and it would only add to Handel's awesome and abiding reputation.

The composition Handel eventually delivered has become legendary, the *Water Music* a perennial favourite to this day. Its premiere was a magnificent and magical event and the barges began their stately journey from Whitehall Palace at 8.00 pm on 17 July 1717, the evening balmy and pleasant. George I's grand barge was laden with a number of hand-picked, illustrious guests though the Prince of Wales was not in attendance, perhaps fearing a dunking by his curmudgeonly father.

With the orchestra safely ensconced on the neighbouring vessel, the historic voyage began. Adding to the party atmosphere were innumerable Londoners who sailed alongside on their own boats, the Thames filled with people eager to hear the new composition, in a celebratory spirit a million miles from the somber mood of the Coronation riots. On arrival at Chelsea the royal party took to the shore and there celebrated a while longer before returning to their barge at 11.00 pm for a moonlit trip home.

In true paparazzi style the press were there for every second of the event, with the *Post Man and the Historical Account* newspaper providing a rather fine summary of the events of the evening:

'On Wednesday Evening at about Eight, the King took Water at Whitehall in an open Barge, where were several Persons of Quality, and went up the River towards Chelsea, attended by a great many Barges full of Persons of Quality, and such a Number of Boats, that the whole River in a manner was cover'd; a City Company's Barge was employ'd for the Musick, wherein were 50 Instruments of all sorts, who play'd all the way from Lambeth (while the Barges drove with the Tide without Rowing, as far as Chelsea) the finest Symphonies, compos'd express for this Occasion, by Mr Hendel [sic]; which his Majesty liked so well, that he caus'd it to be plaid over three times in going and returning. At Eleven his Majesty went a-shoar at Chelsea, where a supper was prepar'd, and then there was another very fine Consort of Musick, which lasted 'till Two; after which, his Majesty came again into his Barge, and returned the Same way, the Musick continuing to play till he landed.'[15]

As the strains of the melody faded away into the summer night, the people of London returned their boats to the riverside and went to their beds.

---

15. *Post Man and the Historical Account* (London, England), July 18, 1717–July 20, 1717; issue 15120, p.1.

Handel's favour at court was set in stone and the composer became an abiding favourite of the king and his successor.

George was no doubt pleased with what had been a successful evening and it was to be the first of many. Strikingly, however, every social engagement was carefully calculated to avoid running into the Prince of Wales. It was a favour that the prince was more than happy to return, having precisely zero desire to encounter the father he loathed.

George knew that there was more to ruling than barge trips with noble pals though, and that the riots at his Coronation had not existed in a vacuum. Not content with winning friends in the upper echelons of society, he decided that he must get out there amongst the ordinary people, hunting, dancing and dining more. And so it was that George I visited not only the great and the good but even Marshalsea, despite a painful attack of piles!

None of this came easily to George I, especially given his difficulties with the English language, but he ploughed on with these schemes as duty dictated. Of course, it couldn't all be fun and river cruises …

It couldn't even all be Marshalsea.

The South Sea Bubble Goes Pop

The reign of George I seemed to be beset by challenges with domestic and political thorns never far from the king's side. In Parliament, he looked increasingly to the likes of Sir Robert Walpole for guidance yet that self-serving politician was ruthless in ambition, and a man who was most definitely not to be trusted. The king did all he could to cultivate the image of someone who loved to socialize, and though he was no longer half as remote as he might first have appeared, trouble was never far behind him. And nothing was more troublesome than the South Sea Bubble.

The South Sea Bubble has become legendary, synonymous with ruin and bankruptcy, with big business running rampantly out of control. It could almost be a story from today's headlines where money reigned supreme, banishing good political sense and it dealt an enormous blow to George's popularity. Yet what were the events that led to this famed scandal and the catastrophic fallout?

It starts with a name, and not a very memorable or succinct name either. The company behind all the trouble was officially known as *The Governor and Company of the Merchants of Great Britain, trading to the South Seas and other parts of America, and for the encouragement of fishing.* Created in 1711, the organization became better known as the South Sea Company, a far more manageable moniker!

The company took a gamble at the outset with much of its business model reliant on monopolizing trade with South America. Although the War of Spanish Succession prevented such schemes at its inception, the company assumed that, once the war ended, they would be free to commence trading. The public shared this confidence and stocks sold well but when peace came, it wasn't quite the bounty the company had hoped for. Nevertheless, the king himself became governor of the South Sea Company in 1718, which did wonders for its reputation.

The following year, the company offered to buy up the national debt of Great Britain, which amounted to £30 million, ploughing funds into the country's war chest. With George already a governor, he didn't need much convincing to champion this audacious plan and after some canny lobbying via his ministers and Melusine, who sang its praises in her lover's ear, the king set his weight behind the proposal. Walpole, on the other hand, had strong and, as we will learn, more than reasonable, reservations, which probably saved him a fortune.

Under the terms of the agreement, the company would underwrite the entire national debt in return for five per cent interest. It was an enormous amount and one that investors could scarcely believe but with the backing of king and Parliament, what could possibly go wrong? With the proposal accepted, the value of stocks in the company skyrocketed and their shares faced unprecedented demand, although it seemed that not everybody was taken in.

'[…] the Payment of the Publick Debts was a Stratagem to cheat the Whole Nation […] the South Sea Company could not answer the Design for which the Credit was raised, and Establishment given to it, the Money of now too many suffering Families, flung in, in hopes of doubling their Money upon Security and Credit of the Stock, not worth half they pretended.'[16]

Those who sat at the head of the the company dangled the carrot of new opportunities for trade and though they might not have a track record of financial acumen, they were born spin doctors. Soon the value of shares in the South Sea Company rose to ten times their initial value and it seemed as though everyone, from the lord in his manor to the tradesman in his corner shop, was buying up stock.

And for the conmen, it was a dream come true.

Those with little experience in dealing with the stock market were easy prey to charlatans and soon there was a brisk trade in all sorts of enterprises. Stocks were sold for companies that never even existed or were fanciful at best, and no doubt those with genuine shares shook their head at the gullibility of those who bought these make-believe investments

However, it was soon apparent that investors in the genuine South Sea Company were not much better off. Of course, nobody knew this at the start and the mania continued as George gadded off to Hanover. As he made his trip to the continent, the market was still rising at an uncontrollable rate, eventually becoming so rampant that Parliament finally passed the Bubble Act, intended to stop the craze for stocks.

The first sign of the trouble ahead appeared in 1720 when the directors of the company, well aware that they were selling shares in an enterprise that had no hope of making anything like the fortune they had been promising, quietly sold off their own stock. No matter how surreptitiously they tried to offload the burden, news leaked out that selling had started and soon other shareholders were following their lead. The more people that sold, the more others joined them as investors panicked. Soon it seemed that everyone was selling and the value of the stock began to plummet at an alarming rate.

Fortunes were lost, the king who had put his support behind the South Sea Company made haste to sail once more for England and in the eyes of the public, his personal stock hit an all-time low. It wasn't only the rich who lost their shirts, people from all ranks and stations were caught up in the

---

16. *Weekly Journal or British Gazetteer* (London, England), Thursday, January 7, 1720, p.2.

investment mania that gripped the country, believing it marked their chance to finally make a mint.

Allegations of corruption were rife and in the face of accusations of bribery the Postmaster-General, James Craggs the Elder, apparently took his own life.[17] The collapse of the market brought with it a rash of suicides and bankruptcies and across both Houses of Parliament, hundreds of members were left in dire straits.

The king and his two lady friends were heckled in the streets and it was left to Robert Walpole to ride to the rescue. Safely in office as First Lord of the Treasury and, in fact, the first British Prime Minister, Walpole took decisive measures that placed the financial meltdown under tight control, narrowly avoiding a complete collapse of the banks.

Ever the self-serving politician though, Walpole did not quite see that everyone who was responsible for the bubble was punished, even when evidence of conspiracy, bribes and all manner of dishonesty was uncovered. Instead he let the names of those who might later prove useful slip through the net unnoticed, logging those favours away to call on later. His own reputation flourished and as the king's public popularity dipped, Walpole's influence knew virtually no bounds.

For commentators and satirists, the affair was a bitter gift; Jonathan Swift composed a poem, *The Bubble*, with its furious swipe at the men who led the catastrophe.[18] More ponderous and considerably less famous but no less angry is Mr Arundell's, *The Directors*, printed by Edmund Curll who was, of course, more notorious for pornography than political poetry.

Addressed to Earl Stanhope, the former First Lord of the Treasury who shouldered much of the blame for the affair, the poem could be yours for sixpence.

'Make us [the directors] your Pilots, place us at the Helm,
And guide we will to Ports of *Indian* Wealth,

---

17. The official verdict was that Craggs had died as a result of a fit brought on by grief at the death of his son, but it appears likely that he took poison.
18. Swift's poem is a masterstroke of commentary, the penalty he suggests for the directors as harsh as any of the ruined investors might wish:

> This tottr'ing Vessel of the Commonwealth:
> Ours be the Task, be ours the welcome Toil,
> To ease its Loads, and save the sinking Isle.'

Stanhope, of course, had more urgent matters to concern him than Mr Arundell's poetry and it might be argued that the affair took a heavy toll on his health. He was not yet 50 when, whilst speaking in Parliament in 1721, he was forced to abandon the debate thanks to a violent headache. The following day, he suffered a fatal stroke. His supporters lauded his political passions, blaming his heartfelt defence of the government for the attack that killed him, though perhaps one might also look to the party of the preceding evening when Stanhope and his guests 'drank excessively of new tokay, champagne, visney and barba water, thirteen hours it is said.'[19]

The South Sea Bubble had very definitely burst and the damage to George's reputation was done. In the wake of the catastrophe he came to rely on Walpole more than ever in Parliament, whilst the Elephant and the Maypole were a constant comfort in matters intimate and domestic. Perhaps, though, he might not be quite so keen to take their advice when it came to stocks and shares ...

A Crown Divided

Even as he tamed the panic that followed the bursting of the South Sea Bubble, Walpole took his not so benign influence and applied it to a little domestic conflict resolution. Of course, his motives weren't entirely altruistic, and nobody stood to benefit more from Walpole's scheme than Walpole himself ...

From his lofty perch at the top of the political tree, Walpole surveyed his position, the ageing monarch and his embittered successor, and began to

---

"Directors, thrown into the sea,
Recover strength and vigour there;
But may be tamed another way,
Suspended for a while in air."

19. Pearce, Edward (2011). *The Great Man: Sir Robert Walpole: Scoundrel, Genius and Britain's First Prime Minister*. London: Random House, p.132.

think of the future. It was all very good being popular with the king, but no monarch lives forever. George Augustus was waiting in the wings, and although estranged from his father, he was more than willing to succeed him on the throne. Walpole had schemed and manoeuvred long enough to gain the highest of offices and now, just as he was about to be swept into power to mop up the mess left by the exploding South Sea Bubble, the time had come to consolidate.

Under Walpole's direction, father and son attempted a tentative and somewhat strained reconciliation, enough water having flowed under the bridge to last them a lifetime. Although the relationship between the king and the Prince of Wales would never be easy, both men seemed resigned to the fact that their war of attrition could not continue forever. Indeed, in the eyes of the public, Walpole had orchestrated a much-needed show of unity. In fact, Walpole's own relationship with George Augustus faltered thanks to his sudden popularity with the king but he had little reason to fear the future now. After all, Caroline of Ansbach, the Princess of Wales, was one of Walpole's most trusting allies and he rightly guessed that, with *her* in his corner, the future George II would never leave him out in the cold.

Just as George II would one day consider splitting the crowns of Great Britain and Hanover for somewhat cynical reasons borne out of a family dispute, so too did George I make enquiries into this unorthodox method of succession. Determined to ensure that both realms would be adequately served in the years to come, he hatched a scheme to ensure that the line of succession would henceforth be divided. As an only boy, George Augustus *must* inherit both Hanover and Great Britain yet when it came to his adored and well-drilled grandson, Frederick, things would be different. Frederick would inherit the crown in Great Britain whilst the second born son of George Augustus, should there be one,[20] would be heir to the Electorate of Hanover. This way, he reasoned, there would be no question of either territory being neglected. Should there only be one son, then *he* would inherit the crown, with the electoral cap passing into the House of Brunswick, the nearest hereditary line.

---

20. Although a second son, George William, had been born to the Prince and Princess of Wales, he died in infancy in 1718.

It was a difficult decision for George but it proves that he was far from disinterested in his British realms. Devoted to Hanover as he was, the king nevertheless recognized the importance of ensuring that all interests were properly taken care of. However, Parliament soon confirmed that this couldn't be done as the cap of Hanover, inherited by primogeniture, couldn't go to anyone other than the eldest son and heir. In theory, that heir could abdicate Hanover and allow the next in line to take the cap, but no constitutional change could be made.

When the king died, his son suppressed the will that might have seen these changes enacted but for now, there was nothing that could be done. Still, while he might not have interfered with Fred's expected succession, when it came to his love life, George I had *plenty* to say.

Family Affairs

History remembers and, let's be honest, mocks George I as a king who spent a lot of time in Hanover and indeed, he was a regular and enthusiastic visitor to his homeland. Though his advancing age meant he could no longer occupy an active role on the battlefield, he continued to be a keen negotiator and to take a very close interest in the affairs of his occasionally wayward family.

In between ruling the nation and nipping over to the continent, George attempted to broker marriages between his granddaughter, Amelia, and her cousin, the future Frederick the Great. He also took an interest in the prospective wife of his adored grandson, Fred, erstwhile son of the Prince of Wales. Indeed, George believed he had found a seemingly perfect match for the young prince as well as Amelia, though in the event neither of those marriages actually got as far as the altar.

The lucky lady George had identified for Fred was the young man's cousin, Wilhelmine of Prussia. In suggesting Wilhelmine, George remembered and rekindled the marital ambitions of Sophia, the late Electress of Hanover, and the mutual grandmother of both the prospective bride and groom. Fred had always been led to believe that Wilhelmine would one day be his and though the couple never met, the young man sent his bride-to-be innumerable letters and gifts, growing ever more enthused with each passing year. In fact, no formal approach towards the betrothal was ever made, though informally discussions took place regarding the possibility of a double marriage. Such a dynastic union would be an ideal opportunity to join not only Wilhelmine and Fred but also the future Frederick the Great and Fred's sister, Amelia.

Young Fred fancied himself as madly in love with Wilhelmine and as the official engagement failed to materialize he became more and more vocal in his wish to finally tie the knot. Let us not forget that this was a boy who had always been sure of his place in the world, whose adoring grandfather had lavished him with praise and affection and who, as figurehead of the House of Hanover from childhood, was possessed with an innate and unshakeable confidence in his own self-worth.

Perhaps it was naive to ever expect such an elaborate scheme, with so many ambitious parties involved, to be successful. After all, Prussian and British interests were not necessarily mutually beneficial and in George and Frederick William, father of the Prussian pair, two monumental egos were at war. Throw in a third not-inconsiderable personality in the shape of Fred's father, George Augustus, and it's hardly surprising that things began to wobble precariously. In the end George II vetoed the marriages once he came to the throne, and Fred, like so many lovesick princes before him, just had to get over it.

The Wild Boy

In 1725, hunters in the forest of Hertswold, Germany found themselves chasing a most unusual prey. What had caught their eye on this occasion wasn't game, it was a child who moved silently on all fours, eating leaves and grass. Unable to communicate verbally, he behaved more like a startled animal than a human. He was completely naked save for the tattered remains of a shirt collar, his skin burnished by the sun and his hair thick and dark. After felling a tree to reach the boy, he was seized and flung into the house of correction where he languished, unclaimed and unwanted.

'On being taken prisoner, he gave the most terrible howls, and could not articulate a single word. His hair was matted and bristling, his nails very long, his skin hardened and tanned by the air-in a word he was a perfect savage, probably born, fed, and brought up with the wild beasts of the forest, and speaking no human language. [...] He frightened me.'[21]

Of course, the fact that he was wearing a tattered collar refutes the rather romantic notion that Peter was born and raised among the animals, but we cannot underestimate what an evocative and unique moment this must have been. His origins remain a mystery, though in recent years, scholars have speculated that Peter might have been suffering with Pitt Hopkins Syndrome (an incredibly rare chromosomal disorder, resulting in severe learning difficulties and an unusual appearance) and was likely abandoned by his parents early in his life. For the people of the Georgian era, however, he was a savage, wild boy, a creature of the woods.

The king was fascinated by news of this remarkable find and summoned Peter to an audience in Herrenhausen, where he was to start his life as a member of the court. When George returned to England he took Peter the Wild Boy with him, thrusting the child into a most Georgian kind of celebrity.

Although the memoirs of the writer and commentator Cesar de Saussure contain a record of the young man's first appearance in England, suggesting that Peter was in his teens, his age was never ascertained. Indeed, when the famed William Kent painted the boy, he appeared to be younger than Saussure believed, possibly 11 or 12.[22] Still, whatever his age, he made quite an impact.

Peter made his grand entrance at St James's Palace on 7 April 1726, where he was carried in to meet the assembled courtiers. He delighted them with his strange behaviour and they clearly regarded him more as a pet than a human, with none more fascinated than the Princess of Wales.

'The Princess of Wales wore [...] a gold watch that struck the hours. The chiming of this watch attracted the young savage, who ran towards

---

21. Saussure, Cesar de (1902). *A Foreign View of England in the Reigns of George I & George II*. London: John Murray, pp.148–9.

22. Saussure also mistakenly writes that Peter died soon after his arrival in England, whereas he lived until 22 February 1785. Peter's death was mistakenly and extensively reported in the British press in May 1727.

the Princess to see from whence the sound came; without permission
he examined the sparkling gems on the Princess's gown and also the
watch, which she made chime several times for his pleasure. For some
time he thus stood, much to the amusement of the whole circle, but
unfortunately he could not be taught good manners, and he had to be
removed.'[23]

On that first meeting, Saussure seems to suggest that the fascination was
entirely mutual, and the princess would soon become Peter's newest keeper.
There can be no doubt of the way he was viewed, more chattel than child,
from the manner in which his change of address was reported:

'His Majesty has been pleased to make a Present of the wild Youth,
taken in the Woods near Hamburgh, during his Majesty's Stay at
Hanover, to her Royal Highness the Princess of Wales, and he is sent
for accordingly.'[24]

Although he took up residence with Caroline, Peter's care was entrusted
to Doctor John Arbuthnot, who is at his side in Kent's painting. Arbuthnot
was not an unkind man and did his best to follow the king's wishes to teach
Peter to speak, as well as educating him, but their progress was agonizingly
slow. Peter had no inclination to do anything other than play outdoors; he
loathed his formal new clothes and the routine of lessons, and would not
sleep in a bed, but only on the floor. Though those who saw him at court
no doubt envied him the freedom he enjoyed. However, the picture that
emerges is of a little boy in need, lost in a strange world of which he had
no experience and in which he was nothing more than entertainment, a
lapdog for his owners.

Swift and Defoe wrote works on Peter and the press, public and cartoonists
found him as fascinating a subject as any they had known. Speculation was

---

23. Saussure, Cesar de (1902). *A Foreign View of England in the Reigns of George I &
    George II*. London: John Murray, p.150.
24. *Weekly Journal or British Gazetteer* (London, England), Saturday, January 22, 1726;
    issue 39, p.2.

rife not only about his origins, but about what this might mean for the natural world. The king had him baptized but debate became increasingly more disturbing, centred around whether this creature was human at all. Did his biology alone make him human, or did his bestial behaviour mean he was more animal than man? And if that was the case, did he have a soul to call his own?

Peter was at the centre of debates on nature and nurture, man versus beast, yet for most people in Georgian London, he was simply a curiosity. From initial reports of a savage boy taken into the king's household at Hanover, he became a regular fixture in the popular press and for a time, fascination with him burned bright.

Public tastes are fickle though, and as quickly as the people fell for him, they began to find his antics increasingly old news. No longer in the limelight, Peter was moved out of London and went to live in rural Hertfordshire, where he worked on a farm and received an annual indemnity. His life, once one of luxury in the care of Caroline of Ansbach, had changed again and he was faced with yet another new start. It was a struggle the young man found difficult and in 1728 he ran away back to the woods, tragically searching for the only real home he had ever known.

'The Wild Youth, (as he is commonly call'd) was in keeping at Bone-End in Hertfordshire, went away from thence about a Fortnight ago; [...] 'twas thought the Fool (who now comes under than Denomination by all that know him) got into the Woods, [...] but he is not like to be so well provided for there as he was before.'[25]

Though he was found and returned to his lodgings, Peter had developed a love for wandering. He even saw a spell in Bridewell for vagrancy, where he was only discovered after a fire saw many inmates escape. Peter remained to gaze at the flames in fascination and a witness recognized him from a description of the missing *wild man* in the press.

The result of these wanderings was that Peter was eventually made to wear a collar so that he could be returned home like a lost animal. Despite

---

25. *Daily Post* (London, England), Wednesday, November 6, 1728; issue 2848, p.1.

developing a love for gin and music, he never did learn to speak and remained that same lost child in an unfamiliar world.

Peter the Wild Boy died in 1785 and was laid to rest beneath a simple stone in Northchurch, near Berkhamstead, his smile captured forever on Kent's remarkable canvas.

Dying to Visit Hanover

'Whereas it hath pleased Almighty God to call to his Mercy our late Sovereign Lord King George, of Blessed Memory, by whose Decease the Imperial crowns of Great Britain, France and Ireland, are Solely and Rightfully come to the high and Mighty Prince George, Prince of Wales [...] God save the King.'[26]

In 1727, with Melusine as ever by his side, 67-year-old George I set out once more for his adored ancestral lands in Hanover. The king endured the journey with good humour and fortune until, on 9 June 1727, he suffered a catastrophic stroke.

Close to death, the ailing king was rushed to Schloss Osnabrück, home of his brother, Ernest Augustus, and made as comfortable as possible. Here he lingered in insensibility for two days until, on 11 June 1727, he died. The devastated Melusine never recovered from the loss of the man she had adored for so many decades and refused to believe that his soul had left her. In fact, in the years that followed, she lavished all of her attention and affection on a pet raven, convinced that it was inhabited by the spirit of her dead lover.

George I was interred in the chapel of the Leineschloss and here he rested peacefully until the Second World War shattered Europe. When bombs rained down and destroyed the castle, the late king's remains were moved to Herrenhausen and this, so far, has served as his final resting place.

In the centuries that have passed since the death of George I, the king who came from Hanover has become something of a figure of fun. He is easy to

---

26. *Whereas It Hath Pleased Almighty God to Call to His Mercy Our Late Sovereign Lord King George* (London, England), Wednesday, June 14, 1727, p.1.

deride, of course, whether for the amount of time he spent in Hanover or the fact that the man who occupied the throne of England could not, apparently, speak English. But are these criticisms entirely fair?

In fact, though George did make long trips to Hanover and certainly loved the place above any other, he was not there as often as has been claimed. Likewise, though his English was sparing upon his arrival in his new land, and he remained an awkward public speaker (as do some members of ruling families to this very day), by the end of his reign he could certainly speak and understand English. His relationship with his son was not good, of course, yet with his daughter he was loving, warm and demonstrative apart from his annoyance when she allowed mourning at her marital court for her late mother. Still, as a rule the ties between fathers and daughters of the House of Hanover were not nearly as fraught as those between the menfolk.

George I was a man of contradictions and a monarch whose life was dictated by circumstances unthinkable upon his birth, when there was little expectation of anyone from Hanover ruling in Great Britain. For all the time he spent in the land of his ancestors, George I devoted himself to his reign in Great Britain. Certainly not universally adored, nor was he universally loathed, and now the people looked to George II to fly the flag for their interests. He seemed the antithesis to his predecessor with his popular and sociable demeanour. The time had finally come for him to prove himself.

George II, so long in the shadow of his father, now had his own chance to shine and perhaps discover that this business of kingship was not half as easy as he might have thought!

George II, King of Great Britain and Ireland

(Hanover, Germany, 9 November 1683 –
London, England, 25 October 1760)

T he story of George II begins in sadness, his conception not one of love, but of duty. The early years of the future king bore unhappy witness to a husband and wife whose only meaningful relationship was to become one of endless mutual loathing.

George I was born to a couple who might not win any prizes for romance, but had long since learned to get along. Each knew their role and played it with aplomb, from the father who planned great things for his son to the mother who set her sights on the highest laurels he might achieve. For George Augustus, however, that sort of parental relationship was naught but a distant dream. The toxic domestic drama that shattered the court of Hanover and saw Sophia Dorothea confined to Ahlden House trickled down from George I and bled into his own son, poisoning their relationship irretrievably. From there, that venom continued to drip into the next generation of the family from Hanover and the one that followed, but those stories are yet to unfold.

So let us delve into the eventful years of George II's life and times. Here a famed mistress takes her first steps on the historical stage, a hernia comes back with a vengeance and a bonnie prince from Scotland is *never* far from trouble.

An Absent Mother

Some people are all about firsts, but George II was more inclined to *lasts*. Many years before he became the last British monarch to lead his troops into battle, he became the last king of Great Britain to be born outside the realm he would one day rule. He gave his first plaintive newborn cries in Hanover, just as his own father had done before him.

When their son was born, George and the ill-fated Sophia Dorothea were still in their honeymoon period, tolerating one another and not *yet* at daggers drawn. There was already trouble brewing in the family though, and it was just as the little boy was born that the House of Hanover began the emotive adoption of primogeniture. As is explored elsewhere in this volume, this was a body blow to the brothers of George I and it would map out the course of his son's inheritance and monarchical life. Should primogeniture be accepted, which it eventually was, then this newborn child would one day be sole heir to the lands and powers that were currently shared. Domestic discord erupted amongst those who stood to lose out and there would eventually be conspiracy, exile and many tears shed. In the end, primogeniture was adopted of course, whether the uncles liked it or not.

Whilst, such power plays are not the concern of royal babies, they *are* the concern of royal fathers, along with all manner of political and military business. As a ruler in waiting, George was often away from Hanover at one battle or another and, since he wasn't yet throttling her, there were occasions when Sophia Dorothea was called to join him. When she did, she left the little boy and his younger sister, also called Sophia Dorothea, at home in the care of their grandparents. As the years passed, the children formed a strong bond with their devoted grandmother, Sophia, who was just as ambitious on their behalves as she had been for her own children. She also took charge of their education and Frau von Harling was once again employed to aid in the upbringing of George Augustus.

The little boy spoke only French until the age of four, when his education began to expand under a team of tutors who had been appointed by his grandfather to ensure that he was raised as a suitable future ruler. George Augustus was to learn the values of kings, to show and expect respect, to be pious and disciplined. He was to eschew disappointment and rebellion, both in himself and others, and to become the sort of man who might one day lead a country.

This was of course easier said than done, especially with regard to the discipline part.

If George Augustus was ever disciplined when it came to controlling his temper, it certainly didn't show in the curmudgeon he became. Even in his early years, George was never exactly *zen*-like.

Despite their distance, the occasional physical conflicts between George and Sophia Dorothea cannot have escaped the little boy's attention. Certainly, his father was not secretive about his affair with Melusine von der Schulenberg and by the time George Augustus was 11, the Hanoverian court rang with gossip about Sophia Dorothea and her lover, Count Philip Christoph von Königsmarck.

Of course, we have already heard the sorry tale that ended with Königsmarck disappearing into thin air and to George Augustus, it must have seemed as though his mother suffered the same fate. She was whisked away from her family and confined to her gilded cage at Ahlden House, never to be allowed her freedom again. All mention of her was outlawed, her portraits removed from the walls and her name confined to history. It must have been utterly baffling for her children and, though George Augustus would dust off and rehang those forbidden portraits in the years after his father died, he never laid eyes on his disgraced mother again. With divorce a foregone conclusion, there was no question of a reunion, nor could he find some small solace in the tragic closure of death, for there had *been* no death to mourn. Instead Sophia Dorothea lived on, but she was no longer part of the life of her children and George Augustus had no choice but to accept this.

If the melodramatic rumours of the little boy trying to swim the moat at Ahlden to meet his mother are more tragic than true, the dreadful wrench of the separation surely cannot be underestimated. It is easy to consider these royal children as somehow *different*, their life of privilege cushioning them from the blow of the separation. But is that really fair? For George and his sister, their mother was suddenly *gone*. This time, there was no understanding that she might return from a trip to see her husband on a campaign or visit her family in Celle, she had simply disappeared, torn away by an often absent father. It is little surprise that, as time passed, George Augustus found his audiences with his maternal grandparents growing less frequent too. The decision to imprison Sophia Dorothea proved a decisive moment in the relationship between the two Georges and one that, as the years wore on, saw their mutual disdain grown deeper and more acrimonious than ever.

Monsieur de Busch Goes to Court

The episode that robbed George Augustus of his mother might, of course, paint George I as something of a monster. Controlling, emotionally distant and often absent, there is no doubt that he was far from the ideal father. However, when it came to the question of his only son's marriage prospects, he *did* take a lesson from his own unhappy experience – sort of...

George had been musing on the matter of the young man's marital status for some time, well aware that there were all sorts of dynastic matters to consider when it came to this most important of unions. The favoured candidate, as far as George was concerned, was Dowager Duchess Hedvig Sophia of Sweden, regent of Holstein-Gottorp. Two years older than the prospective groom, Hedvig Sophia had been widowed in 1702 when her husband, Frederick IV, Duke of Holstein-Gottorp, died in battle at Kliszów.

Hedvig Sophia did not miss her late husband, whose bad behaviour had earned him the nickname, *the Gottorp Fury*. Like George and Sophia Dorothea, their marriage had been one of duty not love, and she hated Frederick's infamous, rakish ways. Intelligent, beautiful and hugely popular, the regent would have made an excellent bride, politically speaking, but she had no wish to be yoked to another man she didn't love. Even as the most eligible men in Europe jostled for her hand in marriage, she fell deeply in love with poet Olof Gyllenborg, and he with her.

No doubt this carried some unwelcome reminders of his own wife's misdemeanours, but still George hoped that he might be able to broker a marriage between his son and Hedvig Sophia, bringing with it all the benefits inherent in uniting Hanover with her ancestral house of Palatinate-Zweibrücken, and marital house of Holstein-Gottorp.

For Hedvig Sophia, however, there was no chance of her submitting to yet *another* marriage. She was happy with Gyllenborg and George Augustus, for all that he stood to inherit, held no interest for her whatsoever.

No matter, decided his father, there were plenty of suitable candidates available from outside Sweden, after all. Mindful of his own disastrous marriage, it was of utmost importance to him that the young man should have a chance to meet the girl in question before the plans were set in stone. This was a wise and, to be fair to George, thoughtful move. After all, the last thing Hanover needed was a repeat performance of the disastrous events seen in recent years.

In the event, the bride was not, in fact, chosen by the groom or his father but by the formidable and influential Dowager Electress Sophia of Hanover, George Augustus' grandmother. She had been aware of the orphaned Princess Caroline of Ansbach for some time and found her enchanting. The daughter of Eleonore Erdmuthe of Saxe-Eisenach and John Frederick, Margrave of Brandenburg-Ansbach, Caroline was considered fine stock. She was cultured, well-schooled, chocolate-loving and, crucially, Protestant. In fact, the Dowager Electress was *so* certain of her suitability that she urged George to do something about it, sure that the young lady would soon be snapped up by an eligible bachelor from elsewhere.

The one worry in Hanover was that Caroline would be *too* mindful of who her suitor was, and what he stood to inherit. It was vital that she be the right girl for George Augustus, not just *appearing* so in order to snare her man.

And so they hatched a cunning plan, one intended to see how Caroline would react to an overture not from a future king and elector, but from a chap with no fine titles and fortunes to his name. Sort of *The Princess and Pea*, if the pea were named George Augustus.

When a polite, attractive and cultured young gentleman by the name of Monsieur de Busch rode into Triesdorf to summer at the Ansbach court in 1705, *supposedly* nobody present knew who they *really* had in their midst. Accompanied by a small retinue of trusted friends, Monsieur de Busch was, of course, young George Augustus in disguise. His intention was simple: he and Caroline were to get to know one another without her being swayed this way or that by his real identity. Happily, the young couple fell in love and when George's true name and purpose were revealed, the engagement was on. The marriage ceremony took place in Hanover on 2 September 1705 and for the rest of her life, Caroline was to wield a subtle but enormous influence over her husband, who looked to her at every decision.

Still, this loving marriage was not enough to fulfil the young groom, who petitioned his father again and again to be allowed to go off to fight. Although he would eventually become the last British monarch to lead troops into battle, George Augustus found permission continually denied until he had provided an heir, his father quite unwilling to risk his son without someone else to take his place in line to the throne.

That longed-for heir finally came along in 1707 with the birth of Frederick, nicknamed *Fritz* by his family and, later, popularly known as *Fred*.[1] Always a sickly child, the frail and fragile boy was laid low by rickets in infancy and for parents who had struggled to conceive in the first place, this was far from ideal. At first they loved their son, though sadly they would not always, and when their relationship splintered, it was to be just one more domestic catastrophe in the history of the family. Of course, given that George Augustus had been kept from his own mother before he even reached adolescence, one might expect him to be keen to form a strong bond with his own son but sadly, the divided duty of the House of Hanover meant that this was not to be.

For now, though, George Augustus just wanted to go off to war and prove his mettle, but circumstances at home would simply not allow it. Weakened by her pregnancy, Caroline contracted smallpox and her husband refused to leave her, just as he would stay by her side many years later when she suffered through a final, horrific illness. The inevitable outcome was that George Augustus contracted smallpox too. Happily, both he and his bride

---

1. In his work, *The Four Georges*, William Makepeace Thackeray quoted the anonymous verse commemorating Frederick's death:

"Here lies Fred,
  Who was alive, and is dead,
  Had it been his father,
  I had much rather,
  Had it been his brother,
  Still better than another,
  Had it been his sister,
  No one would have missed her,
  Had it been the whole generation,
  Still better for the nation,
  But since 'tis only Fred who was alive, and is dead,
  There's no more to be said!"

Thackeray, William Makepeace (1869). *The Works of William Makepeace Thackeray: Vol XIX*. London: Smith, Elder, & Co, p.78.

were young and healthy and within the year, had fully recovered. And he *really* wanted to fight.

In 1708 George Augustus finally received permission to fight in the War of Spanish Succession and he did so with enthusiasm, distinguishing himself on the victorious field of Oudenarde, where his mount was killed beneath him. He returned home a hero to his troops, his people and his family, and celebration was order of the day. Perhaps more intimate congratulations followed the public festivities because in the five years that followed, George became a father to a trio of girls, Anne, Amelia, and Caroline.

The family would not stop growing there, yet for George Augustus, it wasn't *all* about his wife ...

Meeting the Mistress

Some years after George Augustus and Caroline of Ansbach tied the knot, fate threw another lady into the court of Hanover in the shape of the now famed Henrietta Howard. The long, twisting and often unpleasant road that brought her into the arms of the heir to the throne was far from a smooth one.

Born Henrietta Hobart in 1689, the young lady's early life was spent in the idyllic surroundings of Blickling Hall. All of that changed when, following the death of her father in a duel and her mother just three years later, Henrietta was left an orphan. She and her siblings were placed in the care of their relatives, the Earl and Countess of Suffolk, and that perfect childhood ended forever. The price for the guardianship of the Suffolks was a high one for the teenaged Henrietta, for it was decided that she would marry the earl's youngest son, Charles.

Charles was famed for his far from pleasant character, and his taste for alcohol, women and most of all gambling, which he loved above any wife. In Henrietta, however, he saw one thing that he certainly *adored*: money. In fact, there had never been much of a fortune to speak of in the first place and now, apart from her dowry, there was even less. Henrietta's money, or what was left of it after her siblings had been taken care of, was held in trust for the day she married. Then marry they must, Charles decided!

Henrietta was besotted by her fiancé but others, luckily for her, were not. Unfortunately for the scheming groom-to-be, Henrietta's uncle was a lawyer and when he learned the identity of her intended, he took immediate action. As long as she was married to Charles, the money would not be released. Instead, any children born of the marriage would inherit her remaining wealth upon her death. Whatever else might happen, Charles would never see so much as a penny.

Swiftly it became horribly apparent that Charles was no prize. Henrietta's married life was a catalogue of cruelty from which it seemed there would be no escape, even when she gave birth to a son. With their money gambled away by the dissolute Charles as quickly as it came into their hands, a desperate Henrietta began to carefully squirrel away a little here and there, hoping one day for a new start.

From her unhappy, impoverished home in England, Henrietta looked to Hanover with interest. In this faraway land she was sure that the streets might be paved with gold or, at least, with *something* better than she had. Together she and Charles decided to travel to Hanover, win the favour of the elector and, crucially, his mother, charm all with their wit, grace and effervescence and begin life anew as courtiers.

To Henrietta's horror, Charles found her travelling chest and promptly squandered its meagre contents, leaving her right back at square one. Once again, she began to save, going so far as to approach wig-makers to enquire about selling her hair to raise funds. Her straits were dire and she was left, hungry, cold and miserable as her husband lived it up in the brothels of London, the couple forced to rely on charity and even living under an assumed name to escape their creditors. One can only imagine how she must have rued that marriage and as Lord Chesterfield noted, 'Thus they loved, thus they married, and thus they hated each other for the rest of their lives.'[2]

Somehow the couple eventually reached Hanover and suddenly things seemed to get back on track. For George Augustus, Henrietta could not have appeared at a better time. He considered a royal mistress virtually a necessity of the job and was tired of people questioning just how many decisions Caroline made for him. Having a mistress might give him a little bit more of a manly reputation and restore some of the virility that some

---

2. Mahon, Lord (ed), (1845). *The Letters of Philip Dormer Stanhope, Earl of Chesterfield: Vol II*. London: Richard Bentley, p.440.

thought might be lacking. For his wife, the situation was ideal. Henrietta was discrete, trustworthy and the perfect candidate for the job. Just as she had a say in so many of her husband's decisions Caroline gave this one the nod, setting the stage for a long affair.

A Trip to England

The life of George Augustus changed forever in 1714 with the death of his grandmother, the dowager electress and then, just two months later, Queen Anne. Of course, he had known since the Act of Settlement in 1701 that his father would likely one day stand to inherit the throne of Great Britain but now that fateful day had come. In the midst of terrible storms, George I left Hanover to journey to England, where his coronation would herald the dawn of the Georgian era.

Having already established an enormous party of retainers and courtiers who would travel with him, George was keen to make this a family affair and looked to his son and daughter-in-law to join him on the journey to his new kingdom. Caroline was granted a stay of departure so that she might remain with her children a little longer but all too soon, the time had come to depart. For young Fred, there was no room on the voyage. He was left behind in the care of his grand-uncle, Ernest Augustus, Prince-Bishop of Osnabrück, the seven-year-old boy now ceremonial figurehead of the House of Hanover.

The new king and his son battled storms to sail from The Hague in September 1714 and on their arrival in England, the two Georges were finally shown to their eager and somewhat uncertain new subjects. A procession took place before an enormous crowd and the mood was fractious but celebratory, with the people keen to catch a glimpse of this new monarch from across the sea. Young George Augustus immediately endeared himself to the reception committee, showing a naturally friendly and garrulous side that his sombre father could not match. It was a definite hint of things to come and would eventually see the king enter uncharacteristically sociable new waters.

Caroline and the girls found themselves safely on English shores just a month later and among their party was a certain Henrietta Howard, now a trusted member of the household. Whether her affair with George Augustus had already begun by this point is debatable but over the years that followed, it would certainly flourish. For Caroline and George Augustus, their mind was not on reunions, but on partings and no doubt they felt the loss of young Fred now that they were so many hundreds of miles apart. This separation would, in time, lead to another fractured relationship between the menfolk of Hanover, with the bitterness that had come between George I and his son returning with a vengeance down the familial line.

The Son They Left Behind

There was nothing and nowhere that George I loved as much as Hanover and he was determined that *someone* must remain in the land of his birth to fly the ancestral flag. With his son required in England, it was left to grandson Fred to be the ceremonial representative of the family in Hanover. This might seem like quite a demand to place on one so young yet George I had every faith in the boy that he adored. After all, the new king had never *quite* seen eye to eye with his own son, which is hardly surprising given that he locked his mother away for most of her life. Rather than spend precious time trying to rebuild this crumbling bond, he decided that the easiest way forward was to shift the focus onto Fred whilst his relationship with George Augustus imploded.

With his parents safely ensconced in England, little Fred was now the most senior representative of the house on Hanoverian soil and George I lavished attention on him, ensuring he received the best possible education and preparation for his role. Time and again, his mother begged her father-in-law for permission to return to Hanover and see her son and time and again it was denied. When Caroline and George Augustus dared to raise the possibility of Fred being sent to England to join his family, George simply would not even entertain it. For fourteen long years Fred and his parents saw nothing of one another and when they met again, the boy they had last seen at seven had changed beyond recognition.

George I made regular visits to Hanover to see Fred and with each meeting his influence grew until it far outstripped that of the young man's absent parents. Eventually this resentment between father and son spilled over into an all out feud, and we'll learn later of the violent row that broke out over the christening of one of Fred's brothers and the family trouble that followed. Of course, it ended badly, with the children of George Augustus and Caroline taken into the custody of the king and kept from their parents just as George Augustus had been kept from his own mother. Still, as family relations in England fractured, in Hanover, Fred was happily living the high life.

The little boy who was left behind was learning to live without his parents and, as ceremonial figurehead of a powerful family, he was *loving* it.

A Man of Action

Fred might be having a great time as the official figurehead of the House of Hanover, but George Augustus was just as capable of living life to the full. His enthusiasm for the social whirlwind of the London court left his illustrious father in the dust. He dined in public, was a regular at the theatre and attended any glittering occasion he could fit into his packed diary. He was the toast of the town, his reputation as a man of fun increasing with every passing day. At home, things really couldn't be better and the Prince and Princess of Wales lived a settled and happy domestic life with their children, a world away from the misery of his mother and father all those years ago in Hanover.

The role of George Augustus was not confined to the ceremonial and, in the early years of George I's reign, he served as Guardian and Lieutenant of the Realm on the occasions when his father wished to leave the country. The more the public got to know of George Augustus, the more they liked him. Perceived as a man of the people, his popularity soared and whether he was dining in public or meeting his subjects, George Augustus was greeted with cheers of welcome.

No doubt to the irritation of his father, it began to seem as though George Augustus could not put a foot wrong. Sociable and fun, he even proved himself an action man when he helped to extinguish fires in the city as well as a philanthropist happy to donate money to the victims of another fire who had lost their property and livelihoods. However, the prince *really* proved his mettle in 1716 when he took a trip to Drury Lane Theatre and an encounter with a would-be assassin proved a real PR coup.

With the prince looking forward to nothing more dramatic than a little light entertainment, a man by the name of Francis Freeman had other ideas. He arrived at Drury Lane armed with a gun and attempted to force an entry into the prince's box, wounding a member of his guard in the process; reports appear to disagree on whether the wound proved fatal. All around him erupted into panic yet as a bullet flew past, George Augustus remained calm and the would-be assassin was apprehended. George I was not in England at the time of the attack but the public were proud of their prince, wondering how such a stiff and austere man as the king could have such a cheery, lighthearted son.

Detained for his crime, labelled a madman by the press and imprisoned in Newgate, it later came to light that his attempt on the life of George Augustus might not have been Freeman's only misdemeanour after all. In July 1717 his name was once again in the papers and just as it was at Drury Lane, his crime was a violent one.

Now an inmate of Marshalsea, Freeman had been placed on trial for a murder committed in Surrey, before his Drury Lane excursion. The report notes that he was a lunatic, and his defence for this killing was a *very* singular one:

'[Freeman] told the Court, like a Lunatick as he is, That his Family had a Patent from King James I to pardon all Murders they had committed, or that any of their Descendants should commit for the future.'[3]

Sadly, Freeman disappears from the record at this point, his story apparently ending in the unhappy confines of Marshalsea.

Domestic Discord

George Augustus might have survived the attempt on his life, but the deathblow to the relationship between king and prince was finally dealt in 1717. Already at loggerheads on matters political, at home, things were growing increasingly strained. For now at least, the two Georges were still

---

3. *Weekly Packet* (London, England), August 10, 1717 – August 17, 1717; issue 267, p.1.

on speaking terms but even *that* wouldn't last. The final straw came courtesy of what really ought to have been a happy event, accompanying as it did the birth of Prince George William, son of Caroline and George Augustus. Although the little boy lived for just a few months, the events of his birth and christening caused a ruction that echoed on for years.

With the birth of the infant prince, Great Britain rejoiced and the royal family celebrated. His christening was to be conducted in his mother's bedchamber under the auspices of no less a man than William Wake, Archbishop of Canterbury.

So far, so good, but the king couldn't resist the temptation to get involved, and on two matters he was determined to get his way: names and godparents.

Perhaps unsurprisingly, given the fact that *he* was a George and his son was a George, the king decided that there was only one name suitable for a royal boy – *George*.

This particular monicker was not on the shortlist assembled by his new parents but they duly conceded defeat and agreed to take the name. This victory no doubt led the king to believe that he was on a winning streak and he moved straight onto the matter of godparents.

For his money, the *only* people for the job were himself, of course, as well as Thomas Pelham-Holles, 1st Duke of Newcastle, and Diana Beauclerk, Duchess of St Albans. Caroline and George Augustus weren't so sure and proposed a compromise. They were keen to invite the child's paternal great-uncle, Ernest Augustus, Duke of York and Albany, to be godfather and wondered whether Newcastle might serve as proxy for him. The king would have none of *that*. There was to be *no* compromise and no alternative would do. Of course, George got his way and Newcastle was given the prestigious role.

The hot-tempered George Augustus and the ambitious, unctuous duke didn't get on so trouble was inevitable. A confrontation at the baptism ended in raised voices and, according to Newcastle, a threat to his life. The duke maintained that the Prince of Wales had challenged him to a duel and the king duly believed him. George Augustus denied Newcastle's claims, suggesting that perhaps his German accent had meant that the unwanted godparent either misheard or misunderstood a more innocent comment. The prince *did* point out that Newcastle should have refused the king's invitation to serve as godfather either way, since he *knew* that it went against the wishes of the newborn's parents even if the king had wanted it. Still, George Augustus shrugged, what was done was done and even if he was not happy about it, there was no way he had threatened *anyone* to a duel.

The king had other ideas and as a result of the duke's mischievous or, at best, mistaken claim, the Prince of Wales was told to leave St James's Palace and not return. Just in case some courtiers hoped to remain in the favour of both parties, he also made it known that any who chose the company of the prince over the king were likewise to become persona non grata at court. When the Princess of Wales chose to go into exile with her husband their children remained in the care of the king, leaving Caroline utterly distraught and desperate enough to chance secret visits to the palace to see them. Eventually George thawed a *little* and Caroline was given limited access to the youngsters, though George Augustus was not afforded the same privilege.

Imagine then the horror with which the parents greeted the news that their newborn son, George William, was gravely ill. The king finally decreed that the anxious parents could spend as much time with their ailing child as they wished, but the days were painfully scant. George William died at just three-months-old and the following extract from the *Daily Courant* gives an indication of the comings and goings that accompanied his final days.

'His Highness the Young Prince George William, Son of their Royal Highnesses, departed this Life on Thursday Night about Eight a-Clock at Kensington, whither, upon Advice of the Physicians, his Majesty thought fit to send him on Wednesday. Her Royal Highness the Princess of Wales was also with him at St. James's on Wednesday, and also at Kensington the same Day; and both their Royal Highnesses went thither on Thursday and remain'd with the young Prince till he died.'[4]

Grieving for the death of their youngest child, Caroline and George Augustus retreated to their home once more, still unable to bring their other children with them. It would take the near-fatal brush with smallpox of their daughter, Anne, to see their access to them improve.

---

4. *Daily Courant* (London, England), Saturday, February 8, 1718; issue 5087, p.2.

With all that had passed between father and son, the king and the Prince of Wales were no longer simply, *not getting along*; they were now *bitterly* at odds whilst in Hanover, another intrigue was brewing.

The Uneasy Peace

If George Augustus could oppose his father in anything, he did. In his alternative court at Leicester House he gathered opposition politicians to his cause yet he could never hope to command the authority or influence of his father. But he had his allies, namely Robert Walpole, who was as ambitious and Machiavellian as ever, and worked hard to ingratiate himself with Caroline.

Walpole was a seemingly permanent fixture at Leicester House and recognized the influence Caroline wielded over her husband. The king's health was not what it had been, Walpole knew, realizing that it was just a matter of time before George Augustus would become George II. With that in mind, it would surely do no harm to ensure that he was on the right side of *both* Georges and in prime position to make the best of whatever the coming years might bring.

As stubborn as ever, the king was not doing much to help the tense relationship that existed between him and his son. Still he would not release the children to live with their parents and during his trips abroad, there was no question that he would allow George Augustus to serve as regent. On the second of these points he was immovable, but on the first, Walpole suggested, there might be *some* room for manoeuvre. Indeed, should the pair reconcile, he might even be able to convince Parliament to settle the prince's rather *extensive* debts.

It was this that really made George Augustus sit up and take notice. He agreed to apologize to his father though he would *not* return to live at St James's Palace, even if it were the last place left on earth. In reply, George refused all Caroline's petitions to return her children to her care and even Walpole's considerable powers of persuasion would not budge him. Still, with Walpole at the helm, an uneasy peace was negotiated between father and son that, whilst still not awarding any regent powers to George Augustus, *would* ensure that the children could return to the custody of their parents. It took a near tragedy to make this dream come true.

In 1720, 10-year-old Princess Anne contracted smallpox and fell dangerously ill. Happily, the little girl survived the often-fatal infection and her experience would later pave the way for her mother to play her own part in popularizing the lifesaving treatment of variolation.[5] Perhaps realizing how close his son and daughter-in-law had come to losing yet another child, the king finally relented and gave the couple free rein to see their children, much to the relief of both the prince and princess.

His job done and his influence clear to all, Walpole was no doubt delighted with the outcome of what might have been a tragic turn of events. Now George Augustus was left to watch Walpole climb the political ladder, the rungs built on the reunion he had negotiated between king and prince. For the ambitious, ruthless politician, it was nothing personal, it was only politics. For the Prince of Wales, it was a clear sign that Walpole was one to keep a *very* keen eye on when he finally sat on the throne.

A Happy Interlude

With the birth of Prince William, Duke of Cumberland, in 1721, Fred's place in the heart of his parents was finally and irrevocably supplanted. Already indelibly associated with the father George Augustus hated, the king wielded Fred's upbringing as a weapon. Fred had become an instrument of George I, subjected to his malign influence and raised according to his wishes. William, however, was the boy that they craved and they were determined not to lose him to the king.

In time the prince and princess's adoration of the younger boy would grow so complete that George Augustus, when king, went on to make enquiries about splitting his domains. However, unlike George I, he did not do so in the understanding that both realms would be adequately governed, but so he could somehow find a way of disinheriting Fred, the son he hated.

---

5. The practice of variolation involved taking a tiny amount of smallpox-infected tissue and introducing it into the body of a healthy patient. The result was a very mild infection and, subsequently, immunity. The Princess of Wales encountered variolation in the writings of Lady Mary Wortley Montagu and eventually had all of her children variolated by Charles Maitland, a Scottish surgeon whom Lady Mary had met in Turkey, where the practice was common.

With their children once more in their care, the Prince and Princess of Wales added two more daughters to the household, Mary and Louisa. The prince, meanwhile, devoted more time to hobbies such as hunting and less to politics. He looked on disillusioned as Walpole's power grew, unchecked and undisputed, sure that he had once been a pawn in that meteoric rise. George Augustus shouldn't have felt too angry at himself though, few were those who could dare to take on Robert Walpole, fewer still those who might do so and emerge victorious.

At home, things were settled and George Augustus was finally enjoying something of a peaceful interlude. Reunited with the majority of his children and caring for his family, he was also enjoying the company of both wife *and* mistress.

Long since promoted to the role of Woman of the Bedchamber to the Princess of Wales, Henrietta Howard was tending to far more intimate matters on behalf of Caroline's husband. She had made something of an impact on George Augustus during those first meetings in Hanover and, with the blessing of the princess, it was inevitable that she would become mistress to the Prince of Wales.

For over a decade, Henrietta and George were a couple, and Caroline appears to have been perfectly satisfied with their setup. For Henrietta, the arrangement was a world away from her brutish husband and had saved her bacon when all seemed lost. There was no real grand passion between George Augustus and Henrietta or, if there was, as the years passed it understandably faded into companionable affection. What there *was*, however, was the security she had sought all her life, from her early years as an orphan to the moment she made the disastrous decision to marry the cruel and dissolute Charles, the man who had misused and abused her at every opportunity.

With a husband like Charles, Henrietta was not a cheap mistress. It cost George Augustus over a thousand pounds a year to keep Charles from making a fuss about the fate of his wife, yet for the lady, it was a price beyond value. She was free at last of the man she loathed, though being mistress to a king brought with it new challenges. With Caroline's loyalty to Walpole no secret, it was Henrietta who seemed to attract those who sought to influence the prince without going through his wife and as the years passed and he became king, those who looked to Henrietta for a nod, a word in the monarch's ear, only increased in volume. Henrietta, however, was nothing if not discrete and though Caroline pulled rank just a little by making her servant kneel as she performed her toilette, the princess had no interest in ending the affair. Besides, Henrietta's influence over her lover was not *nearly* so great as his wife's and as the wags who penned a rather cheeky poem knew, it was an open secret.[6]

Whilst George and Henrietta settled down, Fred was doing anything but. Treated to the best of everything by his grandfather, Fred was not slow to make the most of his influence and privilege. Tutored in the liberal arts, by the time he was in his teens Fred was already indulging in the sort of behaviour that would no doubt turn his parents grey. He drank, gambled and wenched with abandon, gaining quite a reputation as a high-roller in Hanover, a stranger to those who had left him behind.

Yet just as George I and George Augustus battled, the simmering resentment between George Augustus and Fred would soon burst into flame, for a death was on the horizon …

Walpole's Ruse

On 11 June 1727, George I died in Hanover and his only son, George Augustus, became George II, King of Great Britain and Ireland.

In some ways, the death of his father would have certainly been a weight lifted for the new monarch, removing the wilful and troublesome parent who had blighted so many of his years. Although the ill-fated Sophia Dorothea of

---

6. The verse, which angered George *enormously* when he heard it, went as follows:

You may strut, dapper George, but 'twill all be in vain;
We all know 'tis Queen Caroline, not you, that reign –
You govern no more than Don Philip of Spain.
Then if you would have us fall down and adore you,
Lock up your fat spouse, as your dad did before you.

Hervey, John and Croker, John Wilson (ed.), (1848). *Memoirs of the Reign of George the Second: Vol I*. London: John Murray, p.93.

Celle had died the previous year, now her portraits were once more returned to palace walls from which she had long been absent.

It was Walpole who broke the news to the new king and for this political titan, no doubt, it must have seemed like the end was nigh for his illustrious career. Despite his wife's love of Walpole, George had come to prefer the prime minister's colleague, Spencer Compton, later 1st Earl of Wilmington, and made no secret of the fact.

Hervey paints quite the picture of the early days of the new king's reign, turning his shrewd eye upon what the future might now hold for Walpole. Like the man himself, they reckoned his days were numbered but they had not counted on the freshly-minted queen's devotion to her most canny ally.

> 'The King stayed four days in town [after his father's death], during which period Leicester House, which used to be a desert, was thronged from morning to night like the 'Change at noon. But Sir Robert Walpole walked through these rooms as if they had been empty; his presence, that used to make a crowd wherever he appeared, now emptied every corner he turned to, and the same people who were officiously a week ago clearing the way to flatter his prosperity were now getting out of it to avoid sharing his disgrace.'[7]

With Compton the obvious choice to be named First Lord of the Treasury, he made what would prove to be a fatal error. His first duty was to write a speech for the king and, lacking confidence or experience or perhaps both, Compton approached Walpole and asked if he might help with the composition. Ever the helpful pal, Walpole set to work on the speech yet quite by *accident* included a passage that the king found unpalatable.

Compton whisked the speech away to George, who requested an amendment, leaving the politician floundering. He had not written the speech, of course, so had no idea of how to amend it and just like that, things began to turn sour. Walpole was summoned and Compton, in a monumental moment of misjudgement, sent him in to see the king and argue the virtues of the speech *he* had written and Walpole was quick to galvanize his position.

---

7. Ibid., p.37.

Not content with undermining Compton, Walpole produced another ruse from up his immaculately tailored sleeve in the form of money. He dangled an enormous financial settlement before the nose of the new king that Compton simply could not hope to match. Should Compton take the role on offer, then the king would lose not only the allowance, but the immense influence Walpole wielded in Parliament. The devastated Compton had no choice but to step down and though he would later serve in this role fifteen years later[8], he never forgave Walpole for undermining his earlier opportunity.

Now George finally left his sanctuary at Leicester House and took up residence in St James's Palace, the place from which he had been banished whilst Prince of Wales. The courtiers who had been loyal to the errant prince came with him to form the bedrock of the court, with Henrietta Howard now the most powerful mistress in the land. Finally able to lay his father's wish to split the succession to rest once and for all, George seized a copy of the late king's will from the Archbishop of Canterbury's hand and made sure it was *never* seen again. The known copies that existed in Europe conveniently disappeared and eyebrows were raised all over the continent at this strange turn of events.

At the time, those who believed that the late king would have left them *something* had no doubt that his son had suppressed the will to avoid paying out the bequests therein. In fact, George's intention was to silence his father's enquiries about splitting the succession which favoured the hated Fred.

Whilst intrigues might have been bubbling over privately, in public things were very different. It was time for a party and the royal family was about to put on a *heck* of a coronation show.

Dripping in finery and jewels, when George and Caroline's procession to Westminster Abbey snaked past the thousands who had gathered to watch, it took almost two hours to complete. The traditional ceremony at the abbey did undergo some modernization, the chief change being the premiere of the now legendary strains of George Frideric Handel's *Coronation Anthems*[9].

---

8. Compton became prime minister in February 1742, his time in office ending with his death in July 1743.

9. The anthems were heard in the following order: *Let Thy Hand Be Strengthened* opened the proceedings, followed by *Zadok the Priest* and then *The King Shall Rejoice*. *My Heart is Inditing* was the final anthem, performed to accompany the queen's coronation.

The day was one of immense, expensive celebration, and no one was happier about it than the newly-crowned king.

Of course, the House of Hanover was never happy for long …

Trouble at Home

Under the stewardship of George II, the court that had once been so staid and quiet now rang to the sounds of cheer and socializing. Whilst the public approved of this far more personable king and his entourage, in his tell-all memoirs the waspish courtier, Lord Hervey, had *plenty* to say about life in the heart of the inner circle.

Hervey paints a picture of life at the court of St James's as uncouth, dull and characterized by the sort of compulsive routine that George II adored. With little interest in cultural pursuits beyond the theatre, the king was grumpy and ill-humoured, given to swearing and fits of temper and domestic disputes with family and court alike. The temperamental Sovereign would kick his wig around his apartments when angered, descending into fits of temper better suited to a petulant child than a middle-aged monarch.

He had a mania for order, with everything from clothes to mistresses having their appointed place and hour. When it came to the household and money, his was a very keen eye, sometimes to the point of absurdity.

> 'One evening, as the page was carrying some money to be deposited in an iron chest which the King kept in a closet near his bed-room, the bag burst, and one guinea rolled under the door of a recess where some fire-wood was piled. […] "We must find it now [the king said]; set down that bag there, and assist me in removing the wood." The page obeyed and to work they went: when, after toiling about twenty minutes, the guinea was found.'[10]

Hervey remembers a comical episode in which the queen's domestic schemes were the target of that temper. Having spent some time ruminating on the

---

10. Lloyd, Hannibal Evans, (1830). *George IV.: Memoirs of His Life and Reign, Interspersed with Numerous Personal Anecdotes.* London: Treuttel and Würtz, p.lxxxvi.

king's artworks at Kensington Palace, Caroline decided that she really didn't rate her husband's taste. With Hervey's assistance, she exchanged a number of paintings for canvasses that both she and her favourite decided were far better than the original decor.

Upon his return, the king was horrified and demanded that the original artworks be restored. Ever wielding the wooden spoon, Hervey decided to make his case to the queen but George would have none of it and erupted.

'"Would your Majesty", said Lord Hervey, "have the gigantic fat Venus[11] restored too?"

'"Yes, my Lord; I am not so nice as your Lordship, I like my fat Venus much better than anything you have given me instead of her." […] Lord Hervey told the Queen, next morning at breakfast, what had passed the night before, who affected to laugh, but was a good deal displeased, and more ashamed. […] Whilst they were speaking the King came in, but, by good luck said not one word of the pictures: his Majesty stayed about five minutes in the gallery; snubbed the Queen, who was drinking chocolate, for being always stuffing; the Princess Emily for not hearing him; the Princess Caroline for being grown fat; the Duke [of Cumberland] for standing awkwardly; Lord Hervey for not knowing what relation the Prince of Sultzbach was to the Elector Palatine: and then carried the Queen to walk, and be resnubbed, in the garden.'[12]

Of course, with George's accession to the throne a vacancy had opened up for a new Prince of Wales and into the breach stepped Fred, who was still living it up over in Hanover. When Fred was summoned to England to join a family who were little more than strangers to him, the 21-year-old had no choice but to obey. Elsewhere in this volume we have heard of the abandoned scheme to marry Fred to his cousin, Wilhelmine of Prussia, but the young

---

11. The "fat Venus" is Vasari's 1543 work, *Venus and Cupid*.
12. Hervey, John and Croker, John Wilson (ed.), (1848). *Memoirs of the Reign of George the Second: From his Accession to the Death of Queen Caroline, Vol II*. London: John Murray, pp.34–35.

man might not have been called from Hanover *quite* so urgently in 1728 were it not for an ill-judged ploy that went a long way to ending his prospective relationship with Wilhelmine once and for all.

In the cut and thrust of the royal marriage mart, one thing that was utterly forbidden was for either party to directly initiate contact or any liaison with the other. The impatient Fred was never one for protocol and instead of waiting, he employed his own envoy to visit the Prussian court and let them know that he was most taken with the idea of marriage. He was frustrated with the apparent delays his parents were causing in negotiating the union but to send word directly to Wilhelmine's family was a shocking breach of royal marriage protocol. The king demanded his son join him in England without delay, where he might better be able to keep an eye on his troublesome offspring.

The journey to England was long, rough and dangerous but eventually Fred arrived to find himself thrust into a new land with little celebration. There was no grand reception, no formal ceremony, just a low-key arrival to meet parents who barely knew their child and siblings who didn't much relish being usurped by this stranger.

Still, being championed by George I had left Fred with an unshakeable sense of his own worth and a self confidence that would prove *very* useful now he was in somewhat hostile domestic lands. In London the newly-created Prince of Wales found a whole new sorority of young ladies with whom to fraternize, new opportunities to gamble and new ways to annoy the parents that he had not seen in well over a decade. Though his mother hadn't *quite* developed the loathing of her eldest son that she would later exhibit, his father wasn't keen on him from the very beginning and it was only going to get worse.

Fred lived life to the full and in Georgian London that called for money and plenty of it. Just as George III would later engage in an ongoing war over finance with his own eldest son, so too did George II and the debt-ridden Fred begin to battle over cash, politics and everything in between. History repeated itself again when George II, whose father denied him the right to serve as regent, did exactly the same thing to Fred, handing power to Caroline whenever he was called overseas.

It was not long after he arrived in England that Fred met a man who would become one of his closest friends and, later, one of his greatest enemies.

This was the waspish and indiscrete Baron Hervey, a surprising favourite of the queen who would later publish a brutal court memoir. Hervey was famously bisexual and though historians have not been able to prove once and for all whether the two men were lovers, it is certainly not impossible. Intriguingly, though Hervey pulled no *other* punches when his memoirs were published, the pages that dealt with his early relationship with Fred were removed from the manuscript by the baron. We will never know just how intimate they became but artistically, they were well-matched. The two friends even collaborated on a disastrous theatrical endeavour[13] together that met with derision from both the paying public and the theatre manager at Drury Lane.

Despite Fred's ill-chosen decision to send his envoy to Prussia, the marriage negotiations continued to rumble on and on. With all parties keen to conclude matters, Colonel Charles Hotham was engaged to serve as envoy to the Hohenzollern court and ensure that, according to his employer's wishes, 'both marriages or none' would take place. However, Frederick William, whilst still amenable to a marriage between Wilhelmine and Fred, felt that Crown Prince Frederick, his son, was still too young to be wed to Princess Amelia. Perhaps in a decade or so they might revisit the proposition, he mused, but for now he could not and would not consent.

Although the Prussian court delighted in the idea of Wilhelmine and Fred's marriage, without the promised union of Amelia and the crown prince, all celebrations were put on hold. Obstinate, determined and certain that his wishes should not be undermined, George would not be swayed. His heart heavy, Colonel Hotham declared his endeavours in vain; concurrent with the king's demands of two marriages or none, it was to be the latter. Even now the apparently lovesick Fred clung to the hope that things might change – heartsore and desperate to marry the girl he had never even met. Poor old Hotham was not yet freed from his obligation in Prussia and the talks, already ground into the dust, continued.

Perhaps happily for Hotham's nerves, the final straw came when Frederick William made a demand that George simply would not sanction: he agreed to both weddings on condition that Fred be made regent in

---

13. Fred wrote under the pseudonym, *Captain Bodkin*.

Hanover. There was simply *no* way that George would consent to such a request and all negotiations and prospective marriages were called off once and for all. Wilhelmine soon found another husband[14] and for Fred, the grand passion that had consumed him since his formative years dwindled swiftly away to nothing. After all, there were *plenty* more courtly fish in the sea.

The collapse of the marriage plans fostered by the late George I did nothing to endear his successor and Fred to one another. Just like his own father after his banishment from St James's Palace, Fred established an alternative court at which opposing views could be loudly aired. He actively campaigned against his father's government and perhaps more than anything else, it was this that struck the hammer blow to his relationship with his parents. This gathering of opposition figures was a direct challenge to the authority of his mother's treasured ally, Walpole, with whom it was widely believed that Caroline ruled both the country and the will of the king. When she served as regent, it was Walpole whom she credited with guiding her through occasionally troubled waters so when Fred didn't share her adoration of her favourite, the queen had no intention of choosing son over prime minister.

For Fred, all of this was strictly business. His lifestyle didn't come cheap and he needed to offset his mounting debts. If the king and Parliament wouldn't pay up, then he needed political leverage from somewhere and his friendship with opposition movers and shakers provided this in spades. It was also *very* useful for winding up the parents …

The Search for a Princess

If George II was at least discrete with his affections and his mistresses, without any real supervision in Hanover, Fred had grown to *adore* women. Like so many men of the era, the young prince wasn't averse to paying for their attentions either or frequenting the less salubrious parts of town. However, not all of Fred's liaisons were with ladies of the night and he acquired mistresses with a zeal that George IV would no doubt approve of.

---

14. Wilhelmine married Frederick, Margrave of Brandenburg-Bayreuth in 1731.

By now Prince of Wales, Fred entered into a relationship with one particular mistress who was nowhere *near* exclusive and he shared her affections with his best friend, Hervey. She was Anne Vane, a lady in waiting to the queen who was, to put it mildly, rather generous with her favours. She was also the cousin of Fred's secretary and when she gave birth to a son, FitzFrederick Cornwall Vane, in 1732, the already fractious friendship between Hervey and Fred ended forever. Once closer than brothers, the two had already seen politics and ambition drive a wedge between them, and doubt over the child's paternity was the final straw. The queen, doubtful of her son's fertility thanks to his childhood frailty, believed Hervey to be the father of the boy, but the already debt-ridden prince wouldn't hear of setting his mistress aside.

Instead, Fred threw money at Anne with abandon and set her up in a house in Grosvenor Square despite the incredulity of polite society, all of whom supposed Hervey or even one of a few *other* prospective candidates to be the baby's father. Although both child and mother would live for only a few more years[15], Fred's stubborn attachment to Anne was the final straw for Hervey. He cut his friend off once and for all, turning instead to his allegiance with Caroline and embracing the powerful Walpole faction.

By this time, the Prince of Wales was no longer a boy and though he stood in line to inherit the throne, if he could not find a bride and produce an heir, then one day that same throne would likely be warmed by the bottom of the favoured son, William. Perhaps Fred wasn't that concerned by the prospect and the very idea of it certainly pleased his parents, but to the eligible ladies of Europe, the bachelor prince looked like a very tempting prize.

From her position of high society influence, Sarah, Duchess of Marlborough, regarded Fred with appraising eyes. He would, she was sure, make a perfect match with her beautiful and highly eligible granddaughter, Lady Diana Spencer. Even better, Diana's already considerable selling points were complemented by an eye-watering dowry of a hundred thousand pounds. Fred needed the cash and the duchess fancied the prestige but she had reckoned without Walpole, a political sparring partner of old.

---

15. In 1733 Anne gave birth to a daughter by Fred who was named Amelia and lived for just a day. FitzFrederick died in February 1736, with Anne's death following in March of the same year.

When Walpole's informants told him that secret marriage plans were afoot, he went straight to the king and queen with only one mission in mind: to end the scheme once and for all. His argument was as measured and irrefutable as ever, and he urged them not to rush, counselling the couple to think again on the wisdom of contracting this marriage when there were so many eligible continental royal ladies, with all the influence abroad they could bring with them, just waiting for a husband. Listening as ever to the counsel of this most trusted advisor, George and Caroline vetoed the marriage and both Fred and Diana[16] were back on the market.

Of course, centuries later, another Lady Diana Spencer would become famed as the Princess of Wales, but that is a tale for another time!

'A deaf, peevish old beast'

In 1731, Henrietta Howard's station both in marriage and at court changed when her dissolute husband, from whom she had become legally separated in 1728, became the ninth Earl of Suffolk. Now a Countess, Henrietta was accordingly promoted to the position of Mistress of the Robes, meaning that she no longer had to kneel before the queen's toilette!

While Caroline was not exactly hostile to Henrietta, the two women were never friends and no doubt as Henrietta knelt before her imperious mistress, she was thinking one or two less than noble thoughts of her own. Still, this new role as Mistress of the Robes gave Henrietta more free time and she dreamed of retreating to a new life, which she would eventually realize when she established her own household in her beloved home of Marble Hill. Here she would finally get her fairytale happy ending, but there were a few trials to face before she got there!

Henrietta was growing tired of life at court and longed to be free of both her lover and mistress. After years serving the royal household, she was keen to please herself and, perhaps, that time was nearly upon her. Popular with all who knew her and virtually a fixture in the royal palaces, Henrietta's role in her royal lover's life had changed too and not for the better. Over the

---

16. In 1731, Diana married Lord John Russell and in 1732, the couple became Duke and Duchess of Bedford. The Duchess of Bedford died of tuberculosis in 1735, aged just 25.

years, George and Henrietta had become more like brother and sister, with Henrietta bearing the brunt of George's hot temper. She was a convenient buffer between the ever-plumper queen and her husband, receiving him to her apartments not for passionate assignations, but for conversation and company that often tumbled into arguments.

Once glad of the protection George could offer from her husband, now Henrietta was tired of her station and lamented: 'I have been a Slave 20 years without ever receiving a reason for any one thing I ever was obliged to do.'[17]

Henrietta's fatigue and George's dying enthusiasm for their relationship rang alarm bells for the queen. They must have sounded even more loudly when, as the 1730s dawned, the king withdrew more and more from Henrietta's company.

For Caroline, this was far from ideal. After all, Henrietta was a case of 'better the devil you know', and any new mistress might prove far more troublesome to her than this lady ever had. Likewise, it was no secret that Henrietta's attachment to her royal patron stemmed partially from the protection he offered against Charles, who had even succeeding in turning her only son against her. However, when her loathsome husband died just two years later, Henrietta approached the queen and asked to be released from her duties.

Of course, Caroline was in no mood to let her servant go without a fight. She told Henrietta that she had only imagined George's coolness and that the court was her home. Like a parent desperate to prevent their child from flying the nest the queen tried to reason with Henrietta. Only when she seemed destined to fail did Caroline turn to her husband.

If Caroline expected George to fight to keep Henrietta at court, she was to be sadly mistaken. Instead he railed against his wife, roaring; 'What the devil did you mean by trying to make an old, dull, deaf, peevish beast stay and plague me when I had so good an opportunity of getting rid of her?'[18]

The king was happy to release Henrietta from her role and, with a sigh of relief, she stepped out to enjoy life as a woman with *no* obligations. So

---

17. Borman, Tracy (2010). *King's Mistress, Queen's Servant: The Life and Times of Henrietta Howard*. London: Random House, p.174.
18. Hervey, John and Croker, John Wilson (ed.), (1848). *Memoirs of the Reign of George the Second: From his Accession to the Death of Queen Caroline, Vol II*. London: John Murray, p.179.

significant was her departure from court that mention of it could be found in the press, where regular updates were posted regarding developments in the domestic situation of the Countess of Suffolk and her vacated office in the royal household.

> 'Tuesday the Countess of Suffolk, one of the Ladies of her Majesty's Bed-Chamber, resign'd her Employ, and soon after retired from her Apartments in the Royal Palace, to her Brother, Lord Hobart's, in St. James's-Square.
>
> The Countess of Tankerville is appointed to succeed the Countess of Suffolk in her Place of Mistress of the Robes to her Majesty.'[19]

As George bade his retiring mistress farewell, Henrietta happily retreated to Marble Hill. A quarter of a century later the couple would meet again when they passed in a city street, yet George barely glanced her way. Just days from death, the king didn't deliberately ignore the woman who had shared his life for two decades, he didn't even recognize her.

What though, of the promised fairytale ending?

> 'The Hon. George Berkeley, Esq; is with his new married lady, the Countess Dowager of Suffolk, gone for a few Days to Cranford, the Earl of Berkeley's Seat near Hounslow.'[20]

That happy ending came courtesy of her long-time friend, Member of Parliament, George Berkeley. The marriage surprised everyone and eyebrows were raised as the court tried and failed to find a cynical reason for the union. Perhaps, though, the motive behind the match was simply love. Berkeley's sister, Lady Elizabeth Germain, certainly believed that to be the case. She wrote to Jonathan Swift of her hopes for the new couple and one cannot doubt that her words are honest, if tinged with a good-natured sisterly threat:

---

19. *London Evening Post* (London, England), Tuesday, November 12, 1734; issue 1090, p.1.
20. *Old Whig or The Consistent Protestant* (London, England), Thursday, July 24, 1735; issue 20, p.2.

'… he [George Berkeley] hath appeared to all the world, as well as me, to have long had (that is, ever since she hath been a widow, so pray don't mistake me) a most violent passion for her, as well as esteem and value for her numberless good qualities. These things well considered, I do not think they have above ten to one against their being very happy; and if they should not be so, I shall heartily wish him hanged because I am sure it will be wholly his fault.'[21]

George and Henrietta lived a blissful life, but it was to prove tragically short. Berkeley lived for only eleven years after the marriage yet they were the happiest days of Henrietta's life, the career of this celebrated mistress finally at an end.[22]

A Game of Mistresses and Ladders

As Henrietta settled into her happy new life as a lady of leisure, the king was once again in his homeland of Hanover. It was here that he had his head turned by a lady named Amalie von Wallmoden, who soon began to seem like the perfect candidate to take the place of the recently retired Countess of Suffolk.

Amalie was the niece of a certain Melusine von der Schulenberg, the bird-loving mistress who had been George I's wife in all but name. Rumours even persisted that her grandmother had been a close friend and maybe more to the first King George in his teens,[23] so Amalie was well-versed in the ways and history of Hanoverian mistresses. Still, so far at least, Amalie had kept herself out of royal beds.

That was about to change.

Next to the queen, who grew ever plumper as she indulged her love for chocolate and the finer things in life, Amalie was a glamorous specimen.

21. Swift, Jonathan and Hawkesworth, John (1737). *Letters, Written by Jonathan Swift: Vol III*. London: A Pope, pp.76–77.
22. Henrietta died in 1767; her son, with whom she never reconciled, predeceased her in 1745.
23. Thompson, Andrew C,(2011). *George II: King and Elector*. New Haven: Yale University press, p.113.

More than two decades the junior of the royal couple, Amalie dazzled the king on their first meeting in 1735 and their attraction was instant and mutual.

Amalie had been married to Gottlieb Adam von Wallmoden since 1727 yet this did not stop her embarking on a passionate affair with George that resulted in the birth of Johann Ludwig von Wallmoden in 1736[24].

George fell so heavily for Amalie that one might almost suspect he was a little bit blinded by his passion. Hervey recounts a farcical episode in which a ladder was found propped at Amalie's window and a man, presumed to be a thief, was discovered lurking in nearby bushes. Fearing that her lover might *mistakenly* suspect her of some sort of illicit liaison behind his back, Amalie raced by dawn's first light to the king's residence and threw herself on his mercy. In tears she told him of the ladder, the man and the scandal that she was sure would arise, painting herself as the victim in a jealous and spiteful plot.

George, of course, wiped away his mistress's tears and soothed her troubled brow, but the story was soon the talk of the court. With the support of the king, Amalie's reputation was safe but whom and what was behind that ladder was never really sufficiently explained. Perhaps it *was* a cynical plot to discredit Amalie, perhaps a robbery or perhaps, dare one suggest, she was about to receive a late night visit from a secret paramour?

Hervey notes in his memoirs a few more theories, yet he does not deign to suggest which one strikes *him* as most likely:

'Some people in England thought, but I believe without foundation, that Horace Walpole had a hand in this ladder affair, in order to ruin Madame Walmoden, [sic] and make his court to the Queen. Others said that Monsieur Schulemberg [the chap found lurking in the bushes] had an intrigue with Madame Walmoden's chambermaid; others, that the ladder belonged to the garden, and that one of the workmen had placed it where it was found by accident: what the truth was, I know not; but it had not the effect of weakening Madame

---

24. Johann died in 1811. A noted collector of antiquities, he was an important figure in the world of European art and bequeathed part of his collection to George III.

Walmoden's interest in the King, who continued as fond of her as ever.'[25]

So taken was George with this new mistress that he came up with ever more reasons to visit Hanover. Unlike Henrietta, she was young and a novelty, and the fact that he could still father a robust son despite being in his 50s just puffed out George's chest all the more. Each new absence did little for his popularity back home, though Caroline's fortitude did wonders for *her* standing in the eyes of their subjects.

The public now began to view their king's regular and prolonged jaunts to Hanover with open contempt. As George galavanted on the continent, playing at happy families, wags posted a notice on the gates of St James's Palace:

'Lost or strayed out of this house, a man who has left a wife and six children on the parish. Whoever will give any tidings of him to the churchwardens of St James's parish, so as he may be got again, shall receive *four shillings and sixpence* reward.

N.B. This reward will not be increased, nobody judging him to deserve a crown.'[26]

In fact, it was one of these trips abroad that gave Fred the chance to demonstrate exactly how fractured the relationship with his parents had become. Caroline would not speak to her son and George thought it best to simply pretend he didn't exist, yet things were about to get far, far worse.

When the king was caught in a storm and apparently lost at sea whilst returning from a trip to Hanover, Fred spread a gleeful rumour that his father was dead. A shockwave sounded through the court and Caroline was beside herself, half believing that she was already a widow. In the absence of evidence that her husband was truly dead, the queen held onto the reins of

25. Hervey, John and Croker, John Wilson (ed.), (1848). *Memoirs of the Reign of George the Second: From his Accession to the Death of Queen Caroline, Vol II.* London: John Murray, p.127.

26. Kiste, John van der (2013). *King George II and Queen Caroline.* Stroud: The History Press, p.159.

power even as Fred allowed himself to dream that the throne was within his grasp. In fact, the king was far from dead and was suffering from nothing but a nasty case of piles and a troublesome cold when he finally set foot once more on solid English ground.

Fred wasn't done yet and when the king went to bed to nurse his aching extremities, the prince spread a rumour that his father was at death's door. The ailing king had no choice but to drag himself out to face the public simply to prove that he was still breathing.

Never one to spend when he didn't have to, George repaid Fred's lack of concern and blatant ambition by refusing to increase his son's allowance, though he relented a little when Walpole leaned on him to do so. The queen in turn now looked on Fred with only bitter hatred, focusing her devotion on the adored Cumberland.

So deep was her dislike of the Prince of Wales that the plain speaking Caroline once said of him, 'My dear first born is the greatest ass, and the greatest liar, and the greatest canaille, and the greatest beast, in the whole world, and I most heartily wish he was out of it.'[27]

A dark and cruel wish, to be sure, yet she would not live to see it come true ...

A New Princess

Although George II had been allowed to visit his own bride-to-be whilst cunningly disguised as Monsieur de Busch, for the troublesome Fred, there was to be no such arrangement. In fact, the request for a bride had come from Fred himself, who felt a sharp sting of resentment when his sister, Anne, was married to William, Prince of Orange, in 1734.

This might not seem like an obvious slight but to the prince the meaning was clear: his parents had overlooked him as the source of the Protestant succession and gone straight to the next in line. Although the king and queen consented to his request for a bride, he would not be allowed to choose his own candidate. He would marry as his parents wished and whoever the lucky girl might be, she would be of excellent stock.

---

27. Doran, John (1855). *Lives of the Queens of England of the House of Hanover, Volume 1.* New York: Redfield, p.347.

It was during a Hanoverian jaunt to play at happy families with his beloved Amalie that the king first laid eyes on the teenaged Augusta of Saxe-Gotha. As daughter of Frederick II, Duke of Saxe-Gotha-Altenburg and Magdalena Augusta of Anhalt-Zerbst, the young lady was of excellent pedigree. Though scarred by smallpox, Augusta was a dozen years younger than Fred and brought with her the promise of many childbearing years ahead. Her family name was impeccable, and best of all, the unassuming and demure princess avoided the messy scandals and sordid triangles that came part and parcel of intrigues with the likes of Anne Vane.

Although the debt-laden Fred was wildly in lust with his latest mistress, Lady Jane Hamilton[28], he was all too aware that a marriage meant money and that was the one thing he couldn't get enough of. After receiving confirmation from his own informants that the newly-proposed Princess of Wales was neither ugly nor crazed, he consented to a betrothal to Augusta and the wheels of the royal marriage machine began to turn.

The timid Augusta arrived in England in 1736 as a wide-eyed innocent, clutching her favourite doll and unable to speak a word of English. As far as the king and queen were concerned she was the ideal wife for the forthright and rebellious Fred, her lack of political ambition exactly what they wanted in his spouse. After all, a wife with an eye on the glittering prizes would only have made his own ambitions so much worse than they already seemed to be. Happily, the marriage between Augusta and Fred was to prove very successful and George was so pleased with his matchmaking skills that he offered to raise Fred's allowance. Yet was Augusta as innocent as she seemed? Perhaps not.

Even as the demure princess did her best to smooth the choppy waters between her husband and his parents, Walpole considered her with a knowing air. Both the court and Fred's parents believed that Augusta was utterly in her husband's thrall, yet the canny politician wondered if there might be more to it than that and whether she might, in fact, be the power behind the prince. Walpole had his suspicions that the way to influence with Fred came through Augusta and he confided his beliefs in his ally, Caroline.

---

28. Lady Jane would eventually serve as Mistress of the Robes and Keeper of the Privy Purse to Augusta. She died in 1753.

Walpole advised the queen to tread softly with the princess, and not to attempt to befriend Augusta too quickly lest a burgeoning friendship with Fred's mother turn the prince against his new bride. Instead, the politician urged, Caroline should bide her time and let Augusta settle in. Only when his new wife was irreplaceable in her husband's affections should the queen attempt to build a true relationship with the younger woman. In fact, events were to conspire that would render such schemes pointless and when Fred carried the pregnant Augusta off in the dead of night rather than let her give birth in the king's house, history repeated itself to dreadful effect.

A Flight by Moonlight

Despite his dalliances with Anne Vane, both George and Caroline expected Fred to take his time starting a family, if he was capable of doing so at all. Caroline believed that her son was probably infertile due to his childhood frailty and if truth be told, she certainly hoped he was. After all, should there be no children from the marriage of Fred and Augusta then her favourite son, Cumberland, would be a surefire heir to the throne. Should the couple have a child then Cumberland would slip down the line of succession, probably irretrievably. The queen was to be sorely disappointed though because, within a year of the marriage, Augusta was pregnant.

One thing that Fred was determined to ensure was that his child would not be born beneath his father's roof and when Augusta went into labour at Hampton Court in July 1737, he sprang into action. Under cover of darkness and as her contractions grew ever more regular, Fred spirited his wife into a carriage. Through the dead of night she was forced to ensure a bumpy ride to the unprepared confines of St James's Palace, where she would deliver her firstborn daughter.

Hearing of their escape, the furious king and queen were sure that this was nothing but a scheme; after all, how could the weak, frail Fred father a child? No, they fretted, perhaps he intended to pass off some stranger's bastard as a royal prince, putting paid once and for all to Cumberland's chances. With this terror of a changeling ringing in their ears, the royal party gave panicked chase, determined to prevent the prince's imagined schemes.

Hervey once again lends an invaluable peek into the torments of the queen, relating the king's fury when he learned of his son's flight. His hot temper went into overdrive, and he bellowed furiously at Caroline, berating her even as she prepared to follow after the fleeing couple.

> 'You see, now, with all your wisdom, how they have outwitted you. This is all your fault. There is a false child will be put upon you, and how will you answer it to all your children? This has been fine care and fine management for your son William; he is mightily obliged to you: and for Ann, I hope she will come over and scold you herself; I am sure you deserve anything she can say to you.'[29]

In fact, by the time the pursuing queen and a retinue including Baron Hervey arrived at St James's Palace, Augusta had delivered a healthy baby girl. Although the gender of the child and the fact that others bore witness to the birth silenced rumours of a changeling, the new grandparents were appalled by Fred's behaviour. For the queen, there was to be no question of celebration and she wrote to her son, telling him, 'Your Royal Highness deserves to be hanged'[30] – hardly the last word in motherly love!

Just as George had been banished from court so now did he banish his son, though he *did* allow the children to go with their parents. Now he channelled all his affections and energy into William, Duke of Cumberland, even looking into the possibility of splitting the succession and leaving Fred with Hanover whilst William would take the more prestigious realm of Great Britain.

After decades of disinterest and outright hostility, the exiled Prince of Wales was little bothered by this new turn of events and threw himself into his Leicester House court. The king didn't take this lying down and let it be known that should anyone who professed loyalty to *him* ever join this alternative gathering, they would be forever exiled from his presence. This

29. Hervey, John and Croker, John Wilson (ed.), (1848). *Memoirs of the Reign of George the Second: From his Accession to the Death of Queen Caroline, Vol II*. London: John Murray, p.867.
30. Trench, Charles Chenevix. (1973) *George II*. London: Allen Lane, p.194.

did little to quell things at Leicester House where opposition colleagues and a flamboyant social circle gathered. It was during this period of exile that Augusta later gave birth to George William in 1738, ending Cumberland's hopes of succession forever.

Frail and sickly, the newborn was not expected to live yet live he did, eventually becoming famed as George III. Under the care of his mother and father he lived a contented childhood, taking part in theatricals and entertainments and at least we can happily conclude that the venomous relationship that started with George I and George II did not seep into this particular father-son bond. Of course, though Fred and George partially reconciled following Walpole's death, the prince found his desire to lead the forces against the Pretender at Culloden frustrated and the role of commander went instead to his brother, the sainted Cumberland.

Those tales, however, must wait their turn, and the death of a queen.

Broken-Hearted

'Last Sunday Night at Ten o'Clock died of a Rupture, and Mortification of the Bowels, inexpressibly lamented, Her Most Sacred Majesty, WILHELMINA DOROTHEA CAROLINA, Queen Consort of Great Britain, &c. aged 55 Years, 8 Months, and 13 Days.'[31]

Although George made no secret of his devotion to Amalie, his closest confidante and counsellor was undoubtedly his wife, Caroline of Ansbach. Mistresses may come and go, ministers may move on and the least said about eldest sons, the better, but the queen remained a constant in his life, providing someone to yell at, a listening ear and a trusted regent. Yet despite their trials and the king's tantrums, when his queen took to her bed in 1737 with a horrific final illness, he remained at her side until she took her last, agonized breath

Caroline was no longer the wide-eyed girl she had once been but had flourished into a queen, a regent and a political force to be reckoned with.

31. *Daily Gazetteer (London Edition)* (London, England), Tuesday, November 22, 1737; issue 752, p.2.

She was, however, not the most health conscious lady in the palace and had grown so fat and gouty that she no longer walked, but allowed herself to be pushed around in a wheelchair. Multiple pregnancies had taken their toll and in November 1737, the complications from a birth more than a decade earlier brought tragedy.

When the queen was struck by a violent pain in her stomach, she dismissed it as nothing more serious than colic and took to her bed, expecting to be back on in her feet in no time. Her condition grew worse with each passing day and soon barely an hour passed without Caroline vomiting or retching, her body wracked by untold agony.

Under the care of royal physicians led by John Ranby, Caroline was bled and treated but still she grew weaker, her suffering more acute. In fact, the queen already harboured a suspicion as to the cause of her illness yet neither she nor George thought fit to share it until they realized that there was no other option if she was to have a hope of survival. They admitted to Ranby that Caroline's last pregnancy in 1724 had left her with a hernia. Could this, they ventured, be the cause of the queen's suffering?

Why then did neither Caroline nor George mention this earlier?

The king confided in Hervey that Caroline loathed any discussion of her ill health and reacted furiously when he asked her to seek medical attention; indeed, she forbade any mention of it again. Perhaps it was embarrassment at such an intimate ailment, though this seems unlikely; perhaps she thought it in some way diminished her femininity or even her humanity. Maybe it was simply that she believed that ignoring her condition might make it go away. Whatever the motive, the hernia did *not* go away and when Ranby examined Caroline, he could clearly feel evidence of it beneath the skin. Without delay the doctor, whom Caroline furiously called 'the blockhead', gathered a team of surgeons and physicians to the queen's side and preparations began for the final, terrible days of her life.

With no anaesthetic, the medics cut into Caroline's belly and discovered that the hernia she had sought to ignore had grown much worse over the years, causing part of her now strangulated bowel to decay. The doctors cut out the mortified intestine, which left Caroline's bowels wide open to the elements. Raw excrement flooded into the queen's abdomen and began to ooze from her surgical wounds even after they were dressed, leaving her in unimaginable agony. The queen's last days were a constant and tortuous routine of vomiting and pain, the results of the catastrophic procedure and those that followed filling the palace air with the sickening stench of faeces and decomposition.

The king would not be drawn from the side of his wife and lavished her with affection and praise even as he could not quite curb that temper that had always plagued him.

'[George told Caroline] that if she had not been his wife, he had rather have had her for his mistress than any woman he had ever been acquainted with. [George] said that, joined to all the softness and delicacy of her own sex, [Caroline] had all the personal as well as political courage of the firmest and bravest man; that not only he and her family, but the whole nation, would feel the loss of her if she died [...] and yet so unaccountable were the sudden sallies of his temper, and so little was he able or willing to command them, that in the midst of all this flow of tenderness he hardly ever went into her room that he did not, even in this moving situation, snub her for something or other she said or did.'[32]

As the days passed, the queen's bedchamber hung heavy with the stench of blood, excrement and decay, Caroline's agonies finding no respite. She received visits from family, courtiers and even ministers yet the one constant through all of it was King George II, settled beside the woman he had married all those years earlier. The queen knew that she was dying and entrusted the care of her younger children to their older siblings, begging George to marry again when she was gone. He would take mistresses, the king told her, but there would be no wife to replace her.

Both husband and wife knew that Caroline's time was short yet even as she lay on her deathbed, Caroline did not forgive her son and Fred was not permitted to visit her. Hervey recorded a bitter comment, given in the final

---

32. Hervey, John and Croker, John Wilson (ed.), (1848). *Memoirs of the Reign of George the Second: From his Accession to the Death of Queen Caroline, Vol II*. London: John Murray, pp.532–3.

throes of her life, when she reflected that, 'At least I shall have one comfort in having my eyes eternally closed – I shall never see that monster [Fred] again'.[33] Although he sought leave to visit his mother, the king refused the Prince of Wales permission to attend her in her final, agonized days.

As Caroline's last day on earth drew on into evening, the tortured queen was attended by the king and their daughter, Amelia. Exhausted by agony and barely moving as the night grew ever darker, the queen asked for prayers, taking some comfort in the whispered repetition of the words. Finally, perhaps mercifully, Caroline took her husband's hand in her own and whispered, 'I am going'. With that, she closed her eyes and passed away.

When the queen died, George was left bereft. The woman who had been his closest and most trusted counsel was laid to rest in Westminster Abbey and George kept his promise never to remarry to the end.

The king and queen's relationship was an odd one and like many marriages, it was certainly not without periods of conflict and bad feeling. There is no doubt that George was grief-stricken at Caroline's death though, and one cannot help but wonder whether he ever really recovered from her loss. With precious little emotional stability from his parents, George did not find it easy to relate to anyone but in Caroline he seemed to have truly found the closest he ever came to a soulmate. Now that soulmate was gone.

To the end of his days, Caroline's death left a hole in George's life that he could not fill and when he died, his coffin was set beside hers in Westminster Abbey. According to his wishes, the sides were removed so that they might rest together in eternity, never to be parted again.

Choosing a Mistress

Although George would keep his promise never to remarry to the very end of his days he did not, of course, give up women altogether. With Amalie out of reach in Hanover he turned to the governess of the royal daughters, Mary Howard, Dowager Countess of Deloraine, for comfort. In fact, George had first seduced Mary whilst Caroline still lived and she was a well-known face at court, where her late husband had served as tutor to the royal sons.

---

33. Hervey, John (1963). *Lord Hervey's Memoirs*. London: Batsford, p.241.

Alexander Pope, never a man given to kindness noted that Lady Deloraine was far from pleasant[34] and Robert Walpole was certainly not a fan of the lady. Our old friend, Hervey, meanwhile lamented that such a pretty head was attached to such a vain and wretched countenance. Should Pope be believed, though, there was a *lot* more to Lady Deloraine than a pretty face.

In fact, he believed she was quite deadly.

Pope recounted the sad tale of a Miss Mackenzie, a young lady whose beauty was much admired at court. Lady Deloraine burned with furious jealousy and resentment at this widespread admiration of her rival and determined to put a stop to it, whatever it took. When the beautiful Miss Mackenzie suddenly fell ill and died, it was assumed that she had been the victim of poison administered by none other than Lady Deloraine. Of course, this sort of court gossip should hardly be treated as fact and no charges were ever brought against the supposed murderer, but such rumours do no good for a lady's reputation!

Although Lady Deloraine would do as a temporary stopgap, Walpole decided that someone less divisive and politically interested was required for the role of *maîtresse-en-titre*. It was with Walpole's hearty approval and assistance that Amalie was summoned to England, in the hope that her presence might go some way to settling the king's grief and loosening the grip of that former governess. George's Hanoverian mistress landed on English shores in 1738 and was installed in the former apartments of Henrietta Howard, perfectly suiting the king's love for routine. He could once again make regular trips to those familiar if somewhat shabby rooms to escape the now quieter court and spend some time just being. Of course, such a blatant flouting of the relationship did not go down well with Amalie's husband and the couple were divorced by 1740, leaving Amalie free to be naturalized and awarded the title of Countess of Yarmouth for her 'services' to the crown.

'His Majesty has been pleas'd to grant the Dignities of a Baroness and Countess of the Kingdom of Great Britain, unto Amalie Sophie de

---

34. Pope is believed to have immortalized Lady Deloraine as *Delia* in *The First Satire of the Second Book of Horace*:

"Slander or poison dread from Delia's rage"

Walmoden, by the Names, Stiles and Titles of Baroness and Countess of Yarmouth in the County of Norfolk; and Letters Patent are passed the Great Seal accordingly.'[35]

Although her grand new title was a little way off yet, Amalie's disinterest in politics smoothed her arrival at the British court. She had no care for intriguing and made friends easily so was really the ideal mistress as far as Walpole and his like were concerned. If Lady Deloraine thought she might put up a resistance to this new arrival she was to be sorely mistaken and an embarrassing fracas at Kensington Palace was about to see off the challenge from Pope's *Delia* once and for all.

Horace Walpole wrote to Sir Horace Mann in 1742 of a prank that had far-reaching consequences for Lady Deloraine, from which her relationship with the king would not recover. During a game of cards with George one of the royal daughters – which one, he does not say – pulled the lady's chair out from beneath her, causing her to fall onto the floor and land on her rump. Upon seeing her royal lover's amusement, Lady Deloraine responded by pulling *his* chair out in turn, determined to share the joke. It was an unwise move and one that ended her days as a contender for the role of chief mistress, as Walpole gleefully reports:

'But alas! the Monarch, like Louis XIV. is mortal in the part that touched the ground, and was so hurt and so angry, that the Countess is disgraced, and her German rival [Amalie] remains in the sole and quiet possession of her royal master's favour.'[36]

It was the end of the road for Lady Deloraine and she died in 1744, her career as a royal mistress long since at an end. To Amalie, fate dealt a happier hand and she outlived not only her lover but her rival, passing away in Hanover in 1765.

---

35. *General Evening Post* (London, England), April 5, 1740 – April 8, 1740; issue 1020, p3.
36. Walpole, Horace (1833). *Letters of Horace Walpole, Earl of Orford, to Sir Horace Mann.* London: Richard Bentley, p.242.

War and Rebellion

'His Majesty (God be praised) has this Day gained a very considerable Battle. […] His Majesty was all the Time in the Heat of the Fire; but is in perfect Health.'[37]

In 1743, 60-year-old George II became the last British monarch to lead his troops into battle when he took an impressive victory at the Battle of Dettingen. The death of Holy Roman Emperor, Charles VI, in 1740 had left the powerful Austrian territories up for grabs and with French sabres rattling, the War of the Austrian Succession was in full swing. Although George was firmly of the opinion that the outcome was vital to his own interests, the people of Britain disagreed. Whilst they took no small amount of pride in his triumph at Dettingen, they weren't altogether happy that their king was off to the continent again, apparently putting the interests of Hanover ahead of those of Great Britain.

It wasn't the only opposition that George would face.

A new pretender had risen.

This Young Pretender was Charles Edward Stuart, better known to history as Bonnie Prince Charlie. Set on winning the throne he believed was rightly his, in July 1745 he arrived in Scotland to stake his claim. Clashes followed and when George sent his favourite son, Cumberland, to face the Young Pretender on the field of Culloden in April 1746, the result was a crushing defeat for the Scottish forces.

Although he led British forces to victory, Culloden would not have a happy outcome for Cumberland's reputation. At the end of the battle, as the duke played cards in his tent, he was asked for his orders. In reply, Cumberland wrote 'no quarter' on the back of the nine of diamonds, the card known to this day as 'the curse of Scotland'. Though the nickname predates Cumberland's throwaway note, its appearance at Culloden added one more grisly association to the card.

Cumberland's orders were to leave no rebel unpunished, whether soldier or civilian. Wounded men were slaughtered where they lay and over the

---

37. *Whitehall June 23 1743 This Morning Mr Parker* (London, England), Thursday, June 23, 1743, p.1.

months that followed the pacification of the Highlands made its merciless way across the land. Those who had not been on the field were rounded up, tried and sentenced to execution or transportation. Cumberland's actions earned him the nickname 'The Butcher', and he did nothing to downplay his fearsome reputation. This same reputation would, of course, come back to haunt him one day.

Reviled in the Highlands, Cumberland returned to England to a hero's welcome though his nephew, who would become George III, was less keen and encouraged use of the Butcher nickname. For the people, however, Cumberland was a man to be lauded. His allowance was increased and the man known by some as 'The Butcher' was called by others by the far more charming name, 'Sweet William'.

'We hear that several ingenious Florists are raising in their Green-Houses, that beautiful Flower called the Sweet William, with a View to have it worn the 15th of next Month, being the Birth Day of his Royal Highness the Duke of Cumberland.'[38]

Cumberland's star waned in time thanks to the fact that his hand was firmly on the rudder in 1747 when British forces were defeated at Laffeldt. Still, for the king, things at home and abroad seemed to be settling. Parliament was occasionally stable and the long-troublesome Jacobite hopes lay in tatters, the Young Pretender having fled for France following his routing at Culloden. Handel composed a piece to celebrate the British victory in the War of the Austrian Succession and on the domestic front, routine reigned. With Amalie holding her place both at court and in her lover's heart, for a time, all was steady in the life of George II.

Of course, it couldn't last!

---

38. *George Faulkner the Dublin Journal* (Dublin, Ireland), March 21, 1747 – March 24, 1747; issue 2089, p.1.

The Death of Fred

In 1751, the Prince of Wales died at 44 from a burst abscess in his lung, leaving a pregnant widow and eight children without a father. The king received the news with remarkable sangfroid, commenting coolly as he looked back on the year, 'I have lost my eldest son, but I was glad of it'[39]. The words are hash and stinging and George did not attend his son's funeral, nor ever give any indication that he had spared a moment's thought for Fred's fate, yet he didn't turn his back on the family Fred had left behind.

Fred's life was one marked by conflict and upheaval, by political failure and domestic happiness but ultimately, it was testament to the poor behaviour of a father who really should have known better. After all, George II knew what it was to be at odds with a parent, to never be able to do or say the right thing. In his youth, had he not been just as wilful as his son, hampering rather than helping what slim chance of reconciliation might remain?

Now George offered a hand of friendship to his bereaved daughter-in-law and when Augusta sought his help and support, the king was quick to give it. He took a great interest in the education of her eldest son and was quick to put in place succession plans should he die before his grandson reached majority.

The advancing age of the king, and the fact that his heir was still a child raised a new problem. George II would not live forever yet the people of Britain were uneasy in their opinion of Cumberland, once known so fondly as 'Sweet William.' He was a man of ambition, after all, and there were concerns that he might use a regency to seize power for himself.

The newly widowed Augusta, however, enjoyed great popularity with the public and George eventually decided on an arrangement in which both Augusta and Cumberland might have some power, with neither enjoying it absolutely. It was agreed that, should a regent be required, it would be Augusta. However, she would be steered by a council of advisors with Cumberland at the head.

The death of George II's daughter, Louisa, that same year left the ageing king in a reflective mood and it was with a heavier heart that he went about

---

39. Hibbert, Christopher (1998). *George III: A Personal History*. London: Viking, p. 14.

his business over the months that followed. He still had his beloved William, of course, but 'The Butcher' would soon find his copybook very blotted indeed. First, however, George had a little blotting of his own to do.

To Do His Utmost

At the outbreak of the Seven Years' War in 1756, Admiral John Byng was a naval high flier and a safe pair of hands. When he sailed out of England to join the Battle of Minorca, his orders were not to let the French capture Port Mahon under any circumstances. Yet Byng was plagued by doubts, certain that his vessel was underprepared and sure to be overwhelmed by the forces of the French. Upon his arrival he found the port besieged and knew that his chances of success were slim.

Despite this Byng *did* go into battle in May 1756. With the French forces heavily outgunning their adversaries, Byng's vessel, the *Ramillies*, ended up boxed in towards the back of the British fleet and never came within firing range of another ship. On that unfortunate day, several British vessels suffered serious damage whilst the French remained untouched. The engagement had been a disaster and George furiously declared, 'This man will not fight'.[40] As Byng sailed for Gibraltar, an order was issued to arrest the admiral as a coward who had retreated from the battle without even attempting to play his part.

When Byng returned to England he found his reputation, actions and character in question. The admiral was placed under guard in Greenwich Hospital as a war of words raged, and eventually, it was decided that he must face a court martial. The case opened in late December 1756 at Portsmouth, with Byng charged under the 12th Article of War:

'Every Person in the Fleet, who through cowardice, negligence or dissatisfaction, shall in time of action withdraw or keep back, or not come into the fight or engagement, or shall not do his utmost to take or destroy every ship which it shall be his duty to engage, and to assist and

40. Thompson, Andrew C, (2011). *George II: King and Elector.* New Haven: Yale University press, p.247.

relieve all and every of His Majesty's ships or those of his allies, which it shall be his duty to assist and relieve, every such person so offending, and being convicted thereof by the sentence of a court martial, shall suffer death.'

There was little room for interpretation of the sentence should one be found guilty under the 12th Article. So, with the public demanding answers and Crown and Parliament keen to settle the matter, the court marital set out to ascertain whether the Admiral had 'done his utmost' during the battle.

Byng argued passionately that he had not deliberately kept the *Ramillies* out of the range of enemy fire. He pointed out that the opposing forces were at angles to one another, rendering it virtually impossible for him to engage the French from his position. Serving as his own defence, he countered that he had been sent into battle without resources and that his sailing for Gibraltar after the engagement had not been a matter of retreat, but necessity.

The judges would hear none of it. Although he was absolved of cowardice, they ruled that he had indeed failed to do his utmost. In this case, the mandatory punishment was death.

'We hear that the following is the Sentence upon Admiral Byng, as sent to the Admiralty:

'It appears to this Court, that Admiral Byng did not do his Duty on bearing down to the French; it appears, therefore, to this Court, he hath incurred a Breach of Part of the Twelfth Article of War and we do sentence him to be Shot to Death. But it does not appear to this Court to be done through Cowardice or Disaffection; we therefore unanimously recommend him to Mercy. [...]'

We hear, that when the Admiral had received his Sentence, he behaved extremely calm, and said, that if nothing but his Life would satisfy the Publick, he was ready to forfeit it.'[41]

---

41. *London Evening Post* (London, England), January 27, 1757 – January 29, 1757; issue 4560, p.1.

Despite their verdict, the judges unanimously recommended that George II show clemency and grant the beleaguered admiral a reprieve. Influential figures raised their voices in support of a lighter sentence, with Horace Walpole believing that Byng was being offered up as a public sacrifice to save ministerial skins. Byng's family campaigned tirelessly on his behalf yet it was to no avail. Petitions brought before the king fell on deaf ears and George gave his decision- the death penalty would stand.

Byng was taken from his prison on HMS *Monarque* in the Solent and brought to the quarterdeck at noon on 14 March 1757. Here a firing squad of Royal Marines awaited him alongside an audience of sailors who had gathered to show support for the unfortunate admiral.

'Mr Byng walked out of the great cabin to the quarter deck [...] He threw his hat on the deck, kneel'd on it, tyed one handkerchief over his eyes and dropped the other as a signal; on which a volley from six marines was fired, five of whose bullets went thro' him, and he was in an instant no more. [...] In short, he died with great resolution and composure, without the least sign of timidity.'[42]

At the moment the squad fired, it not only ended the life of Admiral Byng, it also sealed the king's reputation as the monarch who let a loyal man go to an unjust death.

The Butcher's Ruin

Since childhood, Prince William, Duke of Cumberland, had been the favourite of his parents. 'Sweet William' to his Whig friends, 'Butcher Cumberland' to his Tory enemies, William was a ruthless military commander who possessed a keen political mind. As the Seven Years' War raged, the king looked to his favourite son to play his part.

Cumberland keenly agreed, and in 1757 he could be found on the continent, where it was intended that he would rally to the aid of Prussian

---

42. *Evening Advertiser* (London, England), March 15, 1757 – March 17, 1757; issue 472, p.2.

forces under the command of Frederick the Great. Yet things did not go Cumberland's way, and a disastrous engagement at Hastenbeck ended in defeat as the French moved into Hanover.

George was thrown into a panic at the news that his ancestral lands were under occupation. He immediately sent word to his son, granting Cumberland the authority to negotiate with the French. The results would prove to be disastrous.

Cumberland signed the Convention of Klosterzeven, which contained amongst other clauses, an agreement that Hanover would remain partially under French occupation and the promise that Hanover would henceforth remain neutral and offer no further assistance to Prussia. Frederick the Great regarded the agreement as a betrayal and in Parliament, the king came under pressure from Pitt to revoke it. George eventually did so and Cumberland returned home in disgrace.

Once feted by some as the hero of Culloden, when Cumberland returned to England this time, the reception he received was very different. During an audience the king furiously declared that Cumberland had 'ruined me and disgraced himself'[43] and it spelled the end of a once glittering career.

Smarting from the defeat and his father's fury, Cumberland resigned all his offices and never saw service again. Although he did make a return to public life once his nephew, George III, became king, his days on the battlefield were long since finished.

The King is Dead

'This morning about Seven o'Clock to the great Grief of an affectionate People, died his Most August Majesty George II, King and Parent of the British Dominions. His Majesty, it is said, expired in a Fit of Apoplexy, in the 77th Year of his Age, and 34th of his Reign.'[44]

---

43. Campbell, Thomas (1844). *Frederick the Great, His Court and Times. Vol II*. London: Colburn, p.65.
44. *Whitehall Evening Post or London Intelligencer* (London, England), October 23, 1760 – October 25, 1760; issue 2279, p.3.

As the years passed by and the king, now deaf, partially blind and restricted in mobility, grew older, he reflected more and more on the death of his adored Caroline and the family he had lost. Five of George's children predeceased him and as old age crept over the king, he recognized that his health was failing. Though he was as mentally vibrant as ever, the king found his days increasingly frustrated by frailty.

The reign of George II drew to a close on 25 October 1760, not long after he had left his bed at Kensington Palace. George always started the day with a cup of chocolate before retiring to perform his toilet yet on this morning, not long after he entered his closet, his valet heard the sounds of calamity. Alarmed for his master, the valet went to his aid only to find the king on the floor, barely breathing as he clung to the last threads of life. George was carried to his bed and Princess Amelia and the king's physician, Frank Nicholls, were summoned.

Before they arrived, George II was dead.

Nicholls declared that the cause of death had been an aortic dissection, which was neither preventable nor operable. Following an enormous funeral at Westminster Abbey on 11 November 1760, at which Cumberland was the chief mourner, George was laid to rest beside his adored wife. According to his wishes, the sides of their coffins were removed to allow their bodies to rest together for eternity.

Act Three

George III, King of Great Britain and Ireland

(London, England, 4 June 1738 – Windsor, England, 29 January 1820)

Y ou will know him as the mad king, the monarch about whom plays have been written and films made, who has been immortalized as a comedy punchline for centuries, the 'nudge nudge, wink wink' of Britain's royal history. Madness is his stamp, his lasting trademark yet in his time, George III presided over a country as it changed forever.

Known affectionately to his subjects as *Farmer George*, he was the first Georgian king to be born in England, both of his predecessors having come into the world in Hanover. George I and II spent long periods in their native lands and did not necessarily speak English so well, yet *this* George was unmistakably an English king.

However, there was one area in which George III followed those who had gone before him. Both George I and George II had relationships with their sons that might best be described as *difficult* and this, sadly, was a family tradition that George III was destined to repeat, keeping that particular custom well and truly alive.

A boy in *England* born, in England bred'[1]

'Yesterday between the Hours of Six and Seven in the Morning her Royal Highness the Princess of Wales was happily deliver'd of a Prince, at Norfolk-House in St. James's-Square, the Archbishop of Canterbury being present.'[2]

---

1. George spoke these lines at the age of 10, when he performed the new prologue from Joseph Addison's play, *Cato*.
2. *London Evening Post* (London, England), May 23, 1738–May 25, 1738; issue 1642, p.1.

When George William was born to the Prince and Princess of Wales, he entered into the middle of a bitter war of attrition that had left his father Fred, and grandfather, George II, irretrievably estranged. Instead Fred and his wife Augusta established their own court, where opposition figures gathered and raised their voices in sometimes scathing reply to the king and his government.

George William was born at Norfolk House, which the 9th Duke of Norfolk had laid at the disposal of the Prince and Princess of Wales. The property boasted an illustrious St James's Square address and when Norfolk offered Fred the opportunity to use it as his residence he readily accepted.

In the early days of George William's life, the prospects for the newborn prince were far from promising. He was born premature and his proud parents took one look at their frail, tiny son and realized that he very unlikely to see adolescence. Though he was baptized on the day of his birth, fears for the little boy's health were soon proved to be ill-founded. In fact, George William turned out to be something of a fighter, and he defied the naysayers not only to live through those perilous early days, but to become one of the longest reigning monarchs in Great Britain's history, growing into a healthy, contemplative little boy.

George William's early years were not, it must be said, academically outstanding. Though he could read, write and speak English by the time he was 8, George William was a far from inspiring student. Fred was an involved, enthusiastic and loving parent and he took great delight in following the progress of his children, encouraging and chivying them along in their learning. He had no intention of repeating the mistakes of his own father, George II, who had left him in Hanover for so long that the two could never truly be reunited.

And what of the king?

George II took as little interest in his grandson as he did in his son yet George William barely noticed as he delighted in his lessons under the watchful eye of handpicked tutors, including Lord North. He was a timid but loving boy and never happier than when in the company of his younger brother and best friend, Prince Edward, Duke of York and Albany, even if that time was spent in the schoolroom.

Like his father, George William's passions were astronomy, theatre and music, and he enjoyed many other pursuits. It was in childhood that the disapproving piety he later exhibited began to form, and George William developed a deep faith, sometimes lamenting the fact that the rest of the populace didn't necessarily share it. Though timid and eager to please, George William was certainly not without the occasional bout of childhood sullenness but, to all intents and purposes, he was a son to be proud of.

When Fred died unexpectedly in 1751, George William was stricken with grief. Told of the death of his father, he placed his hand over his heart and commented, 'I feel something here, just as I did when I saw the two workmen fall from the scaffold at Kew'.[3] Even as he mourned though, 12-year-old George William had new concerns.

The death of the Prince of Wales catapulted his young son into the position of heir apparent to the throne of Great Britain and Ireland. Just to drive home the weight he now shouldered, Fred left George William a testament in which he wrote, 'I shall have no regret never to have worn the crown, if you but fill it worthily. Convince the nation that you are not only an Englishman born and bred, but that you are also this by inclination'.[4]

This focus on George William's *Englishness* did not abate, and in his pithy summation of the reigns of the first three Georges, no less a commentator than HG Wells surmises:

'[George I] was entirely German, he could speak no English, and he brought a swarm of German women and German attendants to the English court; a dullness, a tarnish, came over the intellectual life of the land with his coming [...] George I was followed by the very similar George II (1727–1760), and it was only at his death that England had again a king who had been born in England, and one who could speak English fairly well, his grandson George III.'[5]

3. Walpole, Horace (1832). *The Letters of Horace Walpole: Vol II*. New York: Dearborn, p.164.
4. Hibbert, Christopher (1998). *George III: A Personal History*. London: Viking, p.11.
5. Wells, HG (1920). *The Outline of History*. New York: Barnes & Noble, pp.311–12.

George William's Englishness would certainly work in his favour, yet this alone doesn't account for the British public's eventual affection for him. Suddenly, however, someone else was also very interested in the young man and that someone was none other than George II. Although he had received news of Fred's death in a manner that might best be described as cool, he recognized the importance of preparing his grandson for the role ahead. The first step was reconciling with his daughter-in-law, Augusta, and mending that burned bridge.

Together the two would ensure that the heir to the throne was properly prepared. Out went his Tory tutor, Lord North, and in came the more politically agreeable Whig, Lord Harcourt, who was the first in a procession of men who would oversee the young man's education.

One in particular would make quite a stir.

A Fine Pair of Lordly Legs

'The King and Princess are grown as fond as if they had never been of different parties, or rather as people who always had been of different.'[6]

The bereaved Princess Augusta and George II had, with the death of Fred, finally found themselves reconciled, their bond strengthened over their shared interest in the heir to the throne. Both agreed that George William's academic performance and direction needed taking in hand, and it seemed as though the fatherless child was in need of a trusted male role model. Augusta was loathe to let the ambitious Duke of Cumberland, George William's uncle, have too much sway and looked elsewhere, mindful of the responsibility that the lucky candidate would hold.

So, what about a chap Augusta trusted above all others, who she just happened to have met during a card game at the races, and who was known for his very fine legs?[7]

---

6. Walpole, Horace (1832). *The Letters of Horace Walpole: Vol II*. New York: Dearborn, p.379.

7. Earl Waldegrave commented that Bute, 'has a good Person, fine Legs, and a theatrical air of the greatest Importance.' Waldegrave, James (1988). *The Memoirs and Speeches of James, 2nd Earl Waldegrave, 1742–1763*. Cambridge: Cambridge University Press, p.163.

Many years earlier, during a sojourn to Egham races, Augusta and Fred found themselves caught in an unexpected downpour. With nothing for it but to seek shelter and pass the time with some other distraction, they had joined friends for a game of whist. The party soon found that they needed one more member to make up the numbers and invited John Stuart, 3rd Earl of Bute, to join them. So began a friendship between Fred and Bute that lasted until the former's dying day. Stern yet fair, highly intelligent and well aware of the protocol and trust that went into such a role, the Scottish Lord Bute was the natural choice to serve as George William's mentor and he accepted the position readily.

Even as the adolescent heir studied under the earl, the people of Britain were watching with narrowed eyes. Who was this man, they wondered, whom Augusta had apparently plucked out of thin air to replace her late husband, and what were his motives? George II had his doubts too, yet by the time it became apparent that Bute's influence over George William exceeded both the king and Cumberland's, it was far too late to intervene.

'When Frederick Prince of Wales died, and the present King George the Third became immediate Heir to the Crown, Lord Bute very prudently attached himself wholly to him, not only with the approbation, but I believe, at the request, of the Princess Dowager. In this he succeeded beyond his most sanguine wishes. He entirely engrossed not only the affections, but even the senses of the young Prince, who seemed to have made a total surrender of them all to Lord Bute.'[8]

Bute's influence over the young Prince of Wales was without a doubt strong, but was it really a negative one? We cannot really know but Bute was not, whatever the press implied at the time, Augusta's lover, nor was George William a brainless drone in the thrall of this confident, cultured statesman. In fact, Bute had lost his own father when he was just 10-years-old and, like his new charge, had been left to navigate the worrying waters of adolescence without him. He was to remain a constant in George William's life, forever

---

8. Stanhope, Philip Dormer (1845). *The Letters of Philip Dormer Stanhope: Vol II*. London: Richard Bentley, p.471.

dogged by accusations that he had secured his power and influence via Augusta's rumpled bedding.

It wasn't only the British press that were suspicious of Bute, with Frederick the Great musing that Bute had, 'more ambition than ability, and [was] desirous to reign himself under the shadow of his sovereign's name'.[9]

Yet this does a disservice to George William. He did *not* follow Bute slavishly and though both Bute and Augusta certainly exerted a great influence over the young man, to suggest that he was a puppet is unfair and inaccurate.

When George William came of age, he was offered and rejected the opportunity to move into his own residence. Instead, he chose to remain with his devoted mother and with Bute. Enduring constant attacks from all sides, the young man and his governor grew closer than ever. George looked up to his 'dearest friend' more than anyone, and sought his guidance and approval. Bute's influence was to persevere for years, but not forever.

Sophie, Frederica, Sarah and Charlotte

There are few bachelors more eligible than the heir to a throne and George William was no exception to the rule. Unsurprisingly, it looked as if the decision on who he should marry would be taken by George II and by 1753, the shrewd king had set his heart on Princess Sophie Caroline of Brunswick-Wolfenbüttel.

As niece to Frederick the Great, a marriage to Sophie Caroline would cement relations between Hanover and its neighbours. George II was keen to nurture such connections yet Augusta would not hear of it, believing her son could make a much more powerful alliance. The young prince accordingly followed suit, and with neither mother nor son willing to budge, the king was forced to abandon his plans.[10]

---

9. Williams, Thomas (1820). *Memoirs of His Late Majesty George III*. London: W Simpkin and R Marshall, p.31.
10. Sophie Caroline married Frederick, Margrave of Brandenburg-Bayreuth, in 1759. Her brother, Charles, Duke of Brunswick-Wolfenbüttel, married George's sister, Princess Augusta of Great Britain. It was their daughter, Caroline of Brunswick, who later wed George IV.

In fact, Augusta had her own preferred candidate in the form of her niece, Frederica of Saxe-Gotha. However, if she thought that her son didn't know his own mind, she was to be surprised because George William didn't like that idea either, raising concerns that Frederica was 'interested in philosophy',[11] which could lead to all sorts of problems. That might sound like an odd reason to reject a possible bride but remember that George William was a man of strong faith who valued piety. To be joined to a wife who might be driven by her philosophy to question that faith would not be a happy situation for the young Prince of Wales.

Perhaps it came as a shock to George II and Augusta that their young charge dared to voice his opinion on the question of brides. Certainly Horace Walpole thought so as he commented that, 'Could she [Augusta] have chained up his body, as she had fettered his mind, it is probable she would have preferred his remaining single'.[12] Walpole saw in the Dowager Princess of Wales a woman of ruthless ambition, dedicated to furthering her own influence and clinging to the reins of power as tightly as she possibly could. She did not quite manage to keep her son single, but when it came to matters of marriage, he didn't get it all his own way ...

The search for a bride moved up a gear in 1760 when George II died and George William inherited the crown. He received the news whilst out riding with Bute, and told his mentor that he would accept the crown on the understanding that he would once again make Great Britain, 'the residence of true piety and virtue'.[13]

As the country hailed its new king and young George III found his feet in the throne room in the midst of the Seven Years' War, domestic matters were pressing, none more so than who would become his wife and queen. In fact, George had already set his heart on one woman in particular, and she was Lady Sarah Lennox.

---

11. Black, Jeremy (2007). *The Hanoverians: The History of a Dynasty*. London: Hambledon and London, p.118.
12. Walpole, Horace (1845). *Memoirs of the Reign of King George the Third: Vol I*. Philadelphia: Lea & Blanchard, p.47.
13. Black, Jeremy (2008). *George III: America's Last King*. New Haven: Yale University Press, p.71.

Lady Sarah was just 15, and already 'a very young lady of the most blooming beauty, and shining with all the graces of unaffected, but animated nature'.[14] In childhood, she had been a popular and familiar face at the court of George II, but was only recently returned to London after an extended trip to Ireland. As daughter of the Duke of Richmond, Sarah had some pedigree, but her suitability as a royal bride would need more than that, and the fact that she was sister-in-law of the outspoken and ambitious Whig politician, Henry Fox, did not help her cause. George made no secret of his attraction to Lady Sarah and her ambitious family pushed her forward whilst Bute and Augusta urged their charge to think again.

Horace Walpole describes the king constantly dropping clumsy hints to Lady Sarah's circle, hoping that she would realize that he adored her. At drawing rooms and gatherings he gazed doe-eyed at the young woman and when he heard that Sarah was to see their mutual friend, Lady Susan Strangeways, he told Lady Susan, 'They talk of a wedding. There have been many proposals; but I think an English match would do better than a foreign one. Pray tell Lady Sarah Lenox [sic] I said so.'[15]

As Lady Sarah's family did all they could to encourage the courtship, the king's inner circle took up an opposing stance. As a result, things began to get a little farcical, with all the ingredients for a romcom other than the happy ending. Walpole recalls Lady Bute attempting to inveigle her way into Lady Sarah's group to ensure that gossip about the king's attachment didn't get out of hand. He also shares the tale of the cunning Fox's decision to take a trip to the coast whilst ensuring that Lady Sarah was left at Holland House in his absence. She was to contrive to keep herself in George's thoughts and 'appeared every morning in a field close to the great road (where the king passed on horseback) in a fancied habit, making hay'.[16]

All the fancied habits and haymaking in the world were to be no match for the combined wills of the king's mother, Lord Bute and Parliament though. After all, this was a *king* for heaven's sake, the sort of chap who should really

---

14. Walpole, Horace (1845). *Memoirs of the Reign of King George the Third: Vol I.* Philadelphia: Lea & Blanchard, p.63.
15. Ibid., p.48.
16. Ibid., p.48.

be looking for a royal bride, not settling for a mere noble. There were few more serious matters of business than the future of the monarchy and a list of possible candidates was given to George, who rejected every single one. The usually timid and compliant fellow wanted only Lady Sarah, no other would do … or so he thought. Bute, the man he trusted so completely, asked if he would look at the list again and George eventually consented as Bute's counsel was one that he would rarely if ever ignore.

In fact, there was one lady on the list who George wasn't entirely ambivalent towards and that was Princess Sophia Charlotte of Mecklenburg-Strelitz. She was young, respectable, reportedly pretty and intelligent and, best of all, apparently completely benign. It was left for Charlotte's mother to agree the match and no sooner was all set than that same mother promptly died, leaving the princess an orphan.

Given Lady Sarah's efforts to catch the eye of the king and his attachment to her in turn, how on earth might one expect young Miss Lennox to take this unhappy news? If you answered 'badly', you'll be surprised to know that she was far more preoccupied with caring for an injured pet. As the Countess of Ilchester recalled, 'To many a girl H.M.'s behaviour had been very vexatious, but Lady Sarah's temper & affections are happily so flexible & light, that the sickness of her squirrel immediately took up all her attention, & when it, in spite of her nursing it, dy'd, I believe it gave her more concern than H.M. ever did'[17]. Happily, Lady Sarah herself 'did not love him, and only liked him'[18], and soon had an injured hedgehog to care for instead![19]

It was probably less trouble than George would turn out to be …

Whatever the new king may have thought about the arrangement, it was too late to go back now and the orphan princess was on her way to England. After a terribly choppy crossing in which the grieving young woman managed to charm everyone she encountered, she finally arrived in her new

17. Ilchester, Countess of & Stavordale, Lord (eds) (1902). *The Life and Letters of Lady Sarah Lennox*. London: John Murray, p.51.

18. Hibbert, Christopher (1998). *George III: A Personal History*. London: Viking, p.39.

19. Lady Sarah eventually married Sir Charles Bunbury, 6th Baronet, in 1762 and, after many years of scandal in which she eloped with Lord William Gordon and bore him a daughter, was divorced in 1776. In 1781, she married the Honourable George Napier, an army officer. Their marriage was a happy one and the couple had eight children.

Plate 1: The Coronation of King George IV in Westminster Abbey. Charles Turner. (*Courtesy of The Yale Center for British Art. Public domain*)

Plate 2: The Grand Coronation Banquet of George IV, in Westminster Hall. W. Read. (*Courtesy of The Yale Center for British Art. Public domain*)

"WHEN WE FORGET HIM MAY GOD FORGET US."

Drawn by M. Wyatt and Engraved by Wilson Lowry. THURLOW.

Nov. 6. 1817.

London, Publish'd as the Act Directs, by T. Sotheran, 4 Little Tower Street.

Op den 22 October 1727. is de Koning en de Koningin van Engeland tot Londen met een onvergelykelyke pragt en zonder enige wanorder tot vreugde van het gemeen en de groten gekroont. *Pet: Schenk exc:*

Die 22 Octob: 1727. Rex et Regina Angliæ Londinii incomparabili apparatu, nullo existente tumultu omnium, ipsorum etiam magnatum applausu coronati sunt: *Amst: cum Pr:*

Leon: Schenk fec:

Plate 4: The Coronation of George II. Adolf van der Laan. (*Courtesy of Rijksmuseum, under Creative Commons Public Domain Dedication CC0 1.0 Universal licence. http://creativecommons.org/publicdomain/zero/1.0/deed.en*)

Plate 5: The Funeral of George I. Adolf van der Laan. (*Courtesy of Rijksmuseum, under Creative Commons Public Domain Dedication CC0 1.0 Universal licence. http://creativecommons.org/publicdomain/zero/1.0/deed.en*)

Plate 6: The South Sea Scheme: speculators ruined by the collapse of the South Sea Company. William Hogarth, 1721. (*Courtesy Wellcome Library, London, under Creative Commons Attribution only licence CC BY 4.0 http://creativecommons.org/licenses/by/4.0/*)

Plate 7: Georgius D.G. Mag. Britanniae Franciae et Hiberniae Rex. John Benson Lossing. (*Courtesy of The New York Public Library. Public domain*)

Plate 8: George I at Newmarket, 4 or 5 October, 1717. John Wootton, 1717. (*Courtesy of The Yale Center for British Art. Public domain*)

Plate 9: George II. Johann Leonhard Hirschmann. (*Courtesy of Rijksmuseum, under Creative Commons Public Domain Dedication CC0 1.0 Universal licence.* http://creativecommons.org/publicdomain/zero/1.0/deed.en)

Plate 10: George I. Johann Leonhard Hirschmann. (*Courtesy of Rijksmuseum, under Creative Commons Public Domain Dedication CC0 1.0 Universal licence.* http://creativecommons.org/publicdomain/zero/1.0/deed.en)

Plate 13: The Pavilion & Steyne at Brighton. James Mitan, after Charles Cracklow, 1806. (*Courtesy of The Yale Center for British Art. Public domain*)

Plate 14: King George III. Thomas Frye. (*Courtesy Wellcome Library, London, under Creative Commons Attribution only licence CC BY 4.0 http://creativecommons.org/licenses/by/4.0/*)

Plate 15: George III and his family visit Dorchester jail. Charles Howard Hodges, 1793. (*Courtesy of Rijksmuseum, under Creative Commons Public Domain Dedication CC0 1.0 Universal licence. http://creativecommons.org/publicdomain/zero/1.0/deed.en*)

CARLETON HOUSE.

Plate 16: Carlton House. Anonymous, 1800. (*Courtesy of The Yale Center for British Art. Public domain*)

Plate 17: Carlton House, North Front. Richard Gilson Reeve, after William Westall. 1819. (*Courtesy of The Yale Center for British Art. Public domain*)

Plate 18: George III, King of Great Britain, France and Ireland etc. Anonymous. (*Courtesy of The New York Public Library. Public domain*)

Plate 19: George III. Anonymous, 1789. (*Courtesy of The New York Public Library. Public domain*)

Plate 20: George the III, King of Great Britain. Anonymous. (*Courtesy of The New York Public Library. Public domain*)

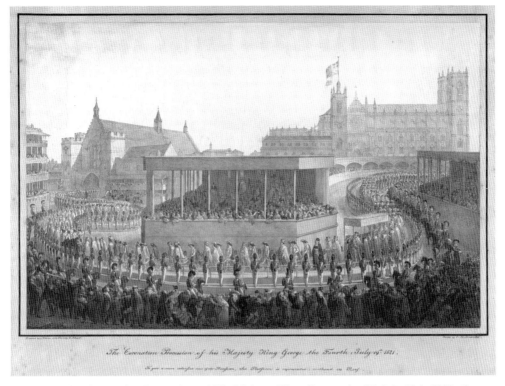

Plate 21: The Coronation Procession of His Majesty King George the IV, July 19th 1821. George Johann Scharf, 1821. (*Courtesy of The Yale Center for British Art. Public domain*)

Plate 22: King George III analyzing the residue from a large glass retort containing a small figure satirizing the English view of Napoleon. T West, 1803. (*Courtesy Wellcome Library, London, under Creative Commons Attribution only licence CC BY 4.0 http://creativecommons.org/licenses/by/4.0/*)

Plate 23: The gouty Prince Regent being helped onto his horse by means of an elaborate contraption outside an oriental pavilion in Kew Gardens. Anonymous, 1816. (*Courtesy Wellcome Library, London, under Creative Commons Attribution only licence CC BY 4.0 http://creativecommons.org/licenses/by/4.0/*)

Plate 24: George IV's Public Entry into the City of Dublin on August 17th 1821. Robert Havell, 1823. (*Courtesy of The Yale Center for British Art. Public domain*)

Plate 25: His Royal Highness George Prince of Wales. Anonymous, 1794. (*Courtesy of The New York Public Library. Public domain*)

Plate 26: Coronation Procession of H. M. George IV, 19 July 1821. William Heath. (*Courtesy of The Yale Center for British Art. Public domain*)

Plate 27: George the Fourth When Prince of Wales. Anonymous. (*Courtesy of The New York Public Library. Public domain*)

GEORGE THE FOURTH WHEN PRINCE OF WALES.

Plate 28: Windsor Castle from the Thames. William Daniell, 1825. (*Courtesy of The Yale Center for British Art. Public domain*)

Plate 30: Windsor Castle View – King George IV Gate and the Round Tower, 28 July 1832, 11.30 am. Dr. William Crotch, 1832. (*Courtesy of The Yale Center for British Art. Public domain*)

Plate 31: Dr Francis Willis, holding a book in his right hand. R Page, 1830. (*Courtesy Wellcome Library, London, under Creative Commons Attribution only licence CC BY 4.0 http://creativecommons.org/licenses/by/4.0/*)

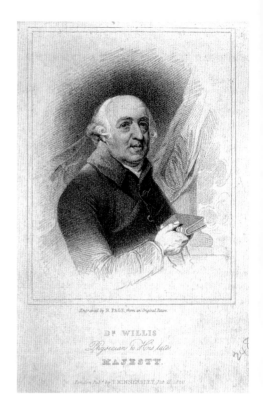

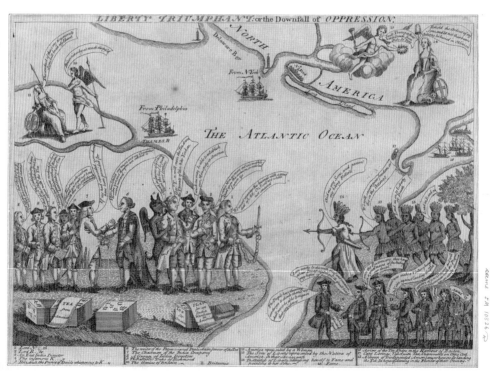

Plate 32: Liberty Triumphant, or The downfall of oppression. Anonymous, 1775. (*Courtesy of The New York Public Library. Public domain*)

land in September 1761 to be the leading lady at a wedding at where Lady Sarah herself was to serve as bridesmaid!

When George and Charlotte met for the first time at St James's Palace on 8 September 1761, she threw herself down at her fiancé's feet. Utterly taken by this enchanting young lady, he raised her to stand and escorted her into the palace to meet the royal family. They were married later that day and would be together for nearly sixty years through all manner of challenges and no less than fifteen children.

'THIS Day His Majesty King George the Third, and Queen Charlotte, were crowned in the Abbey Church of Westminster, with the Ceremonies accustomed upon that Great and Glorious Solemnity'.[20]

Exactly two weeks after their marriage, the couple celebrated the Coronation at Westminster Abbey. Remarkable amongst his fellows, George took no mistresses in the decades that followed, remaining devoted to his bride and the vows that they had made.

The Gentle Shepherd

From that first fateful meeting at Egham races to the moment his former charge ascended the throne, Bute had become so entrenched in the life of George that the two seemed inseparable. It certainly came as a surprise to nobody when, almost as soon as George III was crowned king in 1760, his former tutor began a meteoric rise through the political ranks. Coming to the throne as a war raged, George had to grab the reins with both hands yet even with Pitt never far away and willing to lend guidance, George looked for assurance and advice more from his old friend, Bute.

Bute was a keen and insightful politician and in the second year of George III's reign, he assumed the highest office in the land when he unseated Newcastle as prime minister. Eyebrows were raised in the press where rumours flew that Bute had secured his office not through skill but through

---

20. *London Gazette* (London, England), September 22, 1761 – September 26, 1761; issue 10142, p.3.

nepotism. In Parliament, accusations of a bias against the Whigs were rife. Even worse, the whispers that Bute had gained influence and power through his spirited bedding of George's widowed mother returned full force in the press with *The North Briton*, the newspaper of infamous radical journalist and Member of Parliament, John Wilkes, leading the charge.

The people of Great Britain were not impressed by the thought that their most senior statesman might have slept his way to greatness and the king was deeply wounded by the criticisms and accusations, feeling for the first but by no means last time the sting of royal politics. Ever the realist, Bute recognized that there was little point fighting against the tide, and he was determined to leave before he was pushed. He did not enjoy the vitriol to which his Scottish countrymen were subjected, and found life as prime minster stressful and exhausting. Mocked, heckled and hanged in effigy, it was more than the politician could stand and in April 1763, less than twelve months after he'd assumed office, Bute retired.

George found the departure of his favourite upsetting and he was even more dismayed when Bute was succeeded by George Grenville in the office of prime minister. An elder statesman of British politics, Grenville was a brother-in-law to William Pitt, a man who was both an ally and opponent through their long and historic careers. In fact, it was Pitt who nicknamed Grenville 'Gentle Shepherd', a name which haunted the latter for the rest of his career.

During what was no doubt intended to be a searing speech during a debate on the Cider Bill of 1763, Grenville asked the house that, if a tax could not be set on cider, then where could it be set instead? With no answer forthcoming, he asked again where the money might be found, imploring the House, 'tell me where?', and repeating the request to drive the point home.

As the sitting ended and Pitt left the chamber he was seized by a little devilishness, and began to mimic his opponent, innocently whistling the popular tune of the time, *Gentle Shepherd*, the chorus of which contained the line, 'tell me where?'. Those Members of Parliament in the vicinity found the none-too-subtle dig at Grenville hilarious and the nickname stuck. To this day Grenville is associated with *Gentle Shepherd*, not quite the sort of song that a statesman might want to accompany his name!

Although Bute had thought Grenville was the best man for the job, George and the new prime minister did *not* get on, as the king found Grenville far too forceful. Behind the scenes, George attempted to indulge in some political moving and shaking with his old advisor. He petitioned Bute to approach the deposed Newcastle and even Pitt to ask whether they might be prevailed upon to join the ministry before Grenville had a chance to take office. Pitt *was* willing to assume a position but presented the king with a list of lofty demands that must be satisfied before he would agree once and for all. When no agreement could be reached, Grenville took office and he brought a condition of his own. Bute, Grenville demanded, must resign all of his political positions; it was a condition the king's former mentor willingly fulfilled.

The relationship between Grenville and the king grew no easier and it soon weighed heavily on George. In fact, in 1765 he fell so ill that it was decided that plans for a regent must be drawn up, yet George refused to name a suitable candidate. Grenville, however, was convinced that George intended to choose Augusta as regent, thus handing the power behind the throne directly to her long-time confidante, Bute. This infighting caused George's condition to worsen still further and he looked once again to Pitt and Newcastle, sure that a new prime minister could only improve matters. However, when Pitt continually refused to even discuss the possibility of taking office, George authorized his uncle, the Duke of Cumberland, to negotiate with Newcastle. Until his death in 1765 Cumberland would prove a valuable ally to his nephew and he approached Newcastle with an eye to finally ridding government of the troublesome Grenville.

Thankfully, Newcastle agreed to intervene and in 1765 Grenville was dismissed in favour of Charles Watson-Wentworth, 2nd Marquess of Rockingham.[21] As part of the deal he had brokered, Newcastle would become Lord Privy Seal and though George might have heaved a sigh of relief, it was to be short-lived.

---

21. Ironically, Rockingham had resigned as Lord of the Bedchamber in 1762 in protest at the king's apparent favouritism of Bute.

So Many Governments, So Little Time

Georgian politics was a hothouse of gossip and intrigue and no topic was hotter in the mid-1760s than the Stamp Act. Passed in 1765, the Stamp Act applied a tax to printed matter and marked the first time the colonies had been directly taxed. The money raised would go to meet the costs incurred by Britain's victorious but hugely expensive foray into the Seven Years' War, when Pitt had commanded the rudder of government. The French had been driven from North America and someone had to foot the bill but why, argued the colonists should it be them? After all, they had no direct representation in Parliament and soon unrest was rife, with the protestors upholding their belief of 'no taxation without representation'.

The outcry in America was immense and deafening, with protests and violence on the streets. In the face of this overwhelming anger, the Rockingham ministry proposed that the Stamp Act be repealed, whilst Pitt rounded on Grenville and his apparently shabby treatment of the colonies. Word went round that the king did not support the repeal and Rockingham insisted that George make his support *loudly* known, a command which he obeyed.

In the event, the government won the vote in favour of repeal by a majority of 140 votes, making it a comfortable victory. The repeal made George enormously popular in America and Rockingham felt secure not only in his position but also in the fact that, when he said *jump*, His Majesty enquired politely, *how high?*

Once again, George found his distraction turning to despair. It is a measure of how low he had plummeted that in 1766 he turned to Pitt, cap in hand, and asked for assistance. After two years away from Parliament, Pitt was in a gracious mood and agreed to return to government. It was a development that drove a wedge between the king and Bute, and the situation was not helped by the fact that York, once George's favourite brother, was now regularly dabbling in politics. But not for long.

'His Royal Highness the Duke of York died on the 17th inst. at a village in his way to Venice whither he was travelling from Genoa. His Royal Highness was born March 14, 1738 9 [sic], installed Knight of the Bath on the 4th of June 1752, and created Duke of York and Albany in 1760,

His Royal Highness was embalmed immediately after his decease, and his corpse is bringing over to England with all possible expedition.'[22]

In fact, the freewheeling York, described by Lady Louisa Stuart as, 'silly, frivolous and heartless, void alike of steadiness and principle; a libertine in his practice, and in society one of those incessant chatterers who must by necessity utter a vast deal of nonsense,'[23] died aged just 28 in 1767, leaving George to reflect on the happy times they had known in childhood. Yet even as the court went into full mourning and the king's melancholy deepened, the wheels of Georgian politics continued to grind.

The ministry that Pitt assembled was a curious one. Each member was hand-picked for their personal strengths but this did not necessarily make for a happy combination. Much has been written on this administration but perhaps none summed it up more succinctly than Edmund Burke when he commented:

'He put together (says he) a piece of joinery, so crossly indented and whimsically dovetailed; a cabinet so variously inlaid; such a piece of diversified mosaic; such a tessellated pavement, without cement; here a bit of black stone, and there a bit of white; patriots and courtiers; king's friends and republicans; whigs and tories; treacherous friends and open enemies; that it was indeed a curious show; but utterly unsafe to touch, and unsure to stand on.'[24]

Bute saw Pitt, now Earl of Chatham, slip smartly into the top job that *he* had once occupied and whilst Bute's own loyal followers were not appointed to the ministry, Pitt's were. Little remained of Bute's once pervasive influence and perhaps fortunately so, because this ministry, the fifth in George's six years on the throne, was to prove catastrophic.

Pitt was not a well man and in 1767 he suffered a debilitating nervous collapse. Augustus FitzRoy, 3rd Duke of Grafton, stepped into the breach

---

22. *Gazetteer and New Daily Advertiser* (London, England), Tuesday, September 29, 1767; issue 12034, p.1.
23. Stuart, Lady Louisa (1863). *Some Account of John, Duke of Argyll and His Family*. London: W Clowes & Sons, p.92.
24. Bayley, William (1824). *The Bagman's Bioscope*. Bath: Edward Barrett, p.275.

as, at the time, the youngest Prime Minister Britain had ever known.[25] A long-time opponent of Bute, Grafton struggled from the start with the troublesome administration he had inherited and its vocal opponents. For the early portion of Grafton's time in office he was only acting leader, with Pitt officially the man at the helm, and though both he and George encouraged Pitt's recovery, he seemed to grow more unwell by the day.

'[Pitt's] situation was different from what I had imagined; his nerves and spirits were affected to a dreadful degree: and the sight of his great mind bowed down, and thus weakened by disorder, would have filled me with grief and concern, even if I had not long borne a sincere attachment to his person and character.'[26]

Grafton's interview with his esteemed colleague left him fearing for Pitt's sanity and it was a concern that others shared. Pitt was indeed a man in crisis and in 1768, he resigned. The king initially resisted, writing, 'I think I have a right to insist on your remaining in my service; for I with pleasure look forward to the time of your recovery, when I may have your assistance in resisting the torrent of Factions this country so much labours under'.[27]

The ailing statesman would not be persuaded, however, and his reply to George's letter is almost pitiful in tone, imploring that he be freed from his obligation to the nation. Faced with the passage that follows, George had no choice but to bow to Pitt's request and accept the resignation he had so desperately offered.

'I supplicate again on my knees your Majesty's mercy, and most humbly implore your Majesty's royal permission to resign that high office. Should it please God to restore me to health, every moment of my life will be at your Majesty's devotion.'[28]

---

25. This record was eventually claimed by William Pitt the Younger who came to office in 1783, aged just 24, a full nine years younger than Grafton.
26. Anson, William (ed.) (1898). *Autobiography and Political correspondence of Augustus Henry, Third Duke of Grafton.* London: John Murray, p.137.
27. Taylor, William Stanhope and Prinole, John Henry, (eds.) (1839). *Correspondence of William Pitt, Earl of Chatham: Vol III.* London: John Murray, p.343.
28. Ibid., p.344.

With Pitt gone, Grafton found himself not waving, but drowning. Beset by critics on all sides, his ministry limped along from one disaster to the next. The final nail in the coffin was not hammered home by an enemy, but an old friend.

With all hope seemingly lost for Pitt, an apparent miracle happened in 1770 when he appeared quite unexpectedly in the House of Lords. Here he spoke against Bute and his own old ministry, bringing the tottering Grafton government to its knees. George was quick to respond and approached Lord North, son of his childhood tutor, finding him happy to accept the responsibility of office.

For the first time in what seemed like an age, things were on an even keel in George's Parliament. What, though, of closer to home?

Brothers Banished

So far, you may note that there has been no mention of the sort of domestic strife that characterized the reigns of Georges I and II. George III was a family man, devoted to wife and offspring, and all *seemed* rosy behind the royal closed doors, yet a shattering storm was brewing.

In 1769, George's brother, Prince Henry, Duke of Cumberland and Strathearn, was successfully sued for adultery by Lord Grosvenor, whose wife had been caught *in flagrante* with Henry. The wronged husband was awarded damages of £10,000 and the prince's costs in total reached well over £1million in today's money. The trial records make for melodramatic entertainment, with witnesses cross-questioned on the rumpled nature of the bedding, the disorder of the lady's hair and a mysterious chap employed to drill holes in bedchamber doors so that the liaisons might be observed.

When the full record of the trial was published, complete with lusty letters between the duke and his lover, the pious and reserved king was horrified. To give a flavour of exactly what was reported, here is just a snippet from Cumberland's letter to Lady Grosvenor, she of the not-very-disordered hair!

'I then prayed for you *my dearest love kissed your dearest little Hair* and laye down and dreamt of you, had you on the dear little *couch* ten thousand times, in my arms kissing you, and telling you how much I loved and adored you.'[29]

Of course, the disgraced duke could not hope to pay and went to his crowned brother, cap in hand. George in turn appealed to Lord North and the prime minister approved the payment, with the public purse settling the bill for Henry's fun and games.

Needless to say, George was horrified that his brother should drag the family into such a public spectacle. The press lapped up the gossip with glee and George wondered why it was that his siblings could not behave with the same measure of dignity and regard for duty that *he* managed to. Where was the good royal marriage, the legitimate children and the respectable public persona that he considered so vital? It was almost as though his brothers were intent on being individuals first, and members of the royal family second, a freedom that George had never been afforded.

In 1771, however, Henry had an even bigger shock to share.

No doubt hoping that the stern telling off given to Cumberland on the occasion of his adultery with Lady Grosvenor had hit home, George received a letter from his brother that contained an explosive announcement. In it, Cumberland confessed that he had married Mrs Anne Horton, a widowed commoner, and 'nothing now remains to make me one of the happiest of men but your approbation which I trust the sensibility of your heart and the amiable qualifications of the object of my choice will strongly plead for and fully justify'.[30]

Of course, Cumberland couldn't *really* have expected that his placid brother would be happy to discover not only that he had fallen for a commoner, but that he had already married her. The king was furious. He felt betrayed, humiliated and as though he alone stood for the dignity of the crown he held so dear. There could be no question of his approving the marriage and just as George II and Fred had been banished from the presence of the monarch, so too was Prince Henry.

---

29. Anonymous (1770). *The Trial of His R H the D of C July 5th, 1770. For Criminal Conversation with Lady Harriet G—r*. London: John Walker, p.14.
30. Tillyard, Stella (2007). *A Royal Affair: George III and his Troublesome Siblings*. London: Vintage, p.181.

Along with his wife and any children that might come of the marriage, Henry was exiled and courtiers were warned that they faced the same fate should they choose to keep company with the newly disgraced duke. Not content with this, George also decided that legislation was the only way to prevent such an embarrassment occurring again, and the Royal Marriages Act of 1772 was created. It would be too little, too late.

'[...] no descendant of the body of his late majesty King George the Second, male or female, [...] shall be capable of contracting matrimony without the previous consent of his Majesty, his heirs, or successors, signified under the great seal, and declared in council, [...] and that every marriage, or matrimonial contract, of any such descendant, without such consent first had and obtained, shall be null and void, to all intents and purposes whatsoever.'

The Act ruled that any descendant of George II who wished to marry could not do so without the consent of the monarch. If no such consent was given, no marriage could take place unless the parties were over 25. In that case, the Privy Council must be informed of the wedding and Parliament must not raise any objections. If these conditions were met, then a marriage could go ahead after one year. Life, however, is rarely so simple.

One has to feel for George, beset as he was by siblings who seemed to be a magnet for scandal and whose son, in the years to come, would prove to be more than a match for the lot of them put together. Betrayed, humiliated and furious at Cumberland's behaviour, one wonders whether George was pleased to note that his other surviving brother and trusted friend, Prince William Henry, Duke of Gloucester and Edinburgh, had behaved with a little more circumspection. However, if he did look to Gloucester with the sense of a job well done, pleased to call such a sensible chap *brother*, then he was about to get a rude awakening, because Gloucester had a little announcement of his own to make. He was going to be a father.

Far from being circumspect, William Henry had actually married even earlier than Henry, taking the illegitimately-born widow and Dowager Countess Waldegrave, Maria Walpole, as his bride. Although their relationship was no secret, it was supposed that Maria was nothing more legally binding than a mistress. In fact, the couple had married in 1766 and, mindful that George would likely not be best pleased, they somehow managed to keep the marriage a secret for more than five long years. However, when Maria fell pregnant in 1772, they had no choice but to come clean if her reputation was to remain relatively unsullied.

George was cut to the quick by his brother's lies yet was willing to offer a compromise. If Gloucester would agree never to speak of or allude to his wife or the marriage, then he would continue to be welcome at court. Should these terms be unpalatable to the duke, then both he and his wife would be banished.

What's a duke to do?

Brother or wife?

Gloucester chose Maria and the marriage was soon public knowledge. Just as he had threatened he would, George banished the couple from his presence, wondering what had happened to leave one brother so pious whilst the others were so free with their affections.

In time, both of those banished brothers would be tentatively welcomed back to court but their wives would never be recognized by George with anything but an air of grudging dismissal, never rising much in the estimations of the pious king.

Death of a Dowager

What with one thing and another, it seemed as though 1772 was destined to be George's *annus horribilis* and it began with the death of his mother that February. Augusta had been suffering from throat cancer for some time yet continued to soldier on, determined not to accept the inevitable. Once so popular, her friendship with Bute and the mockery of the press had taken their toll and Augusta was no longer the darling of the people. Her funeral procession was heckled as it passed through the streets and the service was beset with petty crime and disorder.

The *Middlesex Journal or Chronicle of Liberty* offers us a glimpse of the chaotic scenes that accompanied the lying in state of the dowager princess:

'On Saturday morning, about eight 'clock, the doors of the Prince's
Chambers were opened for the admission of company to see the corpse

of her Royal Highness the Princess Dowager of Wales lie in state. The concourse of people, whose curiosity led them to see this awful ceremony, was incredible, and the great difficulty the soldiers met with in keeping off the crowd created the utmost noise and confusion. [...] Upon the whole, the appearance on this occasion was far from magnificent.'[31]

At the loss of his greatest champion, George was heartbroken. He had spent the evening before Augusta's death at her side, his mother unable to speak and wracked with agony. He ordered a deep mourning period of four months yet Horace Walpole reports that 'the mob huzzaed for joy'[32] and 'stripped the black cloth from the platform to the Abbey, before half the procession had passed across'[33], which can't have brought any comfort to her bereaved son.

Whether Augusta was a devoted mother or an ambitious, smothering parent is a matter of opinion, and perhaps she was both. She certainly wielded an enormous influence over her son in his early life and it was her appointee, Bute, who would do much to shape the man George became. With her death and Bute no longer the presence he had once been, the king was now, he hoped, his own man. The years to come would contain many challenges and first among them came courtesy of the affairs of the heart of yet another troublesome sibling. This time, however, it was not a brother, but a sister as the *Time of Struensee* brought intrigue, heartbreak, scandal and death to the Danish royal court.

Drama in Denmark

Princess Caroline Matilda of Great Britain was George's youngest sister and the last child of Frederick, Prince of Wales and Princess Augusta of Saxe-Gotha. Raised without pomp and ceremony away from the court it came as

---

31. *Middlesex Journal or Chronicle of Liberty* (London, England), February 15, 1772–February 18, 1772; issue 450, p.1.
32. Walpole, Horace (1910). *The Last Journals of Horace Walpole During the Reign of George III from 1771–1783*. London: John Lane, p.17.
33. Ibid., p.17.

a rude awakening when, aged just 15, she was packed off to Copenhagen and a new life as wife to her cousin, Christian VII of Denmark. Christian's reputation went before him, and with reports of his *eccentricities* not exactly a well-kept secret, it was surely not a fate any young lady would welcome.

Those eccentricities would eventually explode into a full blown mental illness yet for the time being, Christian contented himself with ignoring his new wife in favour of trips to brothels and the company of Copenhagen's no doubt very enthusiastic prostitutes. All of this wasn't unusual among young royal males and a blind eye was usually turned. However, when a proclivity for ladies of the night began to interfere with the production of an heir, the blind eye could be turned no longer. Whatever else he did and whoever else he did it with, Christian *must* fulfil this most important duty, whether he wanted to or not. The king did not want to, and his queen was less than keen, but the couple finally muddled through and in 1768, a royal son was born.

As Christian's behaviour became more outlandish, the court was hugely relieved when he befriended a Prussian doctor named Johann Friedrich Struensee and brought him home to Denmark. At first appearances, it looked as though Christian was attempting to address his own mental health problems and the far from frivolous Struensee appeared just the tonic, lending a sensible, calming influence to the occasionally flighty young Sovereign.

Unfortunately, he would end up treating *far* more than the king's eccentricities.

At first, the neglected queen did not trust the new arrival, suspicious of his motives when he began to slowly but surely accrue powers at court. Yet when he inoculated her son and saved his life during a smallpox epidemic in Denmark, all of that changed. Lonely, far from home and trapped in the cold Danish court, when Caroline Matilda spied the chance for a little passion with her Prussian doctor, she snatched at it with both hands. As she and Struensee began their heated, deadly affair, Christian descended into madness. In his mania, the king came to believe that the physician was his only friend and awarded him an authority so great that he was a regent in all but name.

The couple made virtually no effort to conceal their romance and we can only speculate if the king knew of the relationship. If he did, he seemed not to care and it might actually have been something of a relief in some ways. After all, he had no wish to spend time in the company of his wife and political business only increased his anxiety, so why not let one man, one trusted friend, take care of both? This was a king who believed it was 'unfashionable to love one's wife'[34], and what was any monarch if not the height of fashion? Of course, there were other players in the game of courtly politics and if Christian didn't lose any sleep over the situation, then his stepmother was a *very* different matter.

Queen Dowager Juliana Maria felt that if her stepson was incapable of ruling then surely *she* should be regent, and properly appointed as such. Struensee's sweeping reforms played right into her hands, infuriating the upper classes with new taxes and taking away their rights and privileges at every turn, leaving them desperate for a return to the status quo. The final straw came when Caroline Matilda gave birth to a daughter who everyone simply assumed *had* to be Struensee's child. With this apparent bastard in the house of the king, the queen dowager took action and marshalled Struensee's enemies against him.

In January 1772, Caroline Matilda and Struensee were arrested and charged with usurping royal authority. Struensee was tortured and the queen was imprisoned and denied access to any counsel. Caroline Matilda initially denied the affair but when her jailer told her that Struensee had admitted it, she too came clean. Even as the queen heard that her marriage had been dissolved a triumphant Christian was paraded through Copenhagen, cheerily greeting his adoring subjects.

As Caroline Matilda languished in Kronborg Castle, Struensee was sentenced to death. On 28 April 1772, before a crowd of thousands, his hand was severed and he was beheaded, drawn and quartered. Though Caroline Matilda's son remained in the custody of his father, her daughter joined her in her prison and the former queen, furious at her fate and grieving for her lover, wrote to her brother, George III, seeking his help.

George stopped short of asking for his sister to be sent home to England and instead negotiated her removal to Celle Castle, where the wife of George I had been born all those years before. Well aware that Augusta's funeral

---

34. Rounding, Virginia (2007). *Catherine the Great*. London: Random House, p.198.

had been a public relations disaster and that his brothers seemed devoted to embarrassing the family, the last thing George needed was *another* scandalous sibling on his hands. No, far better that she be safely in Celle with her daughter, unable to cause trouble for anyone.

Above all else, George urged Caroline Matilda not to try and get involved any further in court politics or to be tempted by promises of power. However, despite his cautionary words she was sure that she could still bring about change in her adopted land and dreamed of the day when Christian might be overthrown and she would rule as regent until her son came of age. Caroline Matilda's dreams never became reality and scarlet fever claimed her life in 1775, when she was only 23.

> 'On Thursday Evening last one of His Majesty's Electoral Messengers arrived from Hanover with the melancholy Account, that Her Majesty Caroline Matilda, Queen of Denmark and Norway, died at Zell on the 10th Instant, about Midnight, of a malignant Fever, after an Illness of Five Days, to the great Grief of Their Majesties and all the Royal Family.'[35]

The fate of George's sister coloured his opinion of arranged, dynastic marriage forever and was to have a dramatic impact on his own daughters. Fearful that they might one day face a similar loveless marriage, when the time came to negotiate their own matches, he was reluctant to marry them off. If he could have arranged the marriages of his wayward brothers, however, George would have been a happy man indeed.

The Trouble with Tea

First brothers, then mothers, then sisters ... whatever would be next? Tea. Really, one has to feel for George sometimes. Here was a chap who seemed ideally suited to a quiet life, a world away from the social whirlwind of George II's early years, with its assassination attempts and fires, or the gritted-teeth gatherings of George I. Instead his court was a traditional,

---

35. *London Gazette* (London, England), May 16, 1775 – May 20, 1775; issue 11562, p.1.

strict place where *all* were expected to abide by the hierarchical rules and his domestic life was one of calm. George wasn't fond of show and his boyhood loves of hunting, astronomy and music were joined by another passion – bookbinding. A man of gentle interests, George was at his happiest tending to his agricultural land at Richmond and Windsor, and he revelled in his nickname, *Farmer George*. There was to be little time for farming in 1773 though, because across the Atlantic a storm was brewing. Discontent in the colonies had been rumbling for a while but things were about to spiral into outright civil disobedience thanks to that most British of traditions – tea.

The Townshend Acts, passed in 1767, were a series of duties placed on the North American colonies. These hugely unpopular acts were repealed bit by bit yet the tax on tea remained resolutely in place. For five years the interests of the East India Company were protected by the Indemnity Act, which gave the company a refund of the duty paid on all tea exported to the colonies but when this expired in 1772, the company was left in a financial hole.

Effectively facing a ten per cent tax on its imported tea, the company raised prices and in response, sales plummeted. Still the East India Company continued to import tea into England where it piled up unsold, leaving the company's accounts seriously in the red. The government could not afford the enormous East India Company to collapse and began to investigate solutions that might set things on an even keel.

With the tax vital in paying the salaries of government employees in the colonies it couldn't be repealed, nor could the tea be offloaded elsewhere, so what could be done? The answer was, of course, to ship the whole lot over to America and Parliament passed the Tea Act of 1773. This permitted the East India Company to export tea direct to North America, where the colonists would have to pay the duty on it. Crucially, the tea would not have to be imported into England first, thus avoiding British taxes and granting the company a monopoly on the North American tea market.

Lord North was urged to reconsider the tax but he refused; after all, the money was needed if the salaries were to be paid. It was a fateful decision and one that would have sweeping consequences for British rule in America. Across the ocean 'no taxation without representation', the call raised against the Stamp Tax in 1765, became a rallying cry once more.

'The tea-tax upon our American brother freeholders, is one of the many errors in government which have unhappily marked the present reign; it is a most daring and flagrant violation of King John's Magna Charta, [...] it is the indispensable duty of the crown to abrogate this tyrannical tax upon the *unrepresented Americans.*'[36]

As America listened with shock to the details of the Tea Act, thousands of crates of tea were already making their way across the ocean towards the colonies and in that faraway land, opposition grew. The Sons of Liberty, a group of American Whigs who had first made their presence felt during protests over Stamp Duty, made as much noise as they possibly could, putting pressure on the consignees who had been officially appointed to sell tea to resign their posts. With officials paid from a tax levied in the English Parliament, how could the colonial governors *possibly* act in the best interests of their people, and who spoke for the colonists in that same Parliament?

Nobody, claimed the Sons of Liberty, and it had gone on for far, far too long.

'It is not the tea-tax that might be of itself so hurtful; but if the Americans admit it, they admit the right of taxation and they will have taxes flung like ropes of onions.'[37]

Tea importers who didn't work for the company would lose their businesses, smugglers would be out of booty, and anyone in the tea trade not from the East India Company would suffer as a result of the new ruling. With the public in uproar, a tea ship was turned away when it landed in Philadelphia whilst the vessel bound for New York arrived to find nobody there willing to act as consignee to its unwanted cargo. It was in Boston, however, that history was made.

When the *Dartmouth* arrived in Boston Harbour on 28 November 1773, its crew found trouble waiting. Under the direction of Samuel Adams, a

---

36. *Morning Chronicle and London Advertiser* (London, England), Tuesday, May 10, 1774; issue 1548, p.1.
37. *Morning Chronicle and London Advertiser* (London, England), Saturday, June 4, 1774; issue 1570, p.2.

politician vehemently opposed to British taxation, who went on to become a founding father of America, local men stood guard at the ship to prevent hundreds of chests of tea from being unloaded, whilst her captain, James Hall, was urged by the Sons of Liberty to turn back and take his tea with him, which would mean that no import duty would have been paid. However, mindful of the disastrous consequences this could have on his own position, Governor Thomas Hutchinson refused permission for the *Dartmouth* to leave Boston until the tea was unloaded and the duty paid.

With armed men patrolling the harbour, the two sides appeared to be at a stalemate. *Dartmouth* was followed by the *Eleanor* on 2 December, and the *Beaver*, which arrived in Boston on 15 December. By the time these vessels arrived, tensions were running high and a seemingly impossible solution was needed. Once the *Dartmouth* arrived, the clock began ticking on a strict deadline of twenty days after which, if the tea had not been unloaded and the duty had not been paid, then the cargo would be confiscated by officials in Boston.

That deadline was due to expire on 16 December and as an enormous crowd of locals and protestors assembled at the Old South Meeting House to hear the decision the three ships languished in their berths, tea still resolutely on board. Finally the word came that the governor would not budge, the ships could *not* leave without unloading their cargo. This was the start of one of the most famous incidents in American history, the *Boston Tea Party*.

With that, the crowd swarmed from the meeting house towards the harbour, some of them disguised as Mohawks to protect their identities. The protestors boarded the three ships and dumped more than 300 chests of tea into the water at Griffin's Wharf. George Hewes, one of the men in disguise, remembered later that, 'in about three hours we had thus broken and thrown overboard every tea chest'[38] and that, apart from a request from the captain not to damage the ship itself, 'no attempt was made to resist us'.[39]

This was the latest and most serious blow to British authority in America and as the king determined that he *must* hold onto the colonies, Parliament

---

38. Barber, John Warner (ed.) (1841). *The History and Antiquities of New England, New York, and New Jersey*. Worcester: Dorr, Howland and Co, p.390.

39. Ibid., p.390.

swung into decisive action. The time for talking was over, and George's advisors had one answer: force. After a meeting with Lieutenant General Thomas Gage, commander in chief of the British forces in America, George wrote to the prime minister and told him:

'Since you left me this day, I have seen Lieutenant-General Gage, who came to express his readiness, though so lately come from America, to return at a day's notice, if the conduct of the Colonies should induce directing coercive measures. [...] He says they will be lyons, whilst we are lambs; but, if we take the resolute part, they will undoubtedly prove very meek. He thinks the four regiments intended to relieve as many regiments in America, if sent to Boston, are sufficient to prevent any disturbance.'[40]

It was to prove a woeful underestimation of the strength of feeling in North America, and things went from bad to worse when North introduced what became known to colonists as the Intolerable Acts and to the British as the Coercive Acts. Intended to make an example of those who had dared go against British authority, the sweeping acts closed the Port of Boston and, amongst other measures, ended self-government in Massachusetts, as well as imposing harsh restrictions on public meetings.

The colonists were outraged, wondering how long it would be before the rest of the country fell under such draconian rule and who would speak for them if it did. Already suspicious of their masters in Britain, the people turned against Parliament and the king, an apparent tyrant who was intent on keeping them firmly in their place with an iron fist. The inevitable outcome was violence and as both sides of the Atlantic reeled, the first blows were struck in the American War of Independence.

The Fallen Idol

Unrest in the colonies did not begin with the Boston Tea Party, but many years earlier, when the Stamp Act was passed. Things had never really settled

---

40. Donne, Bodham W (ed.) (1867). *The Correspondence of King George the Third With Lord North from 1768 to 1783: Vol I*. London: John Murray, p.164.

after that upheaval but the Tea Party was the final straw in the fractious relationship between the stern yet absent parent and its troublesome offspring. In the House of Commons and the royal palaces alike, all were agreed on one thing – that the colonists were getting a little above their station.

> 'I [George III] never doubted of the zeal of the House of Commons in support of the just superiority of the mother-country over its colonies.'[41]

It is outside the scope of this book to examine the details of the years of conflict that ended in America gaining its independence, but for George, they proved exhausting. At first he favoured a softly-softly approach, reserving his strongest feelings for those who, safe in England, raised their voices in favour of the rebelling colonists. Soon though, he had no choice but to agree to a military intervention, and in 1775, the country once again went to war.

Peaceful alternatives were sought, including the so-called Olive Branch Petition, whereby the American colonists promised loyalty to Great Britain in exchange for no further conflict. The king rejected this overture, but when the Declaration of Independence was read out, there could be no doubt that this had become a most serious business. The king must hold firm, he could afford neither doubt nor prevarication.

At the top of government, however, there was a significant wobble and Lord North was having more than a moment of self-doubt. As the war went on, North battled with his confidence as leader, and eventually, in 1778, admitted to the king that he could not go on. The only solution he could suggest was one that sent a chill through George. He wanted to bring Pitt back into the fold and have him at least attempt to replicate his successful navigation of the Seven Years' War. Pitt advocated compromise over military intervention or capitulation, firmly believing that any attempt to win America's loyalty through force was doomed to fail, yet could he be the man of the hour?

41. Ibid., p.232.

The thought of Pitt's return was abhorrent to George and he begged North to reconsider, doing all he could to jolly him along and renew his shattered confidence. Perhaps, he suggested through gritted teeth, Pitt could be part of North's government but not the leader? George would even tolerate Fox being involved in the administration if it meant keeping North in the top job. North's mind was set though, and George reluctantly agreed to let him go, but he would *not* sanction Pitt taking his place. And then the Grim Reaper came calling.

Life had not been kind to Pitt, and a multitude of physical and mental health problems took their toll on the statesman, leaving him frail and reclusive. Yet despite the challenges he faced, the Earl of Chatham maintained a passion for politics. He had heard with horror of General Burgoyne's surrender to the Americans at Saratoga in October 1777, a decision that proved catastrophic for the British cause, and it fired him into action. Just months later, France had unsurprisingly declared itself with America against the British, leading the government's opponents to call for peace at any cost and Pitt could be silent no more.

For Pitt, the events unfolding seemed to be undoing all that he had achieved with his masterful handling of the Seven Years' War. Despite his ill health, he could not sit idly by and do nothing. On 7 April 1778, the very day that the Duke of Richmond intended to speak in the Lords and press for the granting of American independence, Pitt the Younger helped his ailing father into the Lords. None who saw him could fail to recognize that Pitt was incapable of heading a ministry and Lord Camden described the political icon's appearance in a letter laden with pathos.

'The Earl spoke, but was not like himself; his speech faltered, his sentences broken, and his mind not master of itself. [...] His words were shreds of unconnected eloquence and flashes of the same fire which he, Prometheus-like, had stolen from heaven, and were then returning to the place from whence they were taken. Your Grace sees even I, who am a mere prose man, am tempted to be poetical while I am discoursing of this extraordinary man's genius.'[42]

---

42. Campbell, Lord John (1851). *The Lives of the Lord Chancellors and Keepers of the Great Seal of England, Vol. V.* Philadelphia: Blanchard and Lea, pp.253–254.

Frail he might be, but Pitt could not let Richmond's plea for peace and independence go unchallenged. He spoke against the motion yet, when he rose with the apparent intention of speaking again, the elder statesman suffered a seizure and collapsed insensible on the floor of the House of Lords. Witness to the calamity, Camden related the tragic events to Lord Grafton.

'[Pitt] fell back upon his seat, and was to all appearance in the agonies of death. – This threw the whole House into confusion; every person was upon his legs in a moment, hurrying from one place to another, some sending for assistance, others producing salts, and others reviving spirits. Many crowding about the Earl to observe his countenance – all affected – most part really concerned; and even those who might have felt a secret pleasure at the accident, yet put on the appearance of distress, except on the Earl of M.,[43] who sat still, almost as much unmoved as the senseless body itself'.[44]

Pitt was attended by doctors and retired to his seat at Hayes. On 11 May 1778, the man the king believed, 'had the blackest of hearts',[45] died. The press couldn't help but use the opportunity to make a jibe at the members of the House on the occasion, even as it beat its grieving breast and the *General Advertiser and Morning Intelligencer* commented:

'Yesterday morning at eight o'clock, died, at his seat at Hayes in Kent, the Earl of Chatham.

Though the Ministry rejoice at this event, the people at large have reason to be sorry; for never were Shakespeare's words so truly applicable, viz. *Take him for all in all, we ne'er shall look upon his like*

---

43. Lord Campbell did some detective work in the case of the mysterious, unmoved Earl M, having discovered that both Marchmont and Mansfield were present on the occasion of Pitt's collapse. He concluded that it was Mansfield who remained seated, pointing to the evidence of John Singleton Copley's legendary painting, *The Death of Earl Pitt*, that depicts the earl sitting in the chamber as around him, consternation breaks out.

44. Campbell, Lord John (1851). *The Lives of the Lord Chancellors and Keepers of the Great Seal of England, Vol. V*. Philadelphia: Blanchard and Lea, p.253.

45. Hibbert, Christopher (1998). *George III: A Personal History*. London: Viking, p. 28.

again. The services of this great man to his country, are too well known, and too deeply engraven, upon the heart of every Englishman, to need any attempt of repetition here.'[46]

The thorn that had niggled at George's side for his entire political life was gone, though his memory would cast a long shadow through the ages whilst across the ocean, the American War of Independence raged on.

A Family in Mourning

There is much to be said for a loving home and a warm hearth. Whatever challenges he faced in Parliament and no matter how much the government niggled and needled, George could always take comfort in his domestic life. As war raged, he took refuge in the gentle comfort of Charlotte and their growing brood of children, using Richmond Lodge as a family home and commissioning a sweeping programme of renovation and repair at Windsor Castle.

George was devoted to his children who were expected to study hard and behave in a manner befitting the offspring of the very pious king. Still, he was far from the austere, disinterested parent we have seen elsewhere in this volume. George loved to spend time in the company of his children, playing with them and sharing with them his own pastimes. They were permitted to attend the theatre and behind the scenes, all seemed happy. It would not last.

Real life was set to force its way into his family idyll in the most upsetting way and the household would never quite recover from it. So far, George and Charlotte had welcomed fourteen children (the last would be born in 1783) and remarkably, all survived infancy. Tragically, that was about to change and in the space of less than twelve short months, those loving parents would lose not one child, but two.

In the eighteenth century, smallpox was a very real and present threat to the lives of everyone, whether king or pauper. The disease claimed hundreds of thousands and survivors rarely escaped devastating side effects that

---

46. *General Advertiser and Morning Intelligencer* (London, England), Tuesday, May 12, 1778; issue 476, p.3.

ranged from scars to blindness. For any parent, the news that their child had been infected would be terrifying.

In 1782, George and Charlotte took the decision to have their youngest children inoculated against smallpox and by June, they no doubt rued that day. Little Alfred, the couple's youngest son who was a full eighteen years younger than his oldest brother, fell ill not long after receiving the treatment. In order to speed his recovery, he was taken to enjoy the sea air at Deal in the care of Lady Charlotte Finch.

A cheery little boy with a bright disposition, Alfred was nevertheless laid terribly low by his inoculation and began to experience smallpox-like blemishes on his face, whilst his breathing grew ever more laboured. Only when it appeared that the seaside was not working its magic was he returned to Windsor. Here he was attended by court physicians and their conclusion, when it came, was devastating. Little Alfred would be dead within weeks.

'Yesterday morning died at the Royal Palace, Windsor, his Royal Highness Prince Alfred, their Majesties youngest son. The Queen is much affected at this domestic calamity, probably more so on account of its being the only one she has experienced after a marriage of 20 years and having been the mother of fourteen children.'[47]

Prince Alfred of Great Britain passed away on 20 August 1782, just a month shy of his second birthday, and the royal family was rocked by his unexpected death. Protocol did not demand official mourning for one so young but, officially or not, his parents and siblings wept for the cheerful child. He was buried at Westminster Abbey with full honours and though George and Charlotte mourned his loss, they took comfort in their surviving children. The king, in particular, doted on the boy who was now his youngest son, three-year-old Octavius. In his darkest moments he admitted that, should Octavius have died, then he would wish himself dead too. These were to be fateful words.

Despite Alfred's death, it was still reckoned that inoculating the children against smallpox posed less of a risk than leaving them open to the infection

47. *London Chronicle* (London, England), August 20, 1782 – August 22, 1782; issue 4014, p.1.

so little Octavius and his best friend, five-year-old Princess Sophia, were given the treatment. Whilst Sophia suffered no ill effects and would live to a ripe old age, things did not go so well for Octavius.

The queen was pregnant with her final child when, just days after receiving the smallpox inoculation, Octavius grew terribly ill. Unlike Alfred, whose sickness progressed over time, Octavius declined with alarming speed and died on 3 May 1783. The king was beyond devastated, tormented to distraction by grief and as the situation in America neared its endgame, George was perhaps lower than he had ever been.

> 'On Saturday, on the Majesties arriving at Kew, in their way to Windsor, and finding Prince Octavius in a dangerous Way, they determined to stay there all Night and sent an Express to Windsor to acquaint the Attendants of the Reason of their continuing there.
>
> The same Night died at Kew, his Royal Highness Prince Octavius, his Majesty's youngest Son, in the fifth Year of his Age.'[48]

The king brooded on the loss of his children, wondering whether their inoculation against smallpox had contributed to their early deaths. Where once there had been the laughter of infants, the gentle distraction offered when Charlotte and George played adoringly with the youngsters, now there was only silence and grief, the royal household plunged into sadness. A little respite came with the birth of Princess Amelia in August of that same year and George showered her with love, filling the void where his sons had been with the cheer of this new daughter. Little Amelia, or *Emily*, as she was known, lived through childhood but years later it would be *her* death that was to have a catastrophic effect on the father who adored her.

The Land of the Free

Lord North, so set on resignation just a few years earlier, didn't go anywhere until 1782 and even then he was not gone for long. That shattered confidence he so struggled with seemed to crumble often and people had started to

---

48. *Daily Advertiser* (London, England), Monday, May 5, 1783; issue 17249, p.1.

notice. In 1779, Charles Jenkinson, Earl of Liverpool, wrote to the king, to observe, 'I look upon all this as nothing permanent, but as a disaster of the mind which comes and goes'.[49] Indeed, it was still coming and going the following year, causing Liverpool to note with a touch of eye-rolling, '[North] is too fond of having it believed that he continues in office contrary to his inclination'.[50]

In the end, for all his threats, Lord North did not go by choice and was instead forced out by a motion of no confidence that was the result of the catastrophic British defeat at the siege of Yorktown in 1781. This victory, in which forces under the command of General George Washington and the Comte de Rochambeau devastated the troops led by Lieutenant General Charles Cornwallis, was a turning point in the war.

At the end of the three week siege, more than 7,000 British troops were prisoners of the American and French. At home, the British public took the news badly and urged an end to the conflict whilst North recognized, quite rightly, that this sounded the death knell for his own career.

George was at his wits end and as the new Rockingham ministry entered choppy waters, a quiet life in Hanover must have looked very attractive indeed. Although he was taking a second bite of the prime ministerial cherry, Rockingham's moment in the sun was all too brief. Influenza claimed his life after just three months in the job and over the next eighteen months, no fewer than *three* men would hold office. The list culminated with George's own choice, William Pitt the Younger, who managed to stay in the job for almost eighteen years.

Parliamentary shenanigans aside, what mattered now was negotiating a way out of the hostilities that had raged for so long. In 1783, seven years after the Declaration of Independence, the Treaty of Paris was signed and hostilities formally ended, with George writing, 'America is lost! Must we fall beneath the blow?'.[51]

---

49. Namier, Lewis and Brooke, John (1985). *The House of Commons 1754–1790. Vol III, Members K-Y*. London: Secker & Warburg, p.206.
50. Ibid., p.206.
51. Young, Arthur (ed.) (1790). *Annals of Agriculture and Other Useful Arts, Vol I*. Bury St Edmunds: J Rackham, p.11.

So, what should we really make of George III, as the king who lost the colonies? Was he a despot, clinging to a territory that wanted to be rid of its master, flouting the opinions of those who knew better and obstinately hanging onto his empire for grim death? Not quite; the truth was, he was simply a king protecting his lands as rulers had for centuries before and would do for centuries after, just as he had been trained to do since childhood.

Of course we must sympathize with the colonists, ruled from afar with limited input into their own fates and finances, paying taxes without any real representation, yet this not a simple case of good versus evil. George was an over-protective if distant parent, interested not in the day to day, but the overall control and discipline of his charges. The majority of British people rallied behind the monarch even as France and Spain allied with America against Britain, tilting the scales in the balance of independence.

George was not alone in his belief that military intervention was the appropriate solution to the uprising in America and at first, he and Parliament enjoyed great public support. It was only as the years dragged on and the cost of war mounted that the people of Great Britain began to lose their appetite for conflict. By this point, it was far too late to turn back and discontent erupted into violence with the anti-Catholic Gordon Riots of 1780. When independence became inevitable, the king even considered abdicating his throne and retirement must have looked very tempting indeed. Still, he was a man of duty and elected instead to continue, to fulfil his destiny on the throne.

As the smoke cleared from the American War of Independence, it was with a heavy heart that George III surveyed his lot. His heart broken by the deaths of not one but two sons, one might hope that his older children would behave, but the now infamous Prince of Wales was already causing headaches. As we will see, the prince did nothing by halves and the king endured his debts and embarrassments through gritted teeth.

The prince did not redeem himself with his political affiliations either, becoming firm friends with Charles James Fox, son of George's old opponent. Whereas the king was circumspect and considered himself to be a model father, his son lived the highest of high lives and was constantly asking for more money to pay off his enormous debts. Sadly, just as the relationships between George I and George II and George II and Fred were fractured and bitter, the one between George III and the Prince of Wales was going the same way.

The king, who was not exactly *rolling* in money himself, had approved a payment to settle his son's debts in 1783, and when the Prince of Wales came of age, he duly expected that to be an end to the matter. Ever the wishful-thinker, Wales promised that there would be no more profligacy yet almost as soon as the words left his mouth, he was off and spending again. His chosen residence of Carlton House was not at all fit for a man of his breeding, the prince decided, and soon he was renovating and altering the building at enormous cost. We will see more of the profligate prince elsewhere in this volume but for now, he was just one more headache for the king.

An Assassination Hat Trick

'This morning, as his Majesty was alighting from his carriage at the gate of the palace, a woman, who was waiting there under pretence of presenting a petition, struck at his Majesty with a knife; but providentially his Majesty received no injury. The woman was immediately taken into custody; and upon examination appears to be insane.'[52]

George was not a king who enjoyed the public side of monarchy, nor, we might argue, did he particular enjoy the private side either. He wanted a quiet life, a court run on rigidly disciplined lines rather than ostentatious public display, and whilst the press found him a perfect target for satire, for the public *Farmer George* was a very human monarch. He loved books and built a library of more than 65,000 volumes, taking enormous delight in bookbinding, as well as amassing a considerable collection of art. Unlike his predecessors, he never visited his ancestral lands in Hanover, nor did he go to Scotland, Ireland or Wales, and he was therefore, considered more of an *English* king. Of course, no matter how popular you appear to be, being a monarch always carried the risk that someone might take a lethal dislike to you!

---

52. Anonymous (1786). *The Scots Magazine, Vol 48.* Edinburgh: Murray and Cochrane, p.365.

It is rare indeed that an attempted murder has a happy ending for *any* of the parties but for George, a run in with a mentally disturbed woman named Margaret Nicholson in 1786 proved most fortuitous indeed.

It was on 2 August 1786 that Nicholson approached the king as he left his carriage at St James's Palace, claiming to have a petition that she wished to deliver. As he reached to take it, she slashed at him with a dessert knife before being overpowered by his guards. George's first thoughts and sympathies were for the health and welfare of his assailant, saying, 'The poor creature is mad. Do not harm her. She has not hurt me'.[53]

Nicholson, it was concluded, was indeed mad and firmly believed she was the rightful queen of Great Britain. Dismissed from her employment due to a love affair with a man who then abandoned her, the unfortunate woman sank into depression and despair. Later, having recovered her wits somewhat, she claimed that she had no wish to harm the king, only to frighten him. Still, one can't attack a monarch and expect to go free and Nicholson was committed to Bethlem Royal Hospital. She escaped her prison in 1790 and made for the home of her brother yet was swiftly returned to Bedlam, where she remained until her death nearly forty years later.

For George, however, the result was a massive leap in his popularity and paeans to his 'presence of mind, and great humanity'.[54] He was seen as generous, pious and forgiving, never seeking a harsh punishment or penalty for the unfortunate lady. It is an incident in which we clearly see the man behind the title, the gentle character who adored his wife and children and sought only a peaceful existence.

To his opponents, however, the incarceration of Nicholson was the act of an unforgiving brute who circumvented the law for his own vengeful needs. This is hardly fair, for Georgian law offered no clear way to deal with a woman who was guilty of an offence yet had the mitigating circumstance of insanity. In the end, Nicholson was not imprisoned as a result of a guilty verdict, but because she had been declared insane. In 1786 there was no provision for a verdict of 'not guilty by reason of insanity' so off to Bethlem

53. Hibbert, Christopher (1998). *George III: A Personal History*. London: Viking, p.226.
54. Anonymous (1786). *The Scots Magazine, Vol 48*. Edinburgh: Murray and Cochrane, p.366.

she went. In fact, given the era, there could have been no other outcome and had she gone on trial for attempted murder, assault or, after her claims to the throne became louder, treason, Nicholson might have faced a far harsher fate.

Regardless of his increased popularity, in 1788 the illness that came to be synonymous with George III was rearing its head and rumours began to spread that the king was not only unwell, but quite mad. Perhaps, his doctors ventured, a change of air might do the trick and so George travelled to Cheltenham Spa, where it was hoped that he would make a recovery. In fact, his condition worsened.

What started as a violent stomach ache did not remain a physical pain and by autumn the king was at Kew. He barely slept, was often violent and he was always confused. His care was entrusted to Lincolnshire physician and clergyman, Dr Francis Willis, who was known for his treatment of the mad. Willis had been summoned by the queen following a recommendation from a courtier and in his worst moments, George would later rage at his wife for bringing the stern doctor into his life.

Foaming at the mouth and jabbering incoherently for hours on end, the king was subjected to debilitating and brutal treatments. First and foremost, the mad were kept cold in the belief that this would begin to help clear the patient's head. Though Bedlam's patients were hosed down with water, George was given ice-cold baths. Uncomfortable though this would be, the true horrors were yet to come and they began with purging, by which the patient was fed with potions intended to bring on vomiting and diarrhoea. Of course, madness wasn't only to be found in the waste products, but in the blood itself and where there is blood in eighteenth century medicine, leeches are never far away.

Although doctors bled their patients without leeches, no other creature was so industrious when it came to drawing blood and they crop up again and again in the treatment of all manner of conditions. Applied to George's forehead, they hungrily fed on his blood whilst pus was extracted by the agonizing application of hot vinegar and mustard to his shaven head and extremities.

Gagged with a handkerchief when he indulged in violent and obscene outbursts and forcibly restrained in a straitjacket, the king was ruled with a mixture of fear and coercion, Willis giving no quarter to the exalted position of his patient. When the king grew particularly belligerent he was fastened into a specially made chair, which he nicknamed *the coronation chair*, and kept from the company of his family. Eventually, as he submitted to Willis, he was allowed short visits with his beloved spaniel, Badine, and with the queen and Princess Amelia. On occasion, he would speak to his wife so cruelly that she could scarcely hold back her tears and on others he would appear to address Octavius and Alfred, those sons who had died so young.

In Parliament, meanwhile, another problem was looming. With the king in such a desperate condition, he could not possibly *hope* to make the speech that would mark the State Opening. Until the speech was given and Parliament officially convened, no official business could be conducted; it was, to all intents and purposes, a deadlock.

Something had to be done and it was decided that the best way forward was to draw up a Regency Bill, which would place power in the hands of the king's eldest son, the Prince of Wales. As prime minister, Pitt the Younger wrote the bill and proved a powerful friend of the king. With the Prince of Wales allied to his opponent, Fox, it was Pitt who had been a voice of dissent against Fox's claim that *only* the prince could be regent when his father was indisposed. For Pitt, such a forgone conclusion was not set in stone. Though he agreed that the prince was the most obvious candidate, he would not be swayed into the decision. After all, Wales would certainly dismiss Pitt and install Fox, and Pitt's bill included clauses that meant this simply couldn't happen.

'The year opened with an account the most promising of our beloved King. I saw Dr. Willis, and he told me the night had been very tranquil; and he sent for his son, Dr. John Willis, to give me a history of the morning. Dr. John's narration was in many parts very affecting: the dear and excellent King had been praying for his own restoration! Both the doctors told me that such strong symptoms of true piety had scarce ever been discernible through so dreadful a malady. [...] I told the two Dr. Willises that they had given to the whole nation a new year's gift.'[55]

---

55. Burney, Frances (1910). *The Diary and Letters of Frances Burney, Madame D'Arblay, Vol II.* Boston: Little, Brown and Company, p.96.

In the end, negotiations dragged on for so long that the king's recovery rendered the bill unnecessary and his wits returned in early 1789. Now he was able to witness rumours of the Prince of Wales and his Catholic widow, not to mention hearing tales of Gloucester's political schemes and from all sides came requests for increased allowances, grander titles and general complaints, whilst the public received commemorative medals celebrating the king's return to health.

Enter a man with a stone.

John Frith was not, to all intents and purposes, a well chap. He believed himself to have Messianic powers and was sure that military officer, Jeffrey Amherst, had set dark, supernatural forces against him. When Frith was discharged from the army by reason of insanity he was determined to avenge himself on both Amherst and the king. Initially his protests were peaceful if annoying and he bombarded Parliament with petitions but when this scheme proved fruitless, he moved things up a gear.

'Yesterday as his Majesty was passing near the Horse Guards, on his way to the House of Lords, a stone was thrown at the coach, by a tall man dressed in a scarlet coat, black breeches, a striped waistcoat, a cocked hat, with an orange coloured cockade. [...] He proves to be the same person who wrote a libel against his Majesty, and stuck it on the Whalebone in the Court Yard, St James's, about a fortnight since, and signed his name John Frith, Lieutenant of the second battalion of Royals.'[56]

Frith threw a stone at the king's carriage on 21 January 1790, as George made his way to the State Opening of Parliament. To us it sounds like a relatively minor affair and though hurling a stone at a modern monarch's conveyance would likely still meet with raised eyebrows, it's unlikely that it would be considered treason.

If we might suspect that Nicholson had been met with sympathy from her would-be victim because of her gender, such suspicions must now

56. *Whitehall Evening Post (1770)* (London, England), January 21, 1790 – January 23, 1790; issue 6467, p.2.

be set aside. Once again, George heard of his assailant with empathy and understanding and just as Nicholson had been placed in an institution, so Frith duly followed her to Bethlem.

George III, it seemed, had something of an appeal for the most outlandish assassins in the pack. Although Nicholson's butter knife made the tiniest tear in his waistcoat and Frith's stone was no doubt thrown with the aim of catching the attention of the king, neither could realistically be said to pose much of a threat to the monarch.

A gun, however, might prove to be a different matter.

On 15 May 1800, whilst George was inspecting the troops in Hyde Park, there was found to be a live round among the blanks. It went off *by accident*, hitting clerk, William Ongley, in the thigh. It was to be an unlucky day for the king as, that same night, George III followed his grandfather into danger in the royal box. Of course, when he set off for Drury Lane, the king was not expecting to end up as the most talked about show in town, but life on the Georgian throne was never predictable.

'Just as His MAJESTY entered his box, and was bowing to the audience with his usual condescension [...] a person [...] got upon the seat, and levelling a horse-pistol towards the KING'S box, fired it. [...] The audience remained for a second in an agony of suspense. – His MAJESTY showed the most perfect composure, turned his eye towards the man, and continued standing till the QUEEN entered, who displayed also the most dignified courage.'[57]

As the king stood for the national anthem, James Hadfield, another disgruntled former soldier, suddenly drew a pistol and fired at the monarch. Fortunately for George, the bullet went wide and Hadfield was seized before he could try again. When the would-be assassin was dragged off to face charges of attempted murder, Hadfield no doubt thought that he would soon be on the scaffold, yet things would not go quite so badly for him.

Luckily for Hadfield, the famed Thomas Erskine agreed to take his case and defend him against the charge, certain that he could save the defendant's life,

---

57. *Morning Chronicle* (London, England), Friday, May 16, 1800; issue 9667, p.2.

if not secure his freedom. Hadfield had been seriously injured in battle years earlier and, under the changes to the law that had come in since Nicholson wielded her blade, he was found not guilty by reason of insanity. One cannot help but wonder if the king, no stranger to mental disorder himself, felt some sympathy with the unfortunate man who had tried to take his life.

The trial judge, Baron Kenyon, was absolutely clear that Hadfield must not be released and he was committed to Bethlem for life. Although he did make a spirited escape attempt, Hadfield would never regain his freedom and died in Bethlem four decades later.

With George's gentle understanding of Nicholson and Frith's difficulties doing much for his standing and reputation all seemed more settled than it had in a long time. Even without stone throwers, butter knives and messiahs, however, things across the English Channel were getting very worrying indeed.

Revolution

> 'People talk of the French Revolution being injurious to England. We say it never will while our industry remains unchecked. The commercial industry of England turns everything to account. The Governor of the Bastile [sic] had not been executed four days before his head was exhibited in London to the curious at 1s. each.'[58]

Years before Hadfield took aim in Drury Lane, the king and queen of France had fallen victim to a far more fatal fate than a spoiled night at the theatre. In that land, its destiny so tightly and antagonistically intertwined with Great Britain throughout the Georgian era, the Reign of Terror had laid waste to the monarchy. Revolutionary politics and the keen blade of the National Razor made devils or martyrs of Louis XVI and Marie Antoinette and tens of thousands, both rich and poor, followed them to the grave. Revolution, however, did nothing to dim the long-held animosity that bubbled between the neighbouring nations and it was only a matter of time before sabres were rattling once more.

---

58. *Bath Chronicle* (Bath, England), Thursday, July 30, 1789; issue 1451, p.1.

Those sabres were unsheathed in 1793, when France declared war on her old enemy and George turned to Pitt the Younger to deal with the problem from across the sea. Although both king and prime minister were enjoying some measure of popularity at the time, such a situation required very careful handling. After all, one wrong move might see the embers of unrest spread to British shores. There the flames could be fanned by domestic radicals until they burst into the fires of revolution and with the bad behaviour of the Prince of Wales raising eyebrows left right and centre, the last thing the government needed was a reason for the people to turn nasty.

Despite the drama unfolding overseas, the royal family did find time to celebrate the marriage of Charlotte, Princess Royal and the Hereditary Prince Frederick of Württemberg. Though Charlotte might be happy in her new land, the other daughters of George III were to face a more solitary fate. Still grieving for the children he had lost and now feeling Charlotte's departure bitterly, George was also haunted by the unhappy fate of his sister, Caroline Matilda. Perhaps understandably, the king feared what awaited his daughters should they go overseas into an arranged marriage, no doubt very well aware of the tragic events that saw Sophia Dorothea locked away by George I too. Besides these very fatherly concerns, George's health was not what it had been and it was doubtful whether he would be able to withstand the stresses inherent in travelling abroad to negotiate marriages.

The queen, meanwhile, was no keener to see her daughters married off than her husband was. She had drawn the young ladies into a close and secretive circle that would only grow stronger when her husband's illness took hold of him. The thought of sending them away to marry was one that she simply could not countenance, so reliant was she on them as companions and confidantes.

Kept in the Windsor *nunnery*, the girls grew more and more unhappy, with Princess Sophia lamenting many years later in a letter to the Prince of Wales, 'Poor old wretches as we are, four old cats, four old wretches, a dead weight upon you, old lumber to the country, like old clothes. I wonder you do not vote for putting us in a sack and drowning us in the Thames?'.[59]

---

59. Longford, Elizabeth (1989). *The Oxford Book of Royal Anecdotes*. Oxford: Oxford University Press, p.327.

Of course, it was easier to keep Georgian girls in perpetual adolescence than it was boys, and for George's oldest sons, trouble was never far away. They continued to fill the gossip columns and needle for money, for prestige, for anything they might get their hands on. Prevented from marriage without the king's permission by the Royal Marriages Act, George's sons instead acquired mistresses and scandal with a rapacious zeal, setting up home with lovers and, in one shocking and notorious case, even a secret wife.

We shall learn more of the tale of the Prince of Wales and Maria Fitzherbert elsewhere in this volume but rumours of an illegal marriage had grown so loud that an official denial had to be given in Parliament. Both George and Charlotte were left in a state of distraction by the behaviour of their eldest son yet nothing quelled his spending or his partying.

There was nothing else for it but to try a little tough love on Wales and, with all other avenues exhausted, the prince was made an offer that he was loathe to accept but couldn't really refuse. Should he agree to marry his cousin, Princess Caroline of Brunswick, then he would find his debts settled and his allowance increased. Though he abhorred the idea of marriage to Caroline the prince was a realist and, perhaps more importantly, a spoiled brat. For the first time in his life he had to compromise and as we'll learn later, it ended in disaster. The marriage was negotiated, and, as, Parliament rumbled ominously about the largesse of it all, the match was made. That union ended in a war of attrition between husband and wife that would rage for years, but that is a story for elsewhere.

The Mad King

As the eighteenth century ticked over into the nineteenth, George III's realm was a very different place to the one he had inherited. America was gone, Pitt was considering the question of a possible union with Ireland, and the king was ruminating on the matter of Catholic emancipation, a subject guaranteed to fire up strong passions.

Although it was negotiated and drawn up in 1800, the Act of Union did not come into force until 1 January 1801. It united Great Britain and Ireland into the United Kingdom of Great Britain and Ireland and gave George the chance to surrender his ancient title of 'King of France'. Initially members of the Irish Parliament had been suspicious of such a union, fearing what it might mean for their own authority, yet eventually they succumbed to the new order. There were to be no Catholic members for decades though, as their dreams of eventual emancipation remained unfulfilled.

For the British Parliament, however, there was no such doubt. The Irish Rebellion of 1798 had been a worrying foretelling of what *might* come to pass, with the American and French Revolutions inspiring the United Irishmen to rise up against their British rulers with the support of the French. It is beyond of the scope of this book to delve into this tumultuous time but suffice to say, it was decided that the Irish needed to be taken in hand before the unthinkable happened and the country followed France into revolution.

Pitt recognized that concessions must be made to the Catholic majority in Ireland and granted a raft of new rights and privileges for them, which he urged George to support. The conflicted king could not allow himself to do so and returned time and again to the promises he made in the Coronation Oath, when he swore to protect the Church of England. Unable to continue in office without the full support of the ailing king, Pitt resigned in favour of Henry Addington, though he would return to the top job in years to come.

The strain of Pitt's loss along with the worries of the separation of the Prince and Princess of Wales, the Irish Question, war on the continent and just the general business of kingship, combined to bring George once more to the brink of madness.

In the eighteenth century treatment of the mad, whether monarch or maidservant, was brutal by our modern standards. George was fortunate indeed to be a king and thus able to avoid the legendary confines of Bedlam, but even the treatments he received would seem terrible to our eyes. Whether drawing blood, blistering his skin or gagging and restraining him, Dr Willis was not what one might call a sympathetic doctor. Of course, received wisdom now is that George, with his startling and infamous blue urine, was suffering from porphyria, an abnormal metabolism of blood pigment, causing mental instability, though his doctors had no such diagnosis available to them.

Dr Willis now returned to treat his most illustrious patient, accompanied by his sons, John and Thomas. For a time they staved off a complete relapse and the king was able to make public appearances. George even told Willis that his services were no longer required and fled for the sanctuary of Kew. Neither Addington nor Charlotte were convinced, however, and both queen and Parliament readily consented for the doctor to pursue his patient and confine him by any means necessary.

The White House at Kew became George's prison now as surely as Bedlam was for those less well-heeled. Kept in isolation, the treatments began once more. The year 1801 was an exhausting time of illness for George, and the royal household found itself shouldering the burden of dealing with a family member in dire mental straits. Holidays to Weymouth, usually so valued by the family, could not happen whilst the king was ill and the pressure weighed heavy on all. George, however, did realize that he ultimately held the trump card, as there was no provision for a regency, so he told his doctors that unless the queen was permitted to visit him, he would go on strike.

In fact, once he was reunited with his adored family the king did begin to recover, slowly at first but markedly in time. By the time Addington signed the Treaty of Amiens with France in 1802 and brought hostilities to a close, the king was well enough to throw himself back into public life. As the nation readied itself for a Napoleonic invasion, George was perfectly willing to follow his predecessors into battle and made inspections of the troops and volunteers before enormous crowds of his approving subjects.

Of course, the years passed and the invasion didn't come, though if it had, the king would no doubt have taken some convincing not to ride into battle. Stout of heart he might be, but poor old George was to prove no match for the mental illness that continued to plague him.

Domestic Disputes and Dead Valets

At the dawn of 1804 the king was once again quite mad. This time, however, there was to be no coronation chair. Instead, his sons refused permission for the Willis family to attend and summoned Dr Samuel Simmons to treat their father, who had reverted to his old symptoms of endless chatter, interspersed with alarming verbal attacks on his family. George's condition remained inconstant and he was at times utterly coherent, whilst at others he was barely sensible in any sense of the word. Rumours spread that he had behaved improperly towards female domestics and spoke endlessly about which noblewoman he would take for his mistress, all of which did nothing to cheer the increasingly alarmed Charlotte who remained devotedly at his side.

Amazingly, the king remained coherent enough to continue his official duties with the cajolement of family, ministers and medics. When Pitt returned to office in 1804, the king once again found himself mired in Parliamentary disputes whilst overseas, his own daughter, Charlotte, and her husband were firmly allied with Napoleon. This was a difficult pill for her parents to swallow and no doubt they were relieved that her sisters remained safely at home, no troublesome spouses to lead them into bad ways. In this the girls had no say, and with their father's madness now growing more pronounced, Queen Charlotte had no intention of letting her closest confidantes and only comfort leave her bosom.

'The melancholy event of Mr. PITT'S death has left the Country without a Minister, and without a Ministry. It is natural, therefore, that reports as to the formation of a new one should be various.'[60]

In 1806, just one year after the monumental British victory at Trafalgar, Pitt the Younger died. He was just 46, and his death marked a turning point in Parliament. The country was on the brink of what would become the War of the Fourth Coalition and Pitt's successor, Baron Grenville, decided that this was not the time to play party politics. Instead he appointed and sat at the head of the Ministry of All the Talents, an administration appointed not by affiliation, but expertise. So it was that none other than George's old adversary, Charles James Fox, was invited to join.

In fact, George greeted Fox's return to the forefront of politics in a gracious manner. As it was, Fox died later in 1806 and though the politician's final months were not by any means his finest hour, George's acceptance of his appointment did much to increase the monarch's public standing. Compared to the licentious behaviour of his sons, who seemed dedicated to embarrassing their father, the ailing family man was a saint. George remained constant; a gentleman, a devoted husband, the *farmer* who eschewed largesse and scandal in favour of piety and devotion to his realm.

---

60. *The Morning Chronicle* (London, England), Friday, January 24, 1806; issue 11447, p.2.

In stark contrast to their father, George's sons assembled a litany of shocking tales, from the embarrassment of the Delicate Investigation, convened to hear charges against the Princess of Wales, to the Duke of York's involvement with Mary Anne Clarke, who sold army commissions to support herself as the duke's mistress. The Duke of Clarence, later William IV, was openly living with his mistress and a legion of illegitimate children yet perhaps most shocking of all came in 1810 when Ernest, Duke of Cumberland, was implicated in the suicide of his valet, Sellis.

> 'It is with regret and horror we have to announce an horrid attempt which was made, at a very early hour yesterday morning, to assassinate his Royal Highness the Duke of CUMBERLAND, by a villain, an Italian of the name of SELLIS, one of the pages of his Royal Highness.'[61]

According to Cumberland's account, he was contentedly slumbering in his bed in the early hours of 31 May 1810 when he was attacked. Struggling to his feet, the bewildered duke was slashed in the leg by a blade yet managed to raise the alarm and summon his household to his aid. The assailant was nowhere to be seen and, when the staff assembled, neither was his valet, Joseph Sellis. That same morning Sellis was found dead in his own locked room where 'he was found to have cut his throat cut in such a manner, as nearly to have severed his head from his body'.[62]

The public, however, were not so sure and unsurprisingly rumours soon began to spread about the true fate of Sellis. Perhaps the duke had been slipping Mrs Sellis the occasional treat and had her husband killed when they were discovered, or maybe the object of the duke's affections was Sellis himself, who had been slain by his noble lover after he had made an attempt at blackmail. Whatever the truth, it was one more blow to the moral authority of the sons of the king and the public looked to George as the example of how to behave, the paragon of sovereign virtue.

Each fresh scandal dealt a new blow to the royal household and behind closed doors it was not only the king's mental health that was causing

---

61. *The Morning Post* (London, England), Friday, June 01, 1810; issue 12275, p.3.
62. Ibid., p.3.

concern. As George grew older his physicians battled crippling rheumatism and his sight began to fail, cataracts appearing on both eyes. The people were kept informed of the king's health by regular updates in the newspapers, yet nobody could be in any doubt that he had taken a turn for the worst even as he kept battling on. Fate, however, was about to deal a devastating blow and it would be the final straw that broke his already troubled mind.

Losing Amelia

'DEATH of the PRINCESS AMELIA – We have the painful duty to announce the Death of the Princess Amelia, whose affliction has so long excited the lively interest of the public – not merely from her own most amiable qualities, but from the sympathy which they felt in the sufferings of her affectionate parents. She died yesterday noon, and without any pain. She was so totally exhausted by decay, as to make it almost impossible to tell when life was really extinguished.'[63]

On 2 November 1810, George's daughter, Amelia, died.

She was the youngest child of George and Charlotte, the daughter whose birth did so much to help the royal household navigate the crushing grief that came with the deaths of Alfred and Octavius and the object of her father's endless devotion. During his bouts of madness, it was she who often accompanied Charlotte on visits to George, witnessing his worst episodes even as her very presence brought him comfort. The life of Emily, as she was affectionately known, was tragically short and cosseted, yet it was not without drama.

Amelia's health was never strong and in the late eighteenth century she began to develop all the symptoms of tuberculosis, a condition that begged for a change of air. Accordingly, Amelia set off for Weymouth in the company of her father's equerry, the Honourable Sir Charles FitzRoy. Despite her position and the fact that he was more than twenty years her senior, the couple fell in love. Of course, they could not hope for a happy ending and

63. *Hampshire Telegraph and Sussex Chronicle etc* (Portsmouth, England), Monday, November 5, 1810; issue 578, p.3.

when the queen heard of their relationship, she was horrified. FitzRoy was one of the king's most trusted servants and Charlotte flatly refused to tell him of the affair, quashing all dreams of a marriage. Amelia, however, never let go of her affection for her lover and told her siblings that she considered herself to be married, whatever her mother might say.

Perhaps Amelia intended to invoke the Royal Marriages Act and request permission to marry but as it was, she did not live long enough to do so. In 1810 she took to her bed and despite the care and affection of her family, the princess knew that her life was reaching its end. Sure that her father would miss her dreadfully, she had a mourning ring commissioned for him to remember her by. Her beloved FitzRoy was allowed to visit his love in her final days thanks to the schemes of her adoring sisters and as autumn became winter, Princess Amelia died.

The effect of Amelia's death on the king was enormous. Already suffering an episode of madness that further worsened when she placed the mourning ring on his finger just prior to her death, he fell so low that his imminent death was not unthinkable. Increasingly delusional, the king refused to accept that his youngest child was dead and instead created a fantasy in which she was married and living in Hanover with her loving husband and a brood of perfect children. In the bereaved father's mind all was well once more; both Pitt the Elder and Younger still lived and Alfred and Octavius were regular visitors to his chambers.

In these darkest years, George's despair and madness knew no respite and no bounds and he was soon in the straitjacket again. No longer able to cope with his own condition, when the Regency Act was proposed in 1811, the king gladly handed over the reins of government to the Prince of Wales. The Act entrusted George's care to his wife and a committee of privy councillors, whilst the king's physicians were to make regular reports on his condition and ever-decreasing chances of recovery. All of this came not a moment too soon because, by the close of the year, George III was utterly and incurably insane.

The Windsor Years

Over the years of her marriage, Queen Charlotte had grown old and tired, fatigued by the burden of caring for her husband through times both good and bad. Now George hardly recognized her and when he did, he reacted with indifference at best and fury at worse. He blamed her for his treatment at the hands of the Willises, as it had been she who had summoned them in the first place. After 1812 an exhausted Charlotte retreated into her own company and that of her daughters, no longer able to face the changes in the man she had adored.

> 'In pursuance of the commands of his Royal Highness the PRINCE REGENT, acting in the name and on the behalf of his MAJESTY, these are to give public notice, that upon the present melancholy occasion of the death of her late MAJESTY of blessed memory, all persons do put themselves into deep mourning.'[64]

When the queen died in 1818, the Prince Regent held her hand as she passed away. She had longed to join her husband at Windsor but only now did she do so, laid to rest there in the deep winter. Blind, deaf and suffering from dementia, George knew nothing of his wife's death and funeral. Instead, his time was spent in conversation with the dead, moments of lucidity by now virtually non-existent. He held long debates with invisible politicians and paraded with imaginary soldiers, inspecting troops whom appeared to nobody but him. Appointed King of Hanover by the Congress of Vienna, George had no comprehension of this latest honour nor his wife's tragic death, utterly lost in the delusional world of his own madness.

> 'It has pleased the ALMIGHTY to release his MAJESTY from all further suffering. His MAJESTY expired, without pain, at thirty-five minutes past eight o'clock this evening.'[65]

---

64. *The Morning Post* (London, England), Friday, November 20, 1818; issue 14925, p.3.
65. *The Morning Post* (London, England), Friday, January 31, 1820; issue 15299, p.2.

The Duke of York was with his father in his final moments and when news of the late king's death reached the people, they were plunged into mourning. As had been George's wish, the bodies of Octavius and Alfred were moved to rest with him at Windsor, the king reunited at last with the little boys he had so adored and grief fell across the land. In all the long years of George's madness and confinement, the nation to which he had given his oath had not forgotten him but had come to regard him with an unrivalled affection, both in times good and bad. To the people, he was not the man who lost America or the king who went mad, instead he was their talisman, their *farmer* and now, after sixty long and sometimes painful years at the helm, the beloved old king was dead.

Act Four

George IV, King of the United Kingdom and Ireland

(London, England, 12 August 1762 – Windsor, England, 26 June 1830)

Ah, *Prinny*.

The first gentleman of England.

Prince of Wales, Prince Regent and King of the United Kingdom of Great Britain and Ireland, George IV was the punchline to a thousand jokes, the target of a hundred merciless cartoonist's nibs, the price one paid for indulgence.

A man of taste in some things whilst in others he was hideously crass, his personal life is the stuff of tabloid legend with profligacy and widely scattered affections that knew no bounds. George's considerable influence stretched to fashion, art and architecture and can still be felt today.

Still, whatever one may think of him, his eventful life was *never* short on entertainment.

The Son and Heir

'We […] humbly beg Leave to present to your Majesty our sincerest Congratulations on the safe Delivery of the Queen, and Birth of his Royal Highness the Prince, and on the prosperous State of her Majesty's Health since this happy Event.'[1]

---

1. *Public Advertiser* (London, England), Monday, September 6, 1762; issue 8687, p.2.

The man who would one day reign as George IV started life as he meant to go on, as a right royal pain to his parents. His mother, Charlotte of Mecklenburg-Strelitz, underwent a difficult and prolonged labour, suffering through the delivery attended by the Dowager Princess of Wales, the Archbishop of Canterbury and her midwife, Mrs Draper. In the neighbouring room, members of the court waited with bated breath to hear the cries of a healthy and, they hoped, *male* newborn. The prince's birth was announced to the people by the firing of the Tower cannon whilst the Earl of Huntingdon hastened to see the king and let him know that he was father to a healthy, robust baby *girl*. Or perhaps not.

It was an inauspicious start to the life of the boy who would become a notorious libertine. Rather ironically, given the love of spending he would later discover, right from the first second the baby cost his father money. George III had promised to pay the messenger who delivered news of the birth £500 should the newborn be a girl and double that amount if he brought word of a son. The king received Huntingdon with delight and, hearing that he was father to a healthy girl, paid the earl his £500 and set off to see the queen.

Whether Huntingdon ever received the additional £500 once George discovered that the child was a *boy* isn't recorded. Eventually the confusion was ironed out and the court rejoiced in the birth of this child who had been born to a sure destiny: to one day rule as king.

Just as his life would be spent in the crucible of public opinion, within weeks of his debut, the newborn George Augustus, Prince of Wales, was baptized by the Archbishop of Canterbury and placed on public display in St James's Palace. It was the perfect start for a prince who would grow to love drama and the thrill of the limelight and for little George Augustus, *no* expense was spared.

'The ladies who went to see the young prince were admitted into the room, about forty at a time. The cradle in which the royal infant lay was placed on a small elevation, under a canopy of state. The head and the sides, which came no higher than the bed, were covered with crimson velvet, and lined with white satin. From the head rose an ornament of carved work, gilt, with a coronet in the middle. The upper sheet was covered with a very broad, beautiful Brussels lace, turning over at the top, upon a magnificent quilt of crimson velvet, and gold lace; the whole breadth of the Brussels lace appearing also along the sides, and hanging down from underneath. Near the cradle sat the nurse, with a small velvet cushion lying on her knee, for the babe to rest on; and on each side stood a fair mute, employed as occasion required, to rock the infant to sleep.'[2]

Charlotte, it seems, was particularly struck by the beauty of her son and sought some way to keep him like that forever, a newborn babe bedecked in velvet. Of course, being the queen can open all sorts of doors and she *really* went to town …

'[…] her Majesty had a whole length portrait of his Royal Highness modelled in wax. He was represented naked. The figure was half a span long, lying upon a crimson cushion, and it was covered by a bell-glass.'[3]

It sounds like a rather frightful bit of decoration but Charlotte treasured the model all her life, no doubt finding the memory of her perfect little boy rather comforting when the real thing began to grow, drink and wench! For now though, booze, women and gambling were a few years into the future and the young prince was instead living it up in the nursery. He revelled in public appearances in his early childhood and soon proved himself to be bright, intelligent and quick to learn. Indeed, one might conclude that the precocious George Augustus grew up *too* quickly in some ways whilst in others he never really grew up *at all*.

George Augustus was the son of George III, a pious man who enjoyed the simple things in life. Having watched his brothers live high on the hog, the king was determined that his own children, who would eventually number

2. Watkins, John (1819). *Memoirs of Her Most Excellent Majesty Sophia-Charlotte, Queen of Great Britain*. London: Henry Colburn, pp.155–6.
3. Huish, Robert (1830). *Memoirs of George the Fourth: Vol I*. London: Thomas Kelly, p.34.

fifteen, would not fall prey to all the temptations the world would throw in their path. He did all he could to shield them from the vices of eighteenth century society, though as the years passed, it became increasingly apparent that his sons had no interest in being shielded from *anything*.

This loving yet protective father accordingly placed the young Prince of Wales in the care of Lady Charlotte Finch,[4] the governess of the royal house, and under her influence, George Augustus was soon showing a precocious and fierce intelligence. Though his temper might benefit from being somewhat cooler, George Augustus shared the king's passion for music and drama, art and architecture.

The education of the prince was placed in the hands of the experienced courtier, Lord Holdernesse, and a team of suitably learned and pious gentlemen of good breeding. Intensively schooled and disciplined vigorously should he commit a wrong, George and his younger brother, Frederick, Duke of York, spent long hours at their lessons, on pain of harsh punishment should they dare to step out of line. Most important of all was that, to borrow Charlotte Brontë's words, the boys were made useful and kept humble. Every minute of the day was occupied with education and self-improvement and there was an emphasis on Christian piety, with George III lamenting the sorry example of his own brothers.

Charlotte added her own voice to the call for piety and, when her son was just eight-years-old, she advised that his duty must not be underestimated. In instructions that must have been bewildering for one so young, whose concept of *everything* was still being formed, she told George Augustus:

> 'I recommend unto you the highest love, affection and duty towards the King. Look upon him as a friend, nay, as the greatest, the best, and the most deserving of all friends you can possibly find. Try to imitate his virtues, and look upon everything that is in opposition to that duty as destructive to yourself.'[5]

---

4. Lady Charlotte retired in 1793 and received a yearly pension from the Crown. Despite battling ill health, she lived to the proverbial ripe old age of 88 and died in 1813.

5. Aspinall, Arthur (ed.) (1963). *The Correspondence of George, Prince of Wales: Vol I.* London: Cassell, p.6.

The boys, of course, wanted only to indulge in childish pursuits, to play and prank and be children; not for them was the strict schedule imposed by the king and his representatives. In short, they became rather a handful, as the prince's early biographers noted:

> 'The two brothers had passed the joyous days of boyhood together; in their sports they had been inseparable, and in all their mischievous pranks, which drew down upon them, they mutually screened each other; and in those cases where the culprit could not be exactly discovered, each of them was willing to bear the reproach, rather than declare the real offender.'[6]

Refreshment and mealtimes were strictly governed and, in keeping with the king's dislike of largesse, the menu was far from lavish. In adulthood, of course, mealtimes for George Augustus would be all about excess and it is tempting to speculate whether George III's focus on piety and denial, on *not* revelling in the pleasures of the flesh, is exactly what pushed his eldest son to do just that.

When ill health forced Holdernesse to go abroad in 1775, he returned to find that his regime had collapsed, his authority supplanted by the prince's new tutors. Worst of all, without the steadying influence of Holdernesse, the always quick temper of George Augustus had grown far worse. Childhood pranks with his beloved brother had blossomed into a desire to escape his restrictive home and to be allowed into society or even better, to go to war. On the first, some quarter was given and he was *finally* allowed to attend a ball but on the second there was to be no change in parental policy: the Prince of Wales would *never* go into battle.

The newspapers that would later ridicule and taunt the prince were not always so hostile. In fact, in George's youth, the gentlemen of the press championed him, raising their voices in support of his plea. *Give the young man his wish*, they cried, to which the king responded with a resounding *no*!

> 'The Prince of Wales, with a spirit of gallantry that does him great honour, has made three requests relative to a change in that domestic

---

6. Huish, Robert (1830). *Memoirs of George the Fourth: Vol I*. London: Thomas Kelly, pp.37–8.

system which has hitherto environed him; time will shew whether the junto have laid their foundations upon a rock, or upon the sand.'[7]

Whilst the prince's tutors and family friends were pleased at the young man's academic abilities, the God-fearing king suspected that his eldest son was not nearly as interested in his religious studies as he should be. Indeed, as the years passed and he grew into a young man, it became apparent that the almighty really had little place in George's most *passionate* pursuits.

The prince's pleasures were not few and they were not cheap. He loved gambling and finery, burning through his allowance as though there were no tomorrow with more than half his income spent on his stables alone. For all his profligacy though, there was one pastime that outpaced all others, one thing that he could not live without and it was to be the source of gossip, scandal and heartbreak for both the gentleman and his family – women. Combine that with an absolute dedication to getting his own way, and there can only be a recipe for disaster.

An Eye for the Ladies

By the time he was in his late teens, the charming, cultured, intelligent and rather pretty young Prince of Wales had developed an abiding love for the fairer sex. The object of his heated teenage affections was diarist Mary Hamilton, great-granddaughter to the Duke of Hamilton and seven years the senior of the 16-year-old prince. She also happened to be the governess to his sisters.

'Impetuosity, ardour, no word is too strong for my present sentiments. I see Beauty, Person, accomplishments, every thing in Short in you, that could make me happy.'[8]

---

7. *Morning Post and Daily Advertiser* (London, England), Thursday, August 12, 1779; issue 2130, p.1.
8. Dickenson, Mary Hamilton (1925). *Mary Hamilton: Afterwards Mrs. John Dickenson, at Court and at Home*. London: John Murray, p.77.

George pursued Mary tirelessly and passionately, his letters fiery and just as melodramatic as one might expect. She kindly attempted to reject his advances, though she must have been flattered by such an illustrious admirer, even as she told him that she should not 'act so base a part as to encourage such warm declarations'.[9] Undaunted, George sent Mary a lock of his hair and made promises of marriage, of a lifelong ardour that would never cool.

Of course, for the Prince of Wales, a lifelong ardour was something that he would find next to impossible to maintain.

Mary was a little more realistic about such attachments than her excitable suitor and met his declarations of love with pleas for a calmer approach. She could not allow herself to encourage his adoration and instead offered him her friendship and nothing more. In fact, it was lucky that she *didn't* share his passions because that love, born in the first flush of spring, ended as suddenly as it had begun when winter came.

It was a fateful evening indeed when George accompanied his reserved parents to the theatre in December 1779 to take in a command performance of *The Winter's Tale.* The leading lady was Mary Darby Robinson, a young Bristolian actress who had lived a colourful life. Trained by the legendary David Garrick, Mary had been through her share of dramas. These included smallpox and a stint in debtor's prison thanks to her troublesome husband. All of that was behind her now, and the actress was the toast of the London stage and the icon of a whole legion of admirers.

The fact that Mary was married and had been since her mid-teens was not about to stand in the prince's way and when he set eyes on her, he fell in love. Mary herself remembered the night as one of romance and intrigue, recalling that her co-stars had already predicted George's imminent attachment, telling her, 'By Jove, Mrs. Robinson, you will make a conquest of the prince; for to-night you look handsomer than ever'.[10]

Mary, of course, was all starstruck innocence at her illustrious new admirer, bewildered and bedazzled in equal measure. In fact, for one so worldly her wide-eyed wonder seems just a *touch* affected, to put it mildly.

---

9. Ibid., p.76.
10. Robinson, Mary (1827). *Memoirs of the Late Mrs Robinson*. London: Hunt and Clarke, p.99.

'Indeed, some flattering remarks which were made by his royal highness met my ear as I stood near his box, and I was overwhelmed with confusion. The prince's particular attention was observed by every one, and [...] just as the curtain was falling, my eyes met those of the Prince of Wales, and with a look that I *never shall forget*, he gently inclined his head a second time; I felt the compliment, and blushed my gratitude.'[11]

From that moment, the prince was besotted with the leading lady and declared himself to be wildly in love with the woman who was half a decade his senior. He wrote her florid and impassioned love notes addressed to *Perdita* from *Florizel*, which she received with that same blushing bewilderment. Out came the scissors and off went another lock of hair for the object of his affections, who seemed flattered, besotted but, unsurprisingly, nervous.

'However flattering it might have been to female vanity, to know that the most admired, and most accomplished prince in Europe was devotedly attached to me; however dangerous to the heart such idolatry as his royal highness, during many months, professed in almost daily letters, [...] still I declined any interview with his royal highness. I was not insensible to all his powers of attraction; I thought him one of the most amiable of men. There was a beautiful ingenuousness in his language, a warm and enthusiastic adoration, expressed in every letter, which interested and charmed me.'[12]

Mary begged George to do 'nothing that might incur the displeasure of his royal highness's family,'[13] and 'entreated him to recollect that he was young, and led on by the impetuosity of passion; that should I consent to quit my profession and my husband, I should be thrown entirely on his mercy.'[14] Perhaps inspired by Mary's celebrated range of *breeches* roles, the prince

---

11. Ibid., p.99.
12. Ibid., p.102.
13. Ibid., p.103.
14. Ibid., p.103.

invited her to visit him whilst wearing a male disguise and when she refused, George fell into a deep funk.

Throughout this period, Mary's husband seemed determined to sideline her and though this may appear wonderfully convenient, it might also be true. He was hardly a man of great moral fibre, and their marriage had not been a happy one, so let us not be *too* cynical of *Perdita's* recollections. Eventually Mary capitulated and grabbed a very brief moment to say hello to the prince in the presence of chaperones Lord Malden and York, George's favourite brother.

This first meeting was over in minutes but it was not the last by any means and if Mary Hamilton had been circumspect, Mary Robinson was no such thing. George was enraptured and whether Mary was motivated by love or money, she was ready to listen when he dropped a bombshell. Would *Perdita*, the prince ventured, consider leaving her husband and the stage behind in return for a stipend of £20,000 and the role of mistress to this very regal *Florizel?* Indeed she would.

One truism that soon became evident was the fact that George enjoyed nothing more than the thrill of the chase. No matter how grand his passion, the women he set his cap at seemed to lose their lustre once they tumbled into his arms. Mary was the first of many who would discover this yet at the start, all was romance and roses.

When George reached 18, he readily accepted his father's offer of a residence of his own, though he was not yet permitted to fully leave the parental bosom. It is no coincidence that the staid and steady George III declined the same offer when *he* came of age, preparing to stay at home with his mother just as his increasingly wayward son craved the freedom his own household would eventually offer.

Now very much a young man about town, George's relationship with Mary was the talk of society. Already famous in her own right, her celebrity reached stratospheric levels yet was now entirely dependent on staying in the favour of the prince. She had abandoned her career for the life of a professional mistress and those invitations to the best parties, closets full of the finest gowns and, frankly, her notoriety, relied on the Prince of Wales. It was she who really fired his early interest in the Whig politics that opposed his father and rumours persisted that the influential Whig, Charles James

Fox, was her lover. George was revelling in his freedom and when he turned a decidedly critical eye on Mary, he found her wanting. After all, it was *his* turn to be the toast of the town and he really should, he decided, spread his romantic wings a little.

Perhaps unsurprisingly Mary's £20,000 was nowhere to be seen and soon enough, the prince was similarly absent. As the press revelled in the scandal, Mary found her efforts to secure payment frustrated despite the efforts of friends and influential figures who did their best to ensure she received the cash. She demanded £25,000 in return for the letters George had sent her yet the best Fox could eventually negotiate was a lump sum of £5,000 and an income of £500 a year, which Mary grudgingly accepted.

As Mary tried to pick up the tattered threads of her once-celebrated career and gather what was left of her reputation, George had more amorous things on his mind. He turned his appraising eye on celebrated courtesan Elizabeth Armistead, the future wife of Fox, and found her, as so many did, *enchanting*.

Elizabeth was mistress to Lord George Cavendish and it was he who made a rather surprising discovery when visiting his lady's chambers one night.

'Ld George was returning one night to Mrs Armitstead's, rather drunk. In going into her room he perceiv'd some unaccustomed light in another, and much against her entreatys went in. The room seem'd empty, but willing to examine everywhere he soon found there was a man conceal'd behind the door. He stretched out his arm with the candle in his hand close to the person's face, and to his great surprise found it was the P. of Wales.'[15]

In Elizabeth, George had more than met his match and she had little interest in the young prince once the initial ardour had cooled, leaving him behind to travel. George was never alone for long and he brushed off rumours that he had fathered a child with the divorced adventuress, Grace Dalrymple Elliott, happy to let one of her other numerous lovers assume responsibility for her daughter as he went off in search of new romantic pastures.

---

15. Georgiana, Duchess of Devonshire (1955). *Georgiana: Extracts from the Correspondence of Georgiana, Duchess of Devonshire*. London: John Murray, p.291.

He threw money at any number of actresses and courtesans and one of his paramours, Countess von Hardenburg,[16] became so notorious that the king asked her husband to whisk her off to the continent to get her out of his son's hair! It seemed that the prince, to the horror of his pious and frugal father, was determined to live life to the max.

The story of George's reign is a story of affairs, romance and Georgian sauce; rest assured, there's much more scandal where *that* came from!

A Political Prince

Hardly surprisingly for a man who would one day sit on the throne of the United Kingdom, George had many friends in politics and society who were keen to win his trust and patronage. His best and most trusted confidante was his adored younger brother, York, who was always ready with a word of advice to help his elder sibling overcome his latest passion, not that his own personal life was so unblemished that he could afford to do so.

Nevertheless, York had known George longer than almost anyone and recognized in him the flightiness that made him easy prey for those with big ambitions. He saw in his brother a weakness for women and flattery that anyone with a little charm who was seeking to make political capital might exploit and cautioned George against rushing into *any* commitment, whether that of the heart, politics or court. He also warned the young prince, whose dalliance with Mary had proved expensive and embarrassing for the king, *not* to alienate his parents any further.

The high-living George would hear none of it. He loved to party, to spend and to drink, all of the things that his father found abhorrent. Domestic arguments were commonplace and the hot-tempered Prince of Wales had learned nothing from his liaison with Mary. In fact, if anything, it had made him more self-assured. He had wanted Mary, and Mary became his; when he no longer wanted her, he cast her off at seemingly no cost to himself. It seemed that the world bowed before him but when York departed for

---

16. The busy countess also enjoyed an intrigue with George's brother, Frederick, Duke of York.

Germany and a new military career, George lost his best friend and closest counsel in one fell swoop.

It was into this worrying landscape that Charles James Fox strode, a man who shared more than a love of drinking and gaming with the Prince of Wales. Fox had also warmed Mary Robinson's bed and would later secretly marry Elizabeth Armistead, another of George's old flames. Like the Prince of Wales he was a perpetual and proverbial thorn in the political side of George III.

A prominent and leading Whig, Fox was quite the man about town, famed for his high-rolling lifestyle, his charming, witty and intelligent conversation and the fact that he was usually game for anything. He and the prince got on like a house on fire, with George by now a regular favourite of the gossip columnists and constantly before his father, cap in hand, looking for money to throw into his rapidly exhausted coffers. To the king, the prince was a spendthrift, a libertine with perilous morals whereas to the prince, the king was dullness personified, keeping the purse strings too tight and doing all he could to deprive his son of the fun he so adored.

Fox and the Prince of Wales petitioned the king and Parliament for an allowance that would be paid when George reached 21. The initial and mind boggling figure of £100,000 sent the king into an apoplexy of annoyance but eventually it was agreed that George would receive half the requested amount and the use of Carlton House, which would later serve as Fox's election headquarters. After all, what harm could *possibly* come from giving a young man who loved to spend money and have the finest of everything a home that was not in the best of repair? It's hardly as if he would immediately commission an eye-wateringly expensive programme of repairs, renovations and improvements, is it? Of course it is.

Although George III had rejected the opportunity to move away from his own mother, the prince snatched the money with both hands, moving into Carlton House with indecent haste. Here he started spending as though money was no object, commissioning Henry Holland, one of the leading architects of the time, to make extensive and ruinously expensive renovations. It was with some horror that the king learned that the prince, with his £50,000 annual allowance, was spending more than £30,000 of it on stables alone.

Newspapers devoted whole articles to the interior of the magnificent house, taking readers on a room-by-room tour and describing the stunningly rich drapery, the enormity of the chambers and the magnificent decor. It was a world that few could ever dream of being part of but Lady Lyttelton *was* part of that world, and she wrote:

'Carlton House is very beautiful, very magnificent, and we were well amused looking at it yesterday. I don't know whether you are *worthy* of the beauties of old china vases, gold fringes, damask draperies, cut-glass lustres, and all the other fine things we saw there. I can only tell you the lustre in one of the rooms, of glass and ormolu [sic], looking like a shower of diamonds, cost between *two and three thousand pounds*. I write the number at full length, that you mayn't fancy I have put a cypher too many. However, it is such a peculiarly English manufactory that our heir-apparent is right in encouraging it.'[17]

It was to Carlton House that Fox hastened when his coalition with Lord North collapsed in 1783. Over a lavish breakfast prince and politician toasted one another, their guests and the future. The ambitious Fox, of course, would not be out of the spotlight for long.

Scandalous Secrets

At Carlton House, lovers came and lovers went but for all his breast-beating and hair-cutting, none of them tempted the passionate George to the altar except for one, the infamous Maria Fitzherbert. Maria would even make her home at Marble Hill, the former home of George II's lover, Henrietta Howard, but, unlike that royal mistress, Maria was set to bag herself a husband.

Born as Maria Anne Smythe in 1756, the Roman Catholic Mrs Fitzherbert was already a widow at the age of 19, left without anything to call her own by her late husband and within three years, had married and been widowed

17. Spencer, Sarah (1912). *Correspondence of Sarah Spencer Lady Lyttelton 1787–1870.* London: John Murray, p.104.

again. Every cloud has a silver lining as they say, and at her second husband's death Maria was finally left financially secure. She had property, money and some *very* illustrious friends to call her own including the Earl of Sefton, her mother's half-brother. Like any respectable widow she closed herself away for a time but, after a suitable period of mourning, Maria sallied forth into society. She was soon quite the girl about town, mixing with the great and good until she made a fateful trip to the opera and there encountered the starry-eyed Prince of Wales.

Didn't everybody?

Not for the first time George fell madly in love and not for the first time, he was sure that he could not *hope* to live without this perfect goddess.

Maria, however, was a sensible, respectable and perhaps pragmatic Catholic widow, not some romantic young heroine who went starry-eyed when faced with a prince and certainly not one who was willing to risk her reputation for a dalliance. She was also *very* well aware of the prince's reputation with the ladies so, when he set his cap at her, she was not nearly as accommodating as the ill-used Perdita had been. One suspects that she must have been flattered at least, but she had no intention of acquiescing to the Prince of Wales.

Into this maelstrom of young hormones flounced Georgiana, Duchess of Devonshire, one of the prince's closest friends. She knew too well of George's ways, having resisted his advances herself, and she wrote of his attachment to Maria:

> 'Upon coming to town many circumstances had thrown me into an unfortunate intimacy with him and he would not rest till he told me his passion for Mrs. F. and his design to marry her; any remonstrance from me was always followed by threats of killing himself.'[18]

All of that changed in 1784 when news reached Maria that George had attempted suicide and was near death. The lovesick prince had stabbed himself and was asking only for Maria, the woman with whom he wished to spend his final hours. Distraught yet still mindful of her reputation, Maria agreed to attend only on condition that Georgiana would also be there to

---

18. Leslie, Anita (1960). *Mrs Fitzherbert: A Biography.* York: Scribner, p.35.

ensure there could be no whisper of impropriety. She hastened to Carlton House to find the Prince of Wales giving a most melodramatic performance. Pale, weak and languishing beneath bloodstained blankets, he told her that he had chosen to take his own life rather than live without her.

Perhaps, he ventured, she would take his gift of a ring and lend him some comfort in his last moment?

This time, Maria agreed. A doubtful Duchess of Devonshire loaned the prince her own ring and he slipped it onto his beloved's finger, declaring that this was, in his eyes, a symbol of marriage. Suddenly the prince was not nearly so sickly, proclaiming that she was his betrothed and that those present would bear witness to this. Mrs Fitzherbert thought otherwise and fled with Georgiana. Returning the ring, she signed a statement saying that she did not consider herself engaged nor married to *anyone* and immediately quit England for Europe.

> 'On Tuesday the 8th July 1784 Mr Bouverie and Mr Onslow came to me and told me the Prince of Wales had run himself thro' the body and declar'd he would tear open his bandages unless I would accompany Mrs Fitzherbert to him. We went there and she promised to marry him at her return but she conceives as well as myself that promises obtained in such a manner are entirely void.'[19]

However, even his beloved's flight to Europe did not cool George's ardour and still he pursued her, sending heated letters and beseeching representatives. Despite herself, Maria was drawn in and eventually, as letters flew back and forth, she found herself falling under the prince's spell. At home, he gave every indication of a man in deep crisis and Elizabeth Armistead recalled his frequent, hysterical visits to Fox's home. Here he behaved in a most unprincely manner, giving the curtain call to that melodramatic *deathbed* performance.

> '[George] cried by the hour, that he testified the sincerity and violence of his passion and his despair by the most extravagant expressions

---

19. Irvine, Valerie (2007). *The King's Wife: George IV and Mrs Fitzherbert*. London: Hambledon. p, 37.

and actions, rolling on the floor, striking his forehead, tearing his hair, falling into hystericks, and swearing that he would abandon the country, forego the crown, sell his jewels and plate, and scrape together a competence to fly with the object of his affections to America.'[20]

Fox looked on with suspicion and anxiety as George's passion continued to flare. Maria, respectable Catholic that she was, would never consent to become a royal mistress and any attempt to marry her would be illegal under the Royal Marriages Act. Of course, thanks to Maria's faith no consent would have been given by the king so instead, it was simply not sought. That would prove in time to be of utmost importance to George when he carelessly broke his beloved's heart.

To Fox, this attachment could only bring trouble. Should the marriage happen, George's succession to the throne would hang in the balance and with it, his *own* influence on the royal household. As it was, he was a close friend of a future king, yet should George lose or give up his right of succession, then any influence that friendship brought with it would be lost forever. This became horribly prescient with Maria's return to London in 1785, fresh from her European adventures and having secured George's promise of marriage.

After reassuring Fox that there would be no marriage, George promptly went about arranging one. The ceremony took place on 15 December 1785 in Maria's home in Park Street, Mayfair, and was officiated by the Reverend Robert Burt, Chaplain in Ordinary to the Prince of Wales. The marriage was entirely illegal, forbidden by the Royal Marriages Act and only Maria's uncle and brother were present to witness it. Rumours that Burt's debts were paid off and he was released from the Fleet Prison in return for his agreement to officiate are oft-repeated but apparently unsubstantiated. There is no mention of his name in the prison's ledgers yet the story has stuck ... it's nicely scandalous, after all.

When the king refused to fund his son's profligate lifestyle, George had no choice but to move out of the opulent confines of Carlton House and

---

20. Lord Holland (1854). *Memoirs of the Whig Party During My Time: Vol II*. London: Longman, Brown, Green and Longmans, p.126.

into Park Street. Though Maria was not a permanent resident alongside her husband, wherever he went, she joined him. Her movements were of such import to society that even the most inconsequential outing was considered a matter of public interest.

> 'Yesterday Mrs. Fitzherbert took an airing in Hyde-Park for one hour, twenty minutes, and forty-two seconds, attended by her coachman, and one footman.'[21]

No matter what the world might have thought, Maria could now fraternize with her prince in the safe knowledge that they were, in the eyes of the Lord, married. All invitations to George were automatically extended to include Maria and they were a familiar and regular sight on the society scene. Rumours soon began to fly and before long those whispers reached the king. He listened with horror to tales of their open attendance upon one another, saw the caricatures that mocked the couple and finally decided that these rumours must be quashed once and for all.

The Prince of Wales, he decided, needed a princess.

George, however, was not one for doing as his father wished and once again he turned to Fox for a helping hand. He confessed that he was drowning in debt once more and knew that there would be no money from the father with whom he simply could not see eye to eye. Finally, unthinkably for Maria, her husband's debts reached the debating chamber and with the prince's express permission, Fox issued a public denial of the marriage rumours. We cannot know what George told his friend to say on the floor of the House, but Fox told the members:

> '[the rumour of marriage was] proved at once the uncommon pains taken by the enemies of his royal highness to propagate the grossest and most malignant falsehoods, with a view to depreciate [George's] character and injure him in the opinion of his country. [...] The whole of the debt the prince was ready to submit to the investigation of the House; and he was equally ready to submit the other circumstance to which

21. *Public Advertiser* (London, England), Friday, May 12, 1786; issue 16216, p.2.

he had alluded, to their consideration, provided the consideration of a house of parliament could, consistently with propriety and decency, be applied to such a subject. Nay, his royal highness had authorised him to declare, that, as a peer of parliament, he was ready in the other House to submit to any the most pointed questions which could be put to him respecting it, or to afford his majesty, or his majesty's ministers, the fullest assurances of the utter falsehood of the fact in question, which never had, and which common sense must see, never could have happened.'[22]

Although Maria's name was not mentioned, there could be no doubt as to whom the speech alluded. Devastated and betrayed, she looked to George for an explanation. The prince lied to Maria, telling her that he had not authorized the speech and it was duly agreed that his friend, Richard Brinsley Sheridan, would make another statement to clear up the matter. Couched in the most delicate of language and with no names mentioned, Sheridan said:

'[…] a delicate and judicious compliment to the lady to whom it was supposed some later parliamentary allusions had been pointed, affirming that ignorance and vulgar folly alone could have persevered in attempting to detract from a character, upon which truth could fix no just reproach and which was in reality entitled to the truest and most general respect.'[23]

As damage limitation exercises go, it was really the best that Sheridan could hope for if Maria's name was to be spared. Though she was *somewhat* mollified, George was delighted with the outcome of his latest adventures as he pocketed over £150,000 and went home to Carlton House. His relationship with Fox, however, suffered something of a blow as George pointed the finger of blame for Maria's upset at his friend, while Fox told

22. Fox, Charles James (1815). *Speeches of the Right Honourable Charles James Fox in the House of Commons, Vol III*. London: Longman, Hurst, Orme, and Brown, pp.325–6.
23. Leslie, Anita (1960). *Mrs Fitzherbert: A Biography*. York: Scribner, p.72.

him, 'I always thought your father the greatest liar in England, but now I see that *you* are.'[24]

Financially a lot happier, George's much-publicized profligacy meant he was publicly never more unpopular; it was a state of affairs he would have to get used to. Besides, he had other things to attend to, and having learned nothing from the Carlton House renovations, was now about to undertake the same enormous project in Brighton, on what would become the iconic Royal Pavilion. It was in Brighton that he and Maria would be reconciled and where she would live for many years, long after her relationship with George had reached its rocky end.

The Regency Bill

With his time taken up by gadding about, gambling and ladies of all sorts, one thing that the Prince of Wales really *didn't* fancy doing was ruling the country. Of course, he knew that the crown would be his one day but for now, he was rather enjoying being footloose and fancy free.

When George III fell ill in 1788, however, it looked as though the time to grow up had finally arrived. Although the two Georges had never seen eye to eye, the prince was not, as his enemies claimed, unmoved by his father's illness but instead deeply distressed. Both George and York took great interest in the treatment of the king, so much so that it began to cause divisions with their mother, who resented the interference of her sons in her husband's welfare. Whilst it would be easy to speculate that some scheme might be at the root of their interest, it's not so unbelievable to think that they were simply worried for their father and his wellbeing. Let us not forget that for all he had in common with a spoiled brat, the Prince of Wales *was* human.

Human he may be, but he was also the heir apparent and, as such, the natural candidate to fill the role of regent. Unsurprisingly, the ambitious Fox was not about to give up the greatest leverage he had ever held and argued passionately that the regent could *only* be the Prince of Wales. Equally

---

24. Anonymous (1856). *The Rambler: A Catholic Journal and Review, Vol V.* London: Burns and Lambert, p.480.

unsurprisingly, Pitt wasn't so keen, recognizing that his own job hung in the balance. Though he agreed in theory that it would be easier for George to become regent than anyone else, his proposed plan of action put tight limits on the power the prince would be able to exercise. After all, there was more than the country at stake: whole careers, those *legacies* that politicians set so much store by rested on the decisions taken at this delicate stage.

The bill included clauses that restricted the powers of the regent and would not allow him to dismiss the government nor have any rights over the king's estates; in addition, the queen alone would be responsible for her husband's wellbeing. George and York were, of course, outraged at these restrictions yet they weren't fools. They would not, they promised, attempt any action without the full consent and backing of Parliament. It was really all a matter of theory anyway and significant obstacles stood in the way of any Regency Bill, not least the fact that, without that all-important speech from the monarch, the proposed motion could not be passed into legislature. In fact, so long as the king was incarcerated and in treatment, Parliament remained in a deadlock from which there appeared to be no way out.

George hardly cared; he did not lust for power, all too aware of the curtailment it would put on the life he enjoyed leading, though he wouldn't object to the money and influence he would gain should he become regent. Happily, before the prince could be roped into ruling, the king recovered his wits and, with Maria generously forgiving his transgressions and welcoming him back into her arms, all was once again rosy for the Prince of Wales.

From Brighton to Jersey

When the Prince of Wales first visited Brighton in 1783, he took up residence with his uncle, Prince Henry, Duke of Cumberland, and fell head over heels in love. This time the object of his affections wasn't a woman, but the vibrant seaside town itself where he enjoyed the nightlife and the chance to indulge in all his favourite pursuits away from the watchful eye of the king and queen. As the years sped past, Brighton's charms never dimmed in his affections and when he discovered a modest farmhouse close to the Brighton home of Maria Fitzherbert, he knew that he had found his ideal love nest.

Now, one might think or hope that George had learned from his mistakes in the ruinously expensive expansion of Carlton House yet one would be mistaken. Instead, he went and did the same thing all over again.

Under the direction of Henry Holland, the brains behind the Carlton House renovations, that modest farmhouse began to grow in size and grandeur into the Marine Pavilion. George bought up surrounding land so that he might have the stables he believed he deserved and soon it was the most fashionable, fabulous address in Brighton.

Over the next three decades the pavilion became the magnificent Eastern Gothic palace it is today, with the famed John Nash later commissioned to overhaul Holland's work. Once again, the expense knew no bounds and the prince filled the palace with the finest furniture, decoration and guests, who were invited to attend the court of George and the dreadfully forgiving Maria. Not everyone was a fan though, with one of the prince's most scathing biographers describing the pavilion as 'a nondescript monster in architecture, and appears like a mad-house, or a house run mad, as it has neither beginning, middle, nor end'.[25]

For a time, the Prince of Wales and Maria sat at the heart of the most fashionable place in the land, holding court as any king and queen might. Though publicly regarded as nothing more official than a mistress, whilst Maria remained high in her husband's affections, she was untouchable. As so many of George's lovers were to find though, nothing drew him to a woman like her absence, the chance to retain a little mystique. When the *loves of his life* became a permanent fixture, they soon lost their sparkle; for Maria, it would be no different.

Maria could not hold George's passions forever and in 1793 he finally set her aside in favour of Frances Villiers, Countess of Jersey, a woman he had long pursued in vain. The capricious and manipulative countess was a social climber *par excellence* and in Maria she saw a real obstacle to her ambitions to be the prince's number one.

Married to George Bussy Villiers, 4th Earl of Jersey and Gentleman of the Bedchamber to the king, Lady Jersey had clout, cunning and an

---

25. Huish, Robert (1830). *Memoirs of George the Fourth: Vol I*. London: Thomas Kelly, p.272.

acid tongue. She was celebrated for her looks but not so much for her character, and she loved nothing more than gossip and intrigue, which perhaps made her a surprising favourite of the queen. If Maria had attempted to be circumspect in her liaisons with the prince, Lady Jersey would hear none of it. She had no qualms about the affair being public knowledge; indeed, it no doubt did wonders for her already considerable standing in society.

Soon it was *her* movements that were being reported to the public, whether riding in the prince's phaeton or gadding out at the theatre. It was a most public rejection of Maria, yet things were going to get far worse.

It was the conniving Lady Jersey who finally convinced the prince to accept his father's suggestion that he marry his cousin, Caroline of Brunswick, and secure the settlement of his debts. She knew that a marriage for money would be no threat to her position whereas one secured on love, such as that to Maria, could prove dangerous. Accordingly, George wrote to his Catholic bride and told her that their affair was over. Maria was devastated at the end of the marriage yet when the prince wrote his will after that ill-fated *official* marriage had taken place, he left everything he had to 'my Maria Fitzherbert, my wife, the wife of my heart and soul'.[26]

'This day the Nuptials of the PRINCE of WALES to the PRINCESS CAROLINE of BRUNSWICK will be proclaimed in Council at St. James's.'[27]

Meanwhile the king, gentle soul that he was, hoped only that his heir would find the same domestic happiness with which he had been blessed. He was all too aware of George's desire to follow his brothers into military service yet reminded him that, for the other royal sons, this was their *only* duty. The heir to the throne, meanwhile, had far more to concern him than military matters. Nevertheless, he did grant his eldest son a commission on the understanding that the prince would seek no further rank or promotion in

---

26. Leslie, Shane (1939). *Mrs. Fitzherbert: A Life Chiefly from Unpublished Sources*. New York: Benziger Brothers, p.372.

27. *Sun* (London, England), Wednesday, November 5, 1794; issue 657, p.2.

the forces. George, of course, reneged on that understanding and it was left to his father to gently yet firmly remind him of exactly what his station was.

'My younger sons can have no other situations in the State or occupation but what arise from the military lines they have been placed in. You are born to a more difficult one, and which I shall be most happy if you seriously turn your thoughts to; the happiness of millions depend on it as well as your own.

'May the Princess Caroline's character prove so pleasing to you that your mind may be engrossed with domestic felicity, which may establish in you that composure of mind perhaps the most essential qualification in the station you are born to fill, and that a numerous progeny may be the result of this union, which will be a comfort to me in the decline of years [...] rendering [your] subjects prosperous and happy.'[28]

In 1794 the engagement of George and Caroline was confirmed and the bride-to-be set out for England where she would be received by her new Lady of the Bedchamber. That welcoming figure, who arrived an hour late to the appointed meeting, was none other than the scheming Lady Jersey. In her new position she found she could undermine, gossip and bully to her heart's content. It was a bad start … things would only get worse.

A Monstrous Marriage

'The Princess of Wales has ever been known to entertain a strong partiality for England, and frequently to express that she considered herself more of an English woman than a German, her mother being of this country. When she landed at Greenwich, she pleasantly observed, "I now am perfectly happy, for I have reached my country at last."'[29]

---

28. Aspinall, Arthur (1962). *The Later Correspondence of George III.: December 1783 to January 1793, Vol II*. Cambridge:Cambridge University Press, p.329.
29. *London Packet or New Lloyd's Evening Post* (London, England), April 6, 1795 – April 8, 1795; issue 4001, p.1.

Upon her arrival in England, Caroline of Brunswick was well aware of the weight that her forthcoming marriage carried. For her house of Brunswick-Bevern it was something of a coup, and for the royal family she offered stability, respect and, most importantly, succession. With a wife to call his own, George's duty to provide the heir and the spare could finally be done and perhaps he might take the opportunity to really settle down. His bride, who was in her late 20s and without a hint of scandal to her name, was everything that he was not, or so it *seemed*.

Their first meeting was a legendary disaster, with George calling for a strong drink as he claimed that Caroline's hygiene was so poor that she stole his breath, whilst Caroline declared that she had expected something rather better given the portraits she had seen. That famously pretty prince was filling out, high living, feasts and fine wine stealing some of his boyish verve. Not only that, but Caroline was now subject to the constant and unforgiving attentions of Lady Jersey, who watched her every move with a critical eye.

When the wedding day rolled round in the spring of 1795, Caroline swallowed whatever doubts she might have had and dressed for the occasion. Looking every inch the princess in silver, ermine and crimson, she swept into the Chapel Royal of St James's Palace where the Archbishop of Canterbury, the Most Reverend John Moore, waited.

He might have wished he had been *kept* waiting because the groom was not just merry, he was *paralytic*.

Barely able to stand on his own two feet, George staggered and lurched this way and that, clinging to his attendants, the Dukes of Roxburghe and Bedford. When the chance came for those present to speak of any just cause or impediment to the marriage the archbishop gave a dramatic pause that would have made Garrick proud and looked pointedly from the king to the prince. This was the time to mention Maria, the fact that the prince was insensible, *anything…* but of course nobody spoke up and the ceremony proceeded to its close, interrupted only when a confused groom attempted to stagger out during the prayers.

That evening the newlyweds were escorted to their bedchamber and left alone to end the evening however they saw fit. For the Prince of Wales, that meant a collapse into the hearth whilst the newly-minted Princess of Wales climbed into bed alone. She later confirmed that sorry state of affairs when she said, 'what it was to have a drunken husband on one's wedding-day, and one who passed the greater part of his bridal night under the grate where he fell, and where I left him.'[30]

It was an inauspicious start to a disastrous marriage. With Lady Jersey installed as Caroline's Lady of the Bedchamber, she was in a perfect position to watch and undermine, leaving the princess in no doubt that she was *far* from the top of her husband's affections. Of course, given that they barely spoke let alone did anything else, Caroline was probably well aware of where she stood anyway!

George claimed that he and Caroline were intimate only three times, and a year after his wedding night, he wrote:

'I have every reason to believe [that I was not the first], for not only on the first night was there no appearance of blood, but her manners were not those of a novice. In taking those liberties, natural on these occasions, she said, "*Ah mon dieu, qu'il est gros!*," and how should she know this without a previous means of comparison. Finding that I had suspicions of her not being *new*, she the next night mixed up some tooth powder and water, coloured her shift with it ... in showing these she showed at the same time such marks of filth both in the fore and *hind* part of her ... that she turned my stomach and from that moment I made a vow *never to touch her again*. I had known her three times – twice the first and once the second night – it required no small [effort] to conquer my aversion and overcome the disgust of her person.'[31]

Quite apart from the fact that George was too drunk to remember *anything* of his wedding night and the sneaky mention of Caroline's wide-eyed exclamation on his regal endowment, this is hardly gentlemanly behaviour. Of course, these tales of tooth powder and personal hygiene problems should

---

30. Bell, Robert (1955). *The Life of the Rt. Hon. George Canning*. London: Harper, p.304.
31. Robins, Jane (2006), *The Trial of Queen Caroline: The Scandalous Affair that Nearly Ended a Monarchy*. New York: Simon and Schuster, pp.17–8.

probably be taken with a pinch of salt but nobody reading these words could mistake this for a happy husband.

> 'Yesterday morning, at ten minutes past nine o'clock, the PRINCESS of WALES was safely delivered of a PRINCESS at Carlton House.
>
> Her Highness had been dangerously indisposed for three days prior to the happy event.'[32]

George III, however, found his new daughter-in-law charming company and he along with the rest of the country rejoiced when, almost exactly nine months to the day after that unfortunate wedding night a daughter, Princess Charlotte, was born. She was to be the prince's only legitimate child, though rumours flew around about any number of *illegitimate* children. Ironically given his genuine affection for and attachment to Maria, it appeared that the marriage remained childless, though Maria flatly refused to sign any binding document that confirmed she had borne her royal husband no children.

The birth of Charlotte did nothing to bring the royal couple any closer, and society buzzed with gossip at Lady Jersey's appalling treatment of the Princess of Wales. It is, therefore, no surprise to learn that when private letters from Caroline to her family were waylaid and found to contain unflattering remarks about the royal household, it was Lady Jersey who was blamed for opening them.

If the prince and his mistress expected Caroline to face censure for this, they were to be sorely mistaken. Instead the press and public rallied behind the wronged princess, disgusted that even her private correspondence was not beyond the talons of Lady Jersey. If George had been unpopular before, now he was vilified, and he was *furious*. With separation on his mind he wrote to the king in 1796 setting out not only his personal complaints, but darkly hinting that Caroline might bring the monarchy to its very knees.

> 'Misled by advisers in whose hands she is now become an absolute tool, she has flatter'd herself she could reduce me to such a situation as would

---

32. *Oracle and Public Advertiser* (London, England), Friday, January 8, 1796; issue 19 211, p.2.

give her a decided political superiority in this country. This was only to be effected by the degradation of my character. […] Since, therefore, it would now be absolutely ruinous to my character & interest, as well as destructive to my peace of mind, for the rest of my life, to have further communication or intercourse of any kind with so dangerous a person as the Princess, I have only earnestly to supplicate your Majesty to order measures for our final separation.'[33]

The Prince of Wales got his wish and Caroline moved to Montague House at Blackheath, leaving George to rattle around in the company of Lady Jersey and his influential *Carlton House set*.[34] The newspapers were studied in their innocence, musing that 'The PRINCESS of WALES seems to have forsaken the Opera. Her chair latterly has been reversed there.'[35]

If George breathed a sigh of relief at his wife's departure, it wouldn't last long. In her new abode, Caroline was about to paint the town red all over again!

Who's The Mummy?

When Caroline left Carlton House, she was *far* from sorry. Tucked away at Blackheath and free from the husband she had come to loathe, the Princess of Wales decided to go just a little bit wild. Here she found herself an object of curiosity to the movers and shakers of the political world, especially George's opponents. Not only that, but Caroline was soon creating a few intrigues of her own, most notably with dashing naval heroes Sir Sidney Smith and Captain Thomas Manby.

Caroline might have liked her nautical dalliances, but Smith and Manby weren't the only names associated with the lady. As whispers circulated about the identity of various illustrious chaps who beat an eager path to the Princess of

33. Aspinall, Arthur (1962). *The Later Correspondence of George III.: December 1783 to January 1793, Vol II.* Cambridge:Cambridge University Press, p.480.
34. This social circle was made up of highly influential society figures drawn from the worlds of politics, fashion, nobility and beyond.
35. *Oracle and Public Advertiser* (London, England), Wednesday, June 7, 1797; issue 19 642, p.3.

Wales's door and all the way up to her inviting bed, George's blood boiled. For years he seethed and twitched as she made him a laughing stock in the press, the chattering circles and the eyes of those who *mattered*. With the public rallying to his wife's philanthropic calls, Caroline's popularity seemed to grow as his plummeted further with every passing year. He searched for some leverage, some scandal, *anything* to claim the moral high ground and in 1802 it arrived in the unassuming shape of an apparent orphan by the name of William Austin.

Or so he thought.

Caroline had something of a hobby of collecting unfortunate children, and this was one more thing the public liked about her. William, however, would prove to be another matter and not long before he arrived in her household, Caroline began to put on weight. Her concerned friend, Lady Douglas, wondered rather indelicately whether Caroline might be with child and when the infant suddenly appeared, the Princess of Wales laughed off such suspicions. Still, she mused, wouldn't it be a jape to suggest that he was actually the son of the Prince of Wales? Always a joker, the princess had overstepped the mark – she might well have been jesting, but such careless talk could throw the succession into crisis.

As luck would have it, in 1806 George found that he too had a friend in the helpful Lady Douglas. She and Caroline had quarrelled when the princess replaced Smith, a friend of the Douglas family, with Manby. When their friendship ended, Lady Douglas switched her allegiance swiftly and shrewdly. She went straight to the Prince of Wales, finding him *ripe* for her juicy gossip and talk of scandal. Of course, there were plenty of rumours about the prince's own illegitimate offspring but none of *these* ever found their way along the legal path.

The result of this sorry affair was the 1806 *Delicate Investigation*, overseen by Prime Minister, William Grenville. The investigation was charged with determining whether Caroline had *really* given birth to an illegitimate child and if so, what punishment would be appropriate for such a heinous wrongdoing. She in turn retained Spencer Perceval[36] an eminent lawyer and future prime minister, to defend her, which proved to be a very judicious move!

---

36. Perceval retains the dubious honour of being the only Prime Minister of the United Kingdom to be assassinated. He was shot dead on 11 May 1812 by John Bellingham.

George's new and valuable ally was happy to testify that Caroline had told her that William was actually her own illegitimate child, the result of a secret liaison with an unknown man. This was a woman, Lady Douglas told the committee, who *loved* the pleasures of the flesh, delighting in the company of men and willing to sacrifice her morals for pleasure.

The investigation listened to tales of Caroline's busy bedroom, and of the illustrious, suspiciously *Tory* men who seemed to be her beaux of choice. With such allegations more than likely politically motivated, it was telling that many of the names mentioned belonged to senior figures who would undoubtedly call for Caroline to serve as regent should her estranged husband become indisposed.

There could be no question over the gravity of the charges and the *The Morning Post* on 24 June 1806 lends an air of how seriously the matter had to be taken:

> 'The acts charged would, if proved, amount to no less than *high treason* in the illustrious personage: [...] The nature of the accusation, amounting to what might eventually affect the succession of the crown; and the great stake the accusers put to hazard.'[37]

In the end, it was all to naught and the case collapsed beneath the weight of its own pique thanks to two *very* important witnesses: Sophia and Samuel Austin. Far from being an orphan, the child was actually the son of this impoverished couple and they had entrusted his care to Caroline in order to assure a better life for the boy. The revelation was disastrous for George and only enhanced his accused wife's reputation as a lady of selfless philanthropy.

With no other choice open to them, the members of the investigation declared that William Austin was categorically *not* the child of the Princess of Wales. The only victory George won, and it was a small one, came when the commission decided not to quash the charge of adultery, but it was hardly the killer blow he had hoped for. The investigation and its outcome greatly restricted Caroline's access to her daughter and with custody of Charlotte

---

37. *The Morning Post* (London, England), Tuesday, June 24, 1806; issue 12029, p.3.

the next weapon in the war of attrition, the Prince of Wales was certainly the villain of this particular piece.

Perceval, meanwhile, later secured his client's return to court by a rather canny bit of manoeuvring. He wrote down the proceedings of the *Delicate Investigation* in a tome known simply as *The Book* and suggested that, if Caroline were not readmitted to court, then this publication might one day see the open market. In fact, a change of government meant that Caroline got her wish with or without the book, as Perceval made the most of his new office and wrote a cabinet minute that exonerated her and recommended she be received by the king.

With the princess making the most of her return to favour, Perceval supposedly burned all copies of *The Book*, thus saving the prince the bad publicity it might have generated. In fact some copies survived the flames and despite rewards being offered for the return of any rogue volumes, once Perceval was murdered, his *book* went on sale.

The Regent

'THIS day, about 12 o'clock, departed this life, at Windsor, after a long and painful illness, her Royal Highness the Princess Amelia, his Majesty's youngest daughter, to the great grief of all the Royal Family.'[38]

In 1810, Princess Amelia, sister of the Prince of Wales and daughter of George III, died. Elsewhere in this volume we learned how her untimely passing shattered the fragile king's spirit, and as he descended into a madness from which he would never recover, it was obvious that the time had come to find a regent. Thrilled at the idea of their long-term supporter being in power, the Whigs prepared to move into government. Little did they know that the Prince of Wales was wobbling and had become decidedly circumspect about where his allegiances might lie.

---

38. *Hampshire Telegraph and Sussex Chronicle etc* (Portsmouth, England), Monday, November 5, 1810; issue 578, p.3.

Although the king's illness had been an obstacle to the passing of the earlier Regency Bill, Parliament had wisely taken the time to fill in this particular loophole. With the king, to put it politely, indisposed, Lord Commissioners appointed by the Lord Chancellor were granted power to give Royal Assent to what became the Care of King During his Illness, etc. Act 1811, which was ostensibly a Regency Act. In his current mental state, George III could not possibly understand or consent to the act yet now he did not have to, Parliament had taken the necessary steps for him.

> 'This day, at two o'clock, his Royal Highness the Prince of WALES is to be sworn in as Regent of the United Kingdom, in the presence of the whole Privy Council assembled at Carlton House.'[39]

On 5 February 1811, the former Prince of Wales was named as Prince Regent and the Whigs, as well as his Whig sympathizing daughter, Charlotte, rejoiced. George, however, rather overdid the party atmosphere, and instead of displaying a suitable sober and respectful face, held a flamboyant, boisterous party to mark the occasion. With the people of Britain feeling the weight of taxation, this was *not* a wise move. They looked on in distrust, wondering exactly what their beloved old king had been replaced with. The Prince Regent, however, was living it up in style, revelling in his new found power, and the Whigs waited with bated breath to be called. And waited.

Whig celebrations were in fact terribly premature because George, for all his firebrand opposition talk, had undergone a change of heart. Taking counsel from his brothers and his most trusted friends, he decided that the boat of government should remain unrocked. Despite long discussions with the Whigs which they wrongly assumed all but guaranteed them the freedom of the new administration, the new Prince Regent instead took the decision to let the Tories maintain their ministry.[40] Any change, he mused,

---

39. *The Morning Chronicle* (London, England), Wednesday, February 6, 1811; issue 13025, p2.
40. This decision also ended the relationship between the prince and his best friend, Regency style icon, Beau Brummell. Brummell, a sworn Whig, later hammered the final nail into the coffin by publicly referring to the regent's ballooning weight in less than flattering terms.

might be too much for his father to bear in his fevered state; far better to maintain the status quo.

The prince always enjoyed an uneasy relationship with politics and would go on to spurn the Tories too, many years later. Despite his illicit marriage he maintained an absolute distaste of Catholic emancipation right up to his final years of his life, even when popular opinion turned against him. By then of course, neither Whigs nor Tories called him friend, but that was day was yet to come.

Full of political zeal, at 15, Princess Charlotte was fiercely opposed to her father's decision to stick with the Tories, as she believed the Whigs were the best hope for a better future. Although her clout was limited by age, gender and station, her ability to embarrass her father was *not*, and she delighted in doing so. What better way to make your protest, after all, than blowing kisses at the Whig leader in full view of the opera crowd?

'Nor should it be forgot that at the opera, seeing Lord Grey in the box opposite to her, [Charlotte] got up and kissed her hand repeatedly in the sight of the whole opera.'[41]

If 1811 was a year of beginnings; it was also a year for goodbyes as Mrs Fitzherbert finally found herself set aside for good. More concerned with women, architecture and fashion than politics, George could not control that wandering eye that had been apparent since his first youthful dalliances. With Lady Jersey long since and very bitterly consigned to history, the prince was by then head over heels with Isabella Ingram-Seymour-Conway, Marchioness of Hertford, his latest *paramour*. It was an embarrassingly public incident involving that same Lady Hertford that put the final nail in the coffin that was the marriage of the Prince Regent and Maria Fitzherbert.

Both women were invited to a Carlton House dinner in 1811 but George made great show of ensuring that Maria was to be seated at the far end of the table, according to her rank. Rather than face such public embarrassment Maria chose not to attend. She wrote to her husband to tell him that 'I can

41. Pearce, Charles E (1911). *The Beloved Princess, Princess Charlotte of Wales*. London: Stanley Paul & Co, p.279.

never submit to appear in any place or situation but in that where you yourself first placed me many years ago'.[42] After so many years of uncertainty the once passionate marriage of George and Maria was unquestionably finished. Over the years that followed they would never meet again, mutual animosity fuelling the fire of rejection.

Occupied with Lady Hertford, the theatre and living a fabulous, fashionable life, George's reign was not as politically turbulent as that of his father, nor those of the previous Georges. It was without his particular involvement that the War of 1812 came and went, although when the Congress of Vienna decided that in 1814 that Hanover should become a kingdom, he *did* gain something of a promotion in his ancestral homeland, having previously been the Elector rather than the king. His relationship with his daughter, sadly, would never be anything like as easy.

Sepulchral Diversions

In this midst of parties, heartbreak and largesse, let us pause for a moment to consider one of George's more unusual adventures. It is merely an aside yet an occurrence that, I think, rather sums up the prince's love of drama, heritage and excitement. It was not the Prince Regent's finest hour, but it is one that perfectly captures his rather *un*-kingly conduct at times.

As his accounts and the surviving buildings he commissioned attest, George was intent on leaving a legacy that could not be ignored. It was because of this dream that construction work was ongoing in St George's Chapel at Windsor in 1813, where he had commissioned a brand new burial vault. Whilst working on this project, the tombs of Henry VIII, Charles I and Jane Seymour were mistakenly uncovered. Upon hearing of this, the regent was beside himself with fascination and summoned Sir Henry Halford to the scene.

The discovery of Charles I's tomb was a major find, as it was the first time this long discussed resting place had been uncovered. Accounts written at the time of his burial had suggested that Charles was interred beside Henry VIII, but this was an opportunity to prove it once and for all. Mindful of the historic significance of the site, George asked Halford to examine the remains. As Halford recalls, the prince's presence would ensure 'the most

---

42. Irvine, Valerie (2007). *The King's Wife: George IV and Mrs Fitzherbert.* London: Hambledon. p, 136.

respectful care and attention to the remains of the dead during the enquiry'.[43] It didn't, of course.

When the coffin was opened, the prince and Halford were shocked to find that Charles had not fared too badly at all over the years. Though his nose, one eye and one ear were missing and his skin had become discoloured, the king certainly 'bore a strong resemblance to the coins, the busts, and especially to the pictures of King Charles I by Vandyke'.[44] If this was not evidence enough of the identity of the corpse, the fact that his head was severed in a way that perfectly matched accounts of Charles's execution surely provided the final corroborating factor.

There, in the presence of the Prince Regent, it was agreed that this was indeed the corpse of the executed King Charles I, news that excited the British public greatly.

Halford kept some of the remains for his collection of curiosities, including a damaged vertebrae which showed the mark of the axe that had killed the king. After dinner parties, he would produce the bone and hand it around for the amusement of his guests, recounting the tale of the Windsor vault.

The kingly artefacts remained in Halford's family until Queen Victoria's reign and, as has been reported on innumerable occasions, she was *not* amused. Upon learning of the fate of the vertebrae, the queen requested that it be returned to the royal household. This was swiftly done and Charles was reunited with his stolen remains in 1888, the late king resting in peace once again.

A Family at War

Perhaps unsurprisingly for a father in the House of Hanover, George's relationship with his daughter, Charlotte, was never perfect. The problems began early in life when the spiteful prince forbade his loathed wife from anything but the barest contact with her daughter, strictly forbidding mother and child from spending any time alone without chaperones. Still, George was hardly a regular fixture in the royal nursery and in fact, Caroline was able to visit more frequently than he ever realized, spending time with the little girl thanks to the sympathetic scheming of her appointed carers.

---

43. Halford, Sir Henry (1813). *An Account of What Appeared on Opening the Coffin of King Charles the First*. London: Nichols, Son and Bentley, p.7.
44. Ibid., p.7.

When her mother and father became estranged, Charlotte remained in the custody of the royal household at Carlton House. Here the bright and sensitive child charmed all who knew her. Of course, sensitivity is not a quality that does well with constant and fiery conflict, and when her parents were not living separate lives, conflict typified their relationship.

It is unthinkable to us now that any parent might send a child still in single figures to establish their own household and yet, when Charlotte was only eight-years-old, that's just what George did. Reconciled once more with his beloved Maria, he bundled his daughter off to live in Montague House in the care of paid companions. Here she blossomed into a tomboy with a love of adventure, watching the developments between her parents ruefully. Kept from her mother during the Delicate Investigation, it must have been a bewildering time for the little girl.

It would not be her last brush with heartbreak.

Just as George had found himself married to a woman he didn't choose and certainly didn't *want*, history seemed destined to repeat itself. He settled on William, Prince of Orange as a husband for his daughter, a match that Charlotte resisted with all that she was worth, utterly unimpressed by the candidate for her hand. Her complaints were to no avail and in 1814 the marriage contracts were signed and sealed, much to Charlotte's dismay.

With Charlotte making no secret of her dissatisfaction, the prince informed his daughter that she would be moving to Cranbourne Lodge, Windsor. Already lonely and unhappy, Charlotte literally ran away from home, dashing into the street to hail a cab and escape to her mother's residence. Here she was counselled by a number of prominent Whigs, whilst the Duke of York warned that, should she not consent to return, she could be removed by means of a legal warrant.

Aware of the impact this scandal might have on all concerned, Charlotte swallowed her pride and her unhappiness and returned to the custody of her father. Although far from happy with her conduct, she found George perhaps *somewhat* softened towards her as a result of her flight. Perhaps he realized the damage his behaviour was causing the innocent young woman, perhaps he simply relished his victory, but he was also a pragmatist and knew that his daughter's popularity with the public was something that should not be trifled with. When it came to escaping the Prince of Orange, however, Charlotte had something up her immaculate sleeve.

Charlotte cunningly turned to her popular mother, who threw her weight behind her daughter's petitions to be released from the betrothal. The people of Britain joined in the cry to keep the princess in England and George, heels dug firmly in, set his face to the wind and carried on regardless. Charlotte, however, was as bloody-minded as her father and she had fixed her sights firstly on a mysterious and unknown Prussian and then firmly on Prince Leopold of Saxe-Coburg-Saalfeld who she had met several times. *He* was the man that Charlotte had determined she would marry, and she was not about to take no for an answer.

George told his daughter that she could argue all she wanted but there was to be no change. She was promised to Orange and to Orange she would go. One can only imagine his annoyance when Charlotte set a trap for William and he stumbled right into it. She would marry him, she declared, *if* he promised to allow her mother to visit the marital home. Mindful of keeping his future father-in-law on side, William said there was no chance that George's hated wife would *ever* be allowed into their home. That was all Charlotte needed. How could she marry a man who denied her access to her mother, she wailed? What sort of life would that be for her if her husband cared nothing for her finer feelings?

Finally George gave his daughter her wish and called off the engagement, much to William's chagrin. It took some doing but eventually Leopold was summoned to England and an audience with the regent, which must have left both Charlotte and her beloved just a *little* nervous.

In fact, the two men got on famously, and with Caroline having departed for the continent, George agreed to the marriage. Unhappy with her mother's casual leave taking, it proved to be a wonderful boon to Charlotte's low spirits and both she and her betrothed were delighted. The people of Britain shared their joy and even as her mother whooped it up in Europe, on 2 May 1816, Charlotte and Leopold were wed at Carlton House.

'The marriage of the Princess Charlotte of Wales and Prince Leopold of Saxe Cobourg was solemnized yesterday evening at Carlton House, in the presence of the Queen, the Prince Regent, the Royal Dukes, the Princesses, the Cabinet Ministers, the great Officers of the Royal Household, the Foreign Ministers, and a select assemblage of the Nobility.'[45]

The public rejoiced with enormous crowds gathering to see the couple as they made their way to the ceremony and inside Carlton House, the excitement was fizzing. It was a world away from the unhappy union of Charlotte's parents and the newlyweds were ecstatic, embarking on married life in a deep and mutual love. Their happiness was not to last.

'It is this day our melancholy duty to make known to our Readers, the demise of her Royal Highness the Princess CHARLOTTE.'[46]

In November 1817, Princess Charlotte died as she gave birth to a stillborn son,[47] leaving her husband and the people bereft. For her father, *bereft* does not seem strong enough. The Prince Regent received news of his daughter's death with a sorrow so deep and overwhelming that concerns were raised for his health. He barely saw anyone besides his immediate family and those that did meet the prince found him unreachable in his distress. Even then though, he managed to strike out against the wife he had come to so despise.

It was left to George to send word to Caroline that her only child was dead but he did no such thing. Instead, he wrote a letter to the pope and it was only thanks to a coincidence that Caroline met the messenger carrying the note and discovered her daughter's fate. She was devastated and one wonders what George was thinking when he took this decision. Certainly he was grief-stricken but to use the death of a child for revenge is cold in the extreme. Yet the prince never thought clearly when it came to the wife he hated, consumed by thoughts of showing her up once and for all.

In one final torment for the regent, it was just a year later that he lost his mother, with whom he had grieved for the late Princess Charlotte of

---

45. *Jackson's Oxford Journal* (Oxford, England), Saturday, May 4, 1816; issue 3289, p.3.
46. *The Morning Chronicle* (London, England), Friday, November 7, 1817; issue 15138, p.2.
47. Sir Richard Croft, who served as obstetrician to Princess Charlotte, was so distraught at his role in the death of the princess that he committed suicide just three months later.

Wales. The queen was one of the only people who could actually control her son, though even then it was to the barest of degrees. He was holding Queen Charlotte's hand when the end came, the son who had been both thorn in her side and apple of her eye there to comfort her in her final moments.

Assassins on Pall Mall

Through all of his troubles and heartaches, one thing that didn't change was the Prince Regent's passion for spending. Whether at Carlton House or Brighton, whether buying silver, horses or clothes, the prince's debts continued to accumulate at a terrifying rate. The public, exhausted by war, looked on his profligacy with disgust and, united in grief at the passing of Princess Charlotte, asked just *who* had been with her when she died. In fact, she had died with no member of her family present and this was unforgivable, the thought of the prince partying whilst his daughter faced her death, providing just one more reason to loathe him.

Public fury soon bubbled over into action as the walls of Carlton House were daubed with graffiti that read, 'Bread, or the Regent's Head', whilst mobs surrounded and assailed his carriage. George was hissed at, his vehicle stoned and few could be found to sing the praises of the embattled Prince Regent.

Even before Princess Charlotte's untimely death, things had hit a new low earlier in 1817 when the king was returning from the state opening of Parliament. Proceeding along Pall Mall on his way home to Carlton House, a projectile suddenly shot past his face, missing him by a hair. What was initially thought to be a hurled stone was soon revealed to be something just a *little* more worrying.

Lord James Murray, who had been with the prince, reported that the window of the vehicle showed a most peculiar sort of damage in the form of two small holes. These were not the sort of irregular holes that a stone would leave but were, he believed, the result of an air gun pellet piercing the glass.

At the Parliamentary enquiry into the apparent attack, Lord Murray noted that the glass was later completely shattered by a number of large stones hurled by the crowd. He also confirmed that no bullets were discovered in the carriage itself. Indeed, no attacker was ever apprehended and the supposed gunman remained at large.

One or two of George's acquaintances raised an eyebrow at the claims of a shooting, believing it more likely that the panicking prince had merely overstated a stoning for dramatic effect. Still, whatever the truth of the matter, a Prince Regent being stoned, hissed and shot at in the street was *not* the mark of a happy nation!

Could things *really* get any worse?

Oh yes.

'They'll not Peterloo us again ...'[48]

As the years of his reign passed, it seemed as though the Prince Regent was intent on making himself as unpopular as possible. Indeed, the damage already done to his standing with his subjects was compounded when he spoke out in favour of what has become notorious as the *Peterloo Massacre*. This was one more bad call in a run of years that seemed to be full of disastrous decisions, and not ideal for a man who was already being stoned and shot at.

It was a time of great social imbalance, with the whole of Europe rocked by the devastating Napoleonic Wars. Wellington's 1815 victory at Waterloo was now a distant memory and for most, England was a far from green and pleasant land. Only a tiny minority of the population was eligible to vote, jobs were hard to find, taxes were high and people were starving as the Corn Laws of 1815 saw bread prices soar. Protests were rife among the increasingly politicized working classes and called for universal suffrage, determined to make their voices heard. The strength of public feeling caused the people to take to the streets in a series of passionate yet peaceful protests and demonstrations, one of which was scheduled for St Peter's Field, Manchester, on 16 August 1819.

The Manchester Patriotic Union Society organized a rally at which the key speaker would be the famed orator, Henry Hunt, a sure crowd-pleaser. As the summer morning drew on, people from across the north of England assembled at St Peter's Field until the audience numbered over 60,000, much to the horror of watching officials. In fact, those attending did so in a

---

48. *Caledonian Mercury* (Edinburgh, Scotland), Thursday, December 9, 1819; issue 15331, p.2.

highly organized manner, intent on sending a peaceful yet strong message to the government, a plea for suffrage reform. The occasion was particularly notable for the number of women in attendance, represented by members of the northern Female Reform Societies. Dressed in their Sunday best, men, women and children marched together, with the whole event taking on the atmosphere of a festival.

Thrown into a panic at the size of the peaceful crowd, local magistrate William Hulton gave the order to arrest the speakers and disperse the meeting. However, the crowd around the hustings was packed in tight and Hulton issued further orders, this time for armed intervention.

Hundreds of soldiers surrounded the rally both on foot and horseback as the Manchester and Salford Yeomanry, under the command of Captain Hugh Birley and Major Thomas Trafford, moved in to make the arrests. Eye witnesses at the time claimed that many of the yeomen were drunk and that some were even using the opportunity to settle personal scores and vendettas.

Whilst some among the gathering appeared to be attempting to calm the situation, the majority were already set for a fight. The crowd linked arms and held back the advancing yeomanry. Interpreting the resistance as an act of aggression, Lieutenant Colonel Guy L'Estrange led the sabre-wielding Hussars into the crowd and the massacre began.

It was all over in a matter of minutes and by 2.00 pm St Peter's Field had become a scene of horror. Members of the peaceful crowd lay dead beneath the banners of suffrage, blood staining the red caps of liberty. Journalists were arrested and those who reported on the tragedy were imprisoned. As speakers, protesters and organizers were tried for high treason, the magistrates who had ordered the assault and the Hussars who had carried it out were lauded by the Prince Regent as heroes. The strength of public feeling was so great that a test case was eventually brought at Lancaster Assizes against Birley and some of his men, but all were cleared.

More than a dozen people died that day and hundreds more suffered terrible injuries. Nicknamed 'Peterloo' in an ironic response to the courageous acts of soldiers at Waterloo, the atrocity led to rioting in the streets of Manchester and other northern cities. Fearing further unrest, the government clamped down hard on reformers and crushed any suggestion of demonstration or uprising. For a regent already so low in the public estimation, one cannot think of a worse thing to be associated with. George was jeered and hissed at in the streets, furious people crowding around his residences to cry of the shame that the Prince Regent would support what they saw as state authorized murder.

Things were about to get a whole lot worse.

Caroline's Continental Sunset

And where was Caroline while all of this was going on? How about in the arms of a strapping Italian former soldier?

During her extended celebratory jaunt on the continent, Caroline had employed the charming, cultured and handsome Bartolomeo Pergami as her chamberlain. If rumours and appearances were to be believed, he occupied a rather more intimate station too. Caroline had rarely if ever seemed happier, and for George, this new and scandalous attachment was one step too far.

Caroline and Pergami were making a mockery of him, the Prince Regent decided. The cash that his wife was throwing at her Italian lover was British money and if she was intent on making George an even bigger laughing stock than he already was, then she was succeeding. With Charlotte dead and his mother's good counsel lost to him, George's mind was made up once and for all.

He wanted a divorce.

Obtaining a divorce in Regency England was no easy matter and for the man in charge of the country, it was bound to be an embarrassingly public affair. With his increasing ire fuelled by reports of Caroline's adventure with Pergami, not to mention William Austin, the so-called *orphan* who had been the cause of so much drama years earlier, the prince began to gather as much information against his estranged wife as he could. Reports from Europe suggested that the proof required to prove her infidelity would not be hard to come by and, under the auspices of the Milan Commission, George's agents collated all the intelligence they could find, looking for *anything*, no matter how inconsequential, that might be of use in the fight to come.

George was committed to the battle, and only when he was sure that he had gathered enough evidence to prove once and for all that Caroline and

Pergami were lovers did he make his move. If Caroline did not admit adultery and grant him his divorce, then she would be subject to public scrutiny and shame. The strong-willed princess came back fighting and the Commission set to work examining the evidence in the hope of finally settling the fate of this unhappiest of marriages.

Of course, the wronged husband was hardly celibate and it was in that same year that George began the last of his great passions when he fell for Elizabeth, Lady Conyngham. Ambitious for her husband's career, Lady Conyngham could not have chosen a better time to make the prince's acquaintance and was deeply enmeshed in her lover's life when, on 29 January 1820, George III died.

In fact, George IV very nearly didn't make it to the throne because at the moment of his father's death he was dangerously ill himself with a severe cold. Happily, George made a full recovery and had to face a very troublesome truth. Now he was a king, that scandalous, fun-loving wife who was kicking up her heels in Europe was to be his embarrassing, absent queen. A divorce now became of paramount importance and when word reached England that Caroline was on her way back to claim her crown, he hit the roof.

Famously, though possibly not actually true, George so loathed his wife that she even surpassed Napoleon in his hatred. Legend has it that when news of Napoleon's death was circulated George was told, 'I have the pleasure to tell your Majesty that your bitterest enemy is dead.'

'No! Is she, by God?" said the King.'[49]

For their part, Parliament did their best to keep the troublesome queen-in-waiting away, even offering to increase her allowance should she agree to remain abroad. Of course, Caroline would not accept the pay off and early in the summer of 1820, she was back, just in time to be put on trial in Parliament by the Pains and Penalties Bill.

When the queen set foot on English shores she found herself greeted with a public welcome that her husband could never even dream of. However, the king was sure that all of this would be to no avail, now that Parliament was considering the damning evidence of the Milan Commission. Surely,

---

49. Prothero, MA (ed.) (1901). *The Works of Lord Byron, Vol V.* London: John Murray, p.378.

he thought, the forthcoming Pains and Penalties Bill would end Caroline's claims to the throne once and for all.

The Bill placed the queen on trial in the House of Lords and played for the highest stakes. Should she lose, she would be stripped of her British titles, ranks and privileges; her marriage would be over, and her character and reputation would be left in tatters. Witness after witness was called under oath and each was either not that scandalous or, even worse, savaged by Lord Brougham, Caroline's Rottweiler-like counsel. Her advisor for many years, Brougham proved a dangerous opponent and soon the king's plans to rid himself of the troublesome woman were beginning to look very shaky indeed.

With the audacious bill aiming 'to deprive the Queen of her rights and privileges and to dissolve the marriage between her and the King, and [...] set out the adultery of the Queen,'[50] George thought he couldn't fail. Of course, he was wrong.

Instead of being shocked and scandalized, the people of Britain cheered Caroline along, rejoicing in the happy home life she and Pergami seemed to have. They had loved George III and Queen Charlotte for the same reason, for their steadiness and solidity and for being all the things that the flighty George IV never was. Scandalous some of the new queen's behaviour might have been, but she had the good fortune to be held up in comparison to a king who had earned the distrust and dislike of his subjects across a lifetime. Soon Caroline became a rallying point for radicals, and when her defence team tore the prosecution case to shreds, the Bill was doomed to become a messy and very public failure.

Sick of a king who, as Prince of Wales and Prince Regent, had appeared utterly immune to the privations and concerns of his people, the public did not share his disgust at Caroline. They refused to be morally outraged by *any* of the evidence presented, whether it be of baths and carriages shared with Pergami, of shameless galavanting as a couple or of the household they had established together overseas. They had plenty of scandal to disapprove of here at home thanks to George and he did it *all* on the public purse. Nobody stoned and heckled Caroline, after all, and nor would they as the press and people rallied to her call, and what a call it was.

---

50. *Caledonian Mercury* (Edinburgh, Scotland), Saturday, July 8, 1820; issue 15421, p.3.

'Every person who can reflect upon the consequences of passing events, or who can read the danger of the future in the dark aspect of the present, must be convinced that the public welfare is at this moment imminently identified with the preservation of my rights and dignities as the Royal consort of his Majesty. If the highest subject in the realm can be deprived of her rank and title – can be divorced, dethroned, and debased, by an act of arbitrary power, in the form of a Bill of Pains and Penalties, the constitutional liberties of the kingdom will be shaken to its very base.

The rights of the nation will be only a shattered wreck, and this once free people, like the meanest of slaves, must submit to the lash of an insolent domination.'[51]

With his wife becoming a figurehead for political radicals, George realized too late that an ill wind was blowing. No doubt with the utter decimation of the star prosecution witness, Theodore Majocchi, he rightly guessed that his divorce schemes were due to fail. Brougham laid waste to Majocchi's scandalous stories and the servant found himself jeered at by the same public that loved his employer, Queen Caroline. Able to remember the slightest minutiae when being questioned by the prosecution, when he stood before the defence, his memory seemingly deserted him. Majocchi's near-constant answer of, 'non mi ricordo', or, 'I don't remember', in response to Brougham's cross-examination became a national catchphrase, even inspiring poetry in some members of the public.[52]

It was another public relations disaster and one that could, if handled badly, bring Britain to the very edge of revolution.

Despite Brougham's best efforts the Bill *did* pass the Lords by the very narrowest of margins. It would go no further though and the prime minister, Lord Liverpool, put a stop to its progress there and then. He told a packed House that, having only passed by nine votes and in view of the intense public reaction to the Bill, it would not continue to the Commons.

---

51. *The Morning Chronicle* (London, England), Thursday, August 3, 1820; issue 15996, p.3.
52. *The Examiner* of 27 August 1820 features two such spirited poetic works entitled, *Memory and Want of Memory*, by Harry and, *Non Mi Ricordo*, by Brown.

Of course, Liverpool knew that if it *did* make it the House of Commons, the radicals who championed Caroline's cause would use public outcry against the motion to gain ground and his own government might pay the price. Understandably, given the very slight chance of a successful Commons passage for the Bill, Liverpool chose to withdraw rather than risk embarrassment or worse.

> 'Lord Liverpool [...] rose and stated, that whatever his own conviction of the guilt of her Majesty might be, yet looking to the difficulty of impressing that conviction on the public mind [...] he felt it his duty to withdraw the measure.'[53]

The media raised a glass to Caroline and the good sense that had prevailed, revelling in the rather smug defeat of the king, and reflecting on the 'satisfaction of congratulating the Country on the Abandonment of the Pains and Penalties Bill'.[54] George, on the other hand, could not have come out of these 'odious proceedings'[55] more disastrously. Indeed, it appeared to be a spectacular own goal and the press heaved a sigh of self-righteous annoyance and sighed that the Bill had 'done more to withdraw the affections of the people from the Constitutional authorities, than all the Revolutionary writings which ever were'.[56]

The crowd, as the saying goes, went wild, and the press fanned the flames right into George's face. This was not just a victory for Caroline, but for everyone in the United Kingdom. What a triumph it was to score such a public victory over the arrogant and self-centred King George IV.

> 'The triumph of her MAJESTY is also [...] their triumph; for the successful resistance of oppression, the defeat of injustice, are causes for triumph truly worthy of a free and enlightened people'.[57]

---

53. *Caledonian Mercury* (Edinburgh, Scotland), Thursday, November 16, 1820; issue 15477, p.2.
54. *The Morning Chronicle* (London, England), Saturday, November 11, 1820; issue 16082, p.2.
55. Ibid., p.2.
56. Ibid., p.2.
57. Ibid., p.3.

Caroline was feted and pro-George supporters found their premises attacked, their names mocked and their opinions reviled. As the city celebrated, spirits rose, drink flowed and a violent outcome was inevitable.

> 'REMARKABLE OCCURRENCE – A large crowd had assembled, who were discharging fireworks, and applauding such individuals as had lights exhibited in their windows in honour of the Queen. The house of one person [...] became a particular object with the mob, who were a considerable time calling upon the owner to light up; but finding their cries were disregarded, they commenced an attack upon the windows, many of which they demolished.'[58]

The queen, meanwhile, repaid the support of those reformers who had rallied to her by losing her taste for radicalism as quickly as she had embraced it. She had proved her point and scored the victory to end all victories. For Caroline, there was no sense in continuing in politics, she had a coronation to get to.

A Coronation Humiliation

So it was that George, almost 60, parentless, childless and at seemingly endless odds with the wife he had never wanted in the first place, prepared to 'knock 'em dead' at Westminster Abbey on 19 July 1821. Long before he arrived, Caroline was already at the abbey intent on taking her place alongside her husband at this most magnificent occasion. However, by the time George strode proudly onto the greatest stage of his life, Caroline was gone.

Rumours had abounded that the queen might make a surprise visit to the abbey and the pro-George press warned her off, reminding her that such a move would be 'a mediated outrage upon all order and decency'.[59] Happily it seemed that her old defender Brougham had intervened, using his 'wholesome influence [...] to have dissuaded her from the commission of so rash and reprehensible an act'.[60] But his advice hadn't put Caroline off.

---

58. *The Morning Post* (London, England), Saturday, November 11, 1820; issue 15493, p.3.
59. *The Morning Post* (London, England), Thursday, July 19, 1821; issue 15707, p.3.
60. Ibid., p.3.

At 6.00 am, the *almost* queen was touring the abbey doors in the company of Lord Hood and some very vocal supporters, demanding her right to enter. When Caroline was told that entry to the ceremony was by invitation only, she faced the indignity of being offered a ticket by the very gentlemanly Lord Hood, who could not bear to see her so publicly rejected. Caroline turned down his offer and was subject not only to an embarrassing denial of her status but one final humiliation, which Lord Hood recalled:

'Some persons within the porch of the Abbey laughed, and uttered some expressions of disrespect. [...] We expected to have met at least with the conduct of gentlemen; such conduct is neither manly nor mannerly.'[61]

With the sound of laughter ringing in the queen's ears as her supporters melted away, she fled back to her carriage and the lonely sanctuary of Brandenburg House, where she was staying. It was a knockout blow.

In the final moments of the final battle of the war he had fought with Caroline of Brunswick, George had somehow won. Never before had his wife faced such public derision, never before had she misjudged the mood of the people so disastrously. Those who had crowded into the streets to witness the new king's coronation that day didn't want drama, they wanted celebration. For once, the king was not the enemy but the sovereign, and they were fully sold on George's very own brand of extravagance; Caroline was nothing but an unwanted distraction. She didn't give up there, but appealed to direct to the Archbishop of Canterbury, informing him 'of her desire to be crowned some days after the King, and before the arrangements were done away with, so that there might be no additional expense'.[62] The answer was unequivocal, stark and final as Caroline was informed that the archbishop 'could take no part in the ceremony, except in consequence of orders from the Sovereign'.[63] It was the end of a long road for Caroline of Brunswick.

---

61. Urban, Sylvanus (1821). *The Gentleman's Magazine: 1821, Volume 91, Part 2*. London: John Nichols and Son, p.74.
62. Ibid., p.75.
63. Ibid., p.75.

A Coronation Celebration

And what of George, the man of the hour?

What indeed?

For years, the new king had been planning this moment, determined that when his coronation finally came, it would be the greatest Europe had ever seen. He envisioned a themed event with guests dressed in Elizabethan or Jacobean costume and true to form, there was to be no expense spared. After all, the world needed to know that nobody did good old showing off anything like as well as George. Parliament stumped up over £100,000 for the festivities, and a further £138,000 came from France under the terms of a financial indemnity[64] and across the country, a day of celebrations was declared.

> '[George wore] a black hat with a monstrous plume of ostrich feathers, out of the midst of which rose a black heron's plume. His Majesty seemed very much oppressed with the weight of his robes. The train was of enormous length and breadth. It was of crimson velvet adorned with large golden stars, and a broad golden border.'[65]

Ever fabulous, George's togs cost £24,000, the train stretching for twenty seven feet and requiring the attention of eight pages just to lift it. Never one to shirk on luxury, he commissioned a new crown containing over 12,000 diamonds that were on hire from Rundell, Bridge and Rundell. Unfortunately, George grew somewhat fond of his rented diamonds and did his best to hang onto them, only returning them to the jewellers once Parliament rejected his requests for the country to purchase them on his behalf.[66]

At the head of the Coronation procession came Miss Fellowes, the King's herb woman, and her six attendants, scattering flowers and sweet-smelling herbs in a traditional ceremony to ward off plague and pestilence. The procession that followed included the Officers of State who carried the iconic orb, sceptre, crown and sword, bishops bearing chalice, bible and paten and, of course, the

---

64. This is the equivalent of £9.5million in modern money.
65. Gossip, Giles (1828). *Coronation Anecdotes*. London: Robert Jennings, pp.291–2.
66. George had to make do with a gilt bronze cast of his sumptuous new crown, acquired at a cost of £38.

star of the show. George made a splendid sight in his robes, followed by the Barons of the Cinque Ports who carried the Coronation Canopy. Bringing up the considerable rear, were the assembled peers of the realm and other dignitaries, with hired prizefighters playing the role of pages throughout the procession just in case Caroline made another grab for her crown!

Queen or no queen, the monumental procession eventually wound its way through the crowds to Westminster Abbey where the ancient ceremony took place. The summer day was stifling, and George wilted under the weight of his robes, appearing 'distressed almost to fainting'.[67] When the crown was placed on his head, Britain could finally celebrate the coronation of George IV, with the Abbey erupting in a spontaneous hurrah that onlookers said both pleased and perhaps surprised the new Sovereign.

The procession then made its way back to Westminster Hall amid cheering crowds, Caroline's attempted intervention already forgotten. We all know that George liked his food and the coronation banquet was testament to this, consisting as it did of well over a thousand dishes and tens of thousands of pounds of meat alone. The king thanked the assembled guests and did them 'the honour of drinking their health and that of his good people'.[68] It was a night to remember as hundreds of male guests tucked into a vast array of delicacies, whilst the ladies and children were herded into viewing galleries to watch the fun!

Finally, the newly-crowned George IV departed for Carlton House with the people of London joining a fête in Hyde Park, where fireworks were let off throughout the evening. The day had been a flamboyant, excessive triumph and parties went on late into the summer night as the people of the realm celebrated the crowning of the new monarch.

'Yesterday evening, at 20 minutes after ten o'clock, the Queen departed this life, after a short but painful illness at Brandenburgh House, at Hammersmith.'[69]

---

67. Huish, Robert (1830). *Memoirs of George the Fourth: Vol I*. London: Thomas Kelly, p.216.
68. *La Belle Assemblée: Vol XXIV*, 1821. London: J Green, p.45.
69. *The Ipswich Journal* (Ipswich, England), Saturday, August 11, 1821; issue 4346, p.4.

Less than a month later, word reached George that he was finally free: Caroline was dead. In pursuance of her wishes, arrangements were made for her funeral to be held in Brunswick and, perhaps unsurprisingly, George was gadding about within days of her death. He was the first monarch to make a state visit to Ireland in hundreds of years and the first in more than a century to visit Scotland, spending three weeks in Edinburgh at the invitation of Sir Walter Scott, and modelling a rather unflattering kilt and pink tights. Still the man of fashion, he did his bit to popularize tartan once more just as he promoted high collars and dark, forgiving colours, both of which did the world of good when it came to disguising the ever increasing girth of the once slender George.

One cannot, however, hold back the years forever.

'This is Death'

'It has pleased Almighty God to take from this world the King's Most Excellent Majesty. His Majesty expired at a quarter past three o'clock this morning, without pain.'[70]

As George grew older and Caroline faded into the fog of a particularly unhappy memory, his love of trouble did not desert him. Indeed, though his political days were long since over by the time the Duke of Wellington became Prime Minister in 1828, the king was *more* than sniffy and contented himself with sporting with the Iron Duke. To Wellington's dismay and annoyance, George falsely claimed to have been present at Waterloo, even giving *himself* the credit for some decisive victories on the field.

Overweight, a habitual user of laudanum and suffering greatly from the pains that wracked his body, the king began to withdraw from society. As his sanctuary he chose Windsor as his father had before him. Yet whilst George III was unquestionably insane, George IV was mentally *mostly* sound and attended not by the fearsome, mad doctors who had cared for his father but by his devoted companion, Lady Conyngham. From time to time, the king emerged from his seclusion to dabble in politics but his health was in

---

70. *North Wales Chronicle* (Bangor, Wales), Thursday, July 1, 1830; issue 144, p,3.

catastrophic decline, his sight was failing and he was clearly not at all long for the world he had once painted so very red.

The man who had once been the most fashionable and influential in the land was now a recluse, whiling away the hours wandering through the menagerie of exotic beasts that made up his collection. Indeed, it was among these animals that he strolled with his young niece, Victoria, later to rule as queen herself. He delighted in her uncomplicated, childish company, but his had become a melancholy and lonely life.

Those enormous dinners had begun to take their toll many years earlier, and by 1830, the once fashionable, handsome young man was gone for good. In his place was an obese, disease-ridden alcohol and laudanum addict squeezed into a restricting corset and struggling with a body so huge that he could barely breathe when he laid down to sleep. Hearing of his state of health, Maria Fitzherbert sent one last letter to her husband but he was too unwell to reply, leaving her to think herself ignored.[71]

Under the care of his physician, Sir Henry Halford, George now lived out his days in solitude, forced to sleep in a specially adapted chair that could double as a bed. His waking hours were beset by agonizing pain in his limbs and torso that no amount of bleeding could treat, and as he battled discomfort and sleeplessness, deep depression seized the ailing king. In the twilight of his years, he looked back on the wild days of his youth, when he had been the most celebrated young chap in town, and women had fallen at his feet and he had lived the high life with hardly a care in the world. Now though, there was only pain and the slow, creeping deprivations of old age as the world moved on without the increasingly bed bound king.

On the night of his death, George retired to his chambers and that chair-cum-bed in the company of his friend, Sir Jonathan Wathen-Waller. It was in this very chair that the man Byron labelled 'the Leviathan of the *haut ton*' died on 26 June 1830, his body unable to bear the strain any longer. In his final moments, deep in the darkest early hours, George was seized with an attack of breathless agony. He reached out to clutch Wathen-Waller's hand desperately, seeking some comfort in the throes of his fate as he gasped, 'My

---

71. Maria died in Brighton on 27 March 1837. She never remarried.

boy, this is death'.[72] What he saw, heard or perhaps felt in those seconds we cannot know, but moments later, at just before 3.15 am, King George IV died. It was the end of an era.

The king was buried at Windsor with Maria's miniature around his neck and with him, the most controversial monarch of the Georgian era passed into popular legend.

Perhaps we should let his legacy be told by *The Times* and one of the most brutal obituaries the British media has ever seen.

'There never was an individual less regretted by his fellow-creatures than this deceased king. What eye has wept for him? What heart has heaved one throb of unmercenary sorrow? ... If he ever had a friend — a devoted friend in any rank of life — we protest that the name of him or her never reached us'.[73]

---

72. Hetherington Fitzgerald, Percy (1881). *The Life of George the Fourth*. London: Tinsley Brothers, p.908.
73. Morison, Stanley (1935). *The History of the Times: "The Thunderer" in the Making, 1785-1841*. London: The Times (1950), p.268.

Afterword

With the death of the last King George, the Georgian era arguably drew to a close, ending with a breathless whimper rather than a flamboyant bang. George IV's throne was snapped up by his brother, William IV and the scant seven years of William's reign laid the foundations for what would eventually become Victorian Britain.

Taken together, the four Georges made the era what it was, from the upheaval of that first arrival on English soil to the politics of George II, through the loss of America to the birth of the iconic Regency era. In those four men modern Britain found its origins, surviving changes both political and societal that echo into our own century.

The four Georges changed the laws, the land, the *world*, and all whilst living through scandal, drama, romance and tragedy that would make any novelist proud. It was a time of rebirth, renewal and change, and through it all, the four Georges reigned, for better or worse.

Bibliography

Alexander, Marc. *Royal Murder*. UK: Willow Books, 2012.

Angelo, Henry. *Reminiscences of Henry Angelo with Memoirs of His Late Father and Friends*. London: Henry Colburn, 1828.

Anonymous. *La Belle Assemblée*: Vol XXIV. London: J Green, 1821.

Anonymous. *A Brief Account of the Coronation of His Majesty, George IV*. London: D Walther, 1821.

Anonymous. *The Genuine Copies of Letters which Passed Between His Royal Highness the Duke of Cumberland and Lady Grosvenor*. London: J Wheble, 1770.

Anonymous. *George III: His Court and Family, Vol I*. London: Henry Colburn and Co, 1821.

Anonymous. *An Historical Account of the Life and Reign of King George the Fourth*. London: G Smeeton, 1830.

Anonymous. *Letters, in the Original, with Translations, and Messages, that Passed Between the King, Queen, Prince, and Princess of Wales*. London: S Osborn, 1737.

Anonymous. *The Life and Memoirs of Her Royal Highness Princess Charlotte of Saxe Coburg Saalfeld & C*. London: T. Kinnersley, 1818.

Anonymous. *The Rambler: A Catholic Journal and Review, Vol V*. London: Burns and Lambert, 1856.

Anonymous. *The Scots Magazine, Vol 48*. Edinburgh: Murray and Cochrane, 1786.

Anonymous. *The Trial of His R H the D of C July 5th, 1770. For Criminal Conversation with Lady Harriet G—r*. London: John Walker, 1770.

Anson, William (ed.). *Autobiography and Political Correspondence of Augustus Henry, Third Duke of Grafton*. London: John Murray, 1898.

Aspinall, Arthur (ed.). *The Correspondence of George, Prince of Wales: Vol I*. London: Cassell, 1963.

Aspinall, Arthur. *The Later Correspondence of George III: December 1783 to January 1793, Vol II*. Cambridge: Cambridge University Press, 1962.

Aspinall, Arthur. *Letters of the Princess Charlotte 1811–1817*. London: Home and Van Thal, 1949.

Aspinall, Arthur (ed.). *Mrs Jordan and Her Family: Being the Unpublished Correspondence of Mrs Jordan and the Duke of Clarence, Later William IV*. London: Arthur Barker, 1951.

Baker, Kenneth. *George III: A Life in Caricature*. London: Thames & Hudson, 2007.

Baker, Kenneth. *George IV: A Life in Caricature*. London: Thames & Hudson, 2005.

Baker-Smith, Veronica PM. *A Life of Anne of Hanover, Princess Royal*. Leiden: EJ Brill, 1995.

Barber, John Warner (ed.). *The History and Antiquities of New England, New York, and New Jersey*. Worcester: Dorr, Howland and Co, 1841.

Bayley, William. *The Bagman's Bioscope*. Bath: Edward Barrett, 1824.

Bazalgette, Charles. *Prinny's Taylor: The Life and Times of Louis Bazalgette*. British Columbia: Tara Books, 2015.

Beacock Fryer, Mary, Bousfield, Arthur and Toffoli, Garry. *Lives of the Princesses of Wales*. Toronto: Dundurn Press, 1983.

Beauclerk-Dewar. *Royal Bastards*. Stroud: The History Press, 2011.

Bell, Robert. *The Life of the Rt. Hon. George Canning*. London: Harper, 1955.

Belsham, W. *Memoirs of the Kings of Great Britain of the House of Brunswic-Luneburg, Vol I*. London: C Dilly, 1793.

Belsham, William. *Memoirs of the Reign of George III to the Session of Parliament Ending AD 1793, Vol III*. London: GG and J Robinson, 1801.

Benchimol, Alex, Brown, Rhona and Shuttleton, David. *Before Blackwood's: Scottish Journalism in the Age of Enlightenment*. London: Routledge, 2015.

Black, Jeremy. *George III: America's Last King*. New Haven: Yale University Press, 2008.

Black, Jeremy. *The Hanoverians: The History of a Dynasty*. London: Hambledon and London, 2007.

Borman, Tracy. *King's Mistress, Queen's Servant: The Life and Times of Henrietta Howard*. London: Random House, 2010.

Buckingham and Chandos, Duke of. *Memoirs of the Court of George IV, Vol I*. London: Hurst and Blackett, 1859.

Burney, Frances. *The Diary and Letters of Frances Burney, Madame D'Arblay, Vol II*. Boston: Little, Brown and Company, 1910.

Burrows, Donald. *Handel and the English Chapel Royal*. Oxford: Oxford University Press, 2005.

Campbell, Lord John. *The Lives of the Lord Chancellors and Keepers of the Great Seal of England, Vol. V*. Philadelphia: Blanchard and Lea, 1851.

Campbell, Thomas. *Frederick the Great, His Court and Times. Vol II*. London: Colburn, 1844.

Campbell Orr, Clarissa. *Queenship in Europe 1660–1815: The Role of the Consort*. Cambridge: Cambridge University Press, 2004.

Carroll, Leslie. *Royal Romances*. New York: New American Library, 2012.

Chambers, James. *Charlotte & Leopold: The True Story of The Original People's Princess*. London: Old Street Publishing, 2008.

Chauncey Woolsey, Sarah. *The Diary and Letters of Frances Burney, Vol II*. Boston: Little, Brown, and Company, 1910.

Childe-Pemberton, William Shakespear. *The Romance of Princess Amelia*. London: John Lane Company, 1911.

Clark, JCS. *The Memoirs and Speeches of James, 2nd Earl Waldegrave, 1742–1763*. Cambridge: Cambridge University Press, 2002.

Clarke, John, Godwin Ridley, Jasper and Fraser, Antonia. *The Houses of Hanover & Saxe-Coburg-Gotha*. Berkeley: University of California Press, 2000.

Cobbett, William and Jardine, David. *Cobbett's Complete Collection of State Trials, Vol XXII*. London: London, Hurst, Rees, Orme and Brown, 1817.

Coxe, William. *Memoirs of John, Duke of Marlborough, Vol I*. London: Longman, Hurst, Reese, Orme and Brown, 1818.

Coxe, William. *Memoirs of the Life and Administration of Robert Walpole*. London: Longman, Hurst, Rees, Orme & Brown, 1816.

Craig, William Marshall. *Memoir of Her Majesty Sophia Charlotte of Mecklenburg Strelitz, Queen of Great Britain*. Liverpool: Henry Fisher, 1818.

David, Saul. *Prince of Pleasure*. New York: Grove Press, 2000.

Dickenson, Mary Hamilton. *Mary Hamilton: Afterwards Mrs. John Dickenson, at Court and at Home*. London: John Murray, 1925.

Donne, Bodham W (ed.). *The Correspondence of King George the Third With Lord North from 1768 to 1783: Vol I*. London: John Murray, 1867.

Doran, John. *Lives of the Queens of England of the House of Hanover, Volume 1*. New York: Redfield, 1855.

Duggan, JN. *Sophia of Hanover: From Winter Princess to Heiress of Great Britain, 1630 – 1714*. London: Peter Owen, 2013.

Edwards, Averyl. *Frederick Louis, Prince of Wales, 1701–1751*. London: Staples Press, 1947.

Field, Ophelia. *The Kit-Cat Club: Friends Who Imagined a Nation*. London: Harper Press, 2008.

Fox, Charles James. *Speeches of the Right Honourable Charles James Fox in the House of Commons, Vol III*. London: Longman, Hurst, Orme, and Brown, 1815.

Fraser, Flora. *Princesses: The Six Daughters of George III*. Edinburgh: A&C Black, 2012.

Fraser, Flora. *The Unruly Queen: The Life of Queen Caroline*. Edinburgh: A&C Black, 2012.

Georgiana, Duchess of Devonshire. *Georgiana: Extracts from the Correspondence of Georgiana, Duchess of Devonshire*. London: John Murray, 1955.

Gilmour, Ian. *Riot, Risings and Revolution: Governance and Violence in Eighteenth-Century England*. London: Pimlico, 1993.

Gold, Claudia. *The King's Mistress*. London: Quercus, 2012.

Gordon, Peter and Lawton, Denis. *Royal Education: Past, Present, and Future*. London: Frank Cass, 1999.

Gossip, Giles. *Coronation Anecdotes*. London: Robert Jennings, 1828.

Gregg, Edward. *Queen Anne*. New York: Yale University Press, 2014.

Hadlow, Janice. *The Strangest Family: The Private Lives of George III, Queen Charlotte and the Hanoverians*. London: William Collins, 2014.

Hague, William. *William Pitt the Younger*. London: Harper Perennial, 2005.

Halford, Sir Henry. *An Account of What Appeared on Opening the Coffin of King Charles the First*. London: Nichols, Son and Bentley, 1813.

Hansard, TC (ed.). *The Parliamentary Debates from the Year 1803 to the Present Time, Vol XXXV*. London: Hansard, 1817.

Hatton, Ragnhild. *George I*. London: Thames and Hudson. 1978.

Heard, Kate. *High Spirits: The Comic Art of Thomas Rowlandson*. London: Royal Collection Trust, 2013.

Hervey, John. *Lord Hervey's Memoirs*. London: Batsford, 1963.

Hervey, John and Croker, John Wilson (ed.). *Memoirs of the Reign of George the Second: Vol I*. London: John Murray, 1848.

Hervey, John and Croker, John Wilson (ed.). *Memoirs of the Reign of George the Second: Vol II*. London: John Murray, 1848.

Hetherington Fitzgerald, Percy. *The Life of George the Fourth*. London: Tinsley Brothers, 1881.

Hibbert, Christopher. *George III: A Personal History*. London: Viking, 1998.

Hibbert, Christopher. *George IV*. London: Penguin, 1998.

Holland Lord. *Memoirs of the Whig Party During My Time: Vol II*. London: Longman, Brown, Green and Longmans, 1854.

Holt, Edward. *The Public and Domestic Life of His Late Most Gracious Majesty, George the Third, Vol I*. London: Sherwood, Neely and Jones, 1820.

Holt, Edward. *The Public and Domestic Life of His Late Most Gracious Majesty, George the Third, Vol II*. London: Sherwood, Neely and Jones, 1820.

Home, James A. *Letters of Lady Louisa Stuart to Miss Louisa Clinton*. Edinburgh: D Douglas, 1901.

Horrins, Johan. *Memoirs of a Trait in the Character of George III. of These United Kingdoms*. London: W Edwards, 1835.

Huish, Robert. *Memoirs of George the Fourth: Vol I*. London: Thomas Kelly, 1830.

Hunt, Margaret. *Women in Eighteenth-Century Europe*. New York: Routledge, 2010.

Ilchester, Countess of & Stavordale, Lord (eds.). *The Life and Letters of Lady Sarah Lennox*. London: John Murray, 1902.

Inglis, Lucy. *Georgian London: Into the Streets*. London: Viking, 2013.

Irvine, Valerie. *The King's Wife: George IV and Mrs Fitzherbert*. London: Hambledon, 2007.

Jerrold, Clare. *The Story of Dorothy Jordan*. London: Eveleigh Nash, 1914.

Jesse Heneage, J. *Memoirs of the Life and Reign of King George the Third, Vol II*. London: Tinsley Brothers, 1867.

Kiste, John van der. *King George II and Queen Caroline*. Stroud: The History Press, 2013.

Knight, Charles. *The Popular History of England: Volume VI*. London: Bradbury, 1860.

Lancelott, Francis. *The Queens of England and Their Times: Volume II*. New York: D Appleton and Co, 1859.

Langdale, Charles. *Memoirs of Mrs. Fitzherbert*. London: Richard Bentley, 1856.

Laquer, Thomas W. *The Queen Caroline Affair: Politics as Art in the Reign of George IV. The Journal of Modern History*. Vol. 54, No. 3 (Sep., 1982), pp. 417–466

Lehman, H Eugene. *Lives of England's Reigning and Consort Queens*. Bloomington: AuthorHouse, 2011.

Leslie, Anita. *Mrs Fitzherbert: A Biography*. York: Scribner, 1960.

Leslie, Shane. *Mrs. Fitzherbert: A Life Chiefly from Unpublished Sources*. New York: Benziger Brothers, 1939.

Lloyd, Hannibal Evans. *George IV: Memoirs of His Life and Reign, Interspersed with Numerous Personal Anecdotes*. London: Treuttel and Würtz, 1830.

Longford, Elizabeth. *The Oxford Book of Royal Anecdotes*. Oxford: Oxford University Press, 1989.

Lovat-Fraser, JA. *John Stuart Earl of Bute*. Cambridge: Cambridge University Press, 1912.

Mahon, Lord (ed). *The Letters of Philip Dormer Stanhope, Earl of Chesterfield: Vol II*. London: Richard Bentley, 1845.

Marschner, Joanna. *Queen Caroline: Cultural Politics at the Early Eighteenth Century Court*. New Haven: Yale University Press, 2014.

Mitford, Nancy. *Frederick the Great*. London: Random House, 2011.

Morand, Paul. *The Captive Princess: Sophia Dorothea of Celle*. Florida: American Heritage Press, 1972.

Morison, Stanley. *The History of the Times: "The Thunderer" in the Making, 1785–1841*. London: The Times, 1935.

Mounsey, Chris. Christopher Smart: *Clown of God*. Lewisburg: Bucknell University Press, 2001.

Namier, Lewis and Brooke, John. *The House of Commons 1754–1790. Vol III, Members K-Y*. London: Secker & Warburg, 1985.

Nicholls, John. *Recollections and Reflections, Personal and Political, Vol I*. London: Longman, Hurst, Rees, Orme, and Brown, 1822.

Nightingale, Joseph. *Memoirs of the Last Days of Her Late Most Gracious Majesty Caroline, Queen of Great Britain, and Consort of King George the Fourth*. London: J Robins and Company, 1822.

Oulton, CW. *Authentic and Impartial Memoirs of Her Late Majesty: Charlotte Queen of Great Britain and Ireland*. London: Kinnersley, 1819.

Peakman, Julie. *Peg Plunkett: Memoirs of a Whore*. London: Quercus, 2015.

Pearce, Charles E. *The Beloved Princess, Princess Charlotte of Wales*. London: Stanley Paul & Co, 1911.

Pearce, Edward. *The Great Man: Sir Robert Walpole: Scoundrel, Genius and Britain's First Prime Minister*. London: Random House, 2011.

Plowden, Alison. *Caroline and Charlotte*. Stroud: The History Press, 2011.

Poole, Steve. *The Politics of Regicide in England, 1760–1850*: Troublesome Subjects. Manchester: Manchester University Press, 2000.

Pope, Alexander. *The Poetical Works of Alexander Pope, Vol IV*. London, Nathaniel Cooke, 1854.

Prothero, MA (ed.). *The Works of Lord Byron, Vol V*. London: John Murray, 1901.

Quackenbo, John D. *Illustrated School History of the World*. New York: American Book Company, 1904.

Reeve, Henry (ed.). *A Journal of the Reigns of King George IV and King William IV, Vol II*. London: Longmans, Green, and Co, 1874.

Richardson, Joanne. *The Disastrous Marriage*. London: Jonathan Cape, 1960.

Robins, Jane. *The Trial of Queen Caroline: The Scandalous Affair that Nearly Ended a Monarchy*. New York: Simon and Schuster, 2006.

Robinson, Mary. *Memoirs of the Late Mrs Robinson*. London: Hunt and Clarke, 1827.

Rounding, Virginia. *Catherine the Great*. London: Random House, 2007.

Saussure, Cesar de. *A Foreign View of England in the Reigns of George I & George II*. London: John Murray, 1902.

Sebag Montefiore, Simon. *The Romanovs 1613–1918*. London: Weidenfeld & Nicolson, 2016.

Shawe-Taylor, Desmond and Burchard, Wolf. *The First Georgians: Art and Monarchy 1714–1760*. London: Royal Collection Trust, 2014.

Smith, EA. *George IV*. New Haven: Yale University Press, 1999.

Spencer, Sarah. *Correspondence of Sarah Spencer Lady Lyttelton 1787–1870*. London: John Murray, 1912.

Stevens Cabot Abbott, John. *History of Frederick the Great*. New York: Harper & Brother, 1871.

Stuart, Lady Louisa. *Some Account of John, Duke of Argyll and His Family*. London: W Clowes & Sons, 1863.

Suffolk, Henrietta Hobart Howard. *Letters to and from Henrietta, Countess of Suffolk, Vol I*. London: John Murray, 1824.

Swift, Jonathan and Hawkesworth, John. Letters, *Written by Jonathan Swift: Vol III*. London: A Pope, 1737.

Taylor, William Stanhope and Prinole, John Henry (eds.). *Correspondence of William Pitt, Earl of Chatham: Vol III*. London: John Murray, 1839.

Thackeray, William Makepeace. *The Works of William Makepeace Thackeray: Vol XIX*. London: Smith, Elder, & Co, 1869.

Thompson, Andrew C. *George II: King and Elector*. New Haven: Yale University press, 2011.

Thoresby, Ralph. *The Diary of Ralph Thoresby, Vol II*. London: Henry Colburn and Richard Bentley, 1830.

Tillyard, Stella. *A Royal Affair: George III and his Troublesome Siblings*. London: Vintage, 2007.

Trench, Charles Chenevix. *George II*. London: Allen Lane, 1973.

Urban, Sylvanus. *The Gentleman's Magazine: 1821, Volume 91, Part 2*. London: John Nichols and Son, 1821.

Waldegrave, James. *The Memoirs and Speeches of James, 2nd Earl Waldegrave, 1742–1763*. Cambridge: Cambridge University Press, 1988.

Wallace, William. *Memoirs of the Life and Reign of George IV., Vol I*. London: Longman, Rees, Orme, Brown, and Green. 1831.

Wallace, William. *Memoirs of the Life and Reign of George IV., Vol III*. London: Longman, Rees, Orme, Brown, Green, & Longman. 1832.

Walpole, Horace and Doran, John (ed.). *Journal of the Reign of King George the Third*. London, Richard Bentley, 1859.

Walpole, Horace. *The Last Journals of Horace Walpole During the Reign of George III from 1771–1783*. London: John Lane, 1910.

Walpole, Horace. *Letters of Horace Walpole, Earl of Orford, to Sir Horace Mann*. London: Richard Bentley, 1833.

Walpole, Horace. *The Letters of Horace Walpole: Vol I*. Philadelphia: Lea and Blanchard, 1842.

Walpole, Horace. *The Letters of Horace Walpole: Vol II*. New York: Dearborn, 1832.

Walpole, Horace. *Memoirs of the Reign of King George the Second: Vol I*. London: Henry Colburn, 1846.

Walpole, Horace. *Memoirs of the Reign of King George the Third: Vol I*. Philadelphia: Lea & Blanchard, 1845.

Ward, AW, Prothero, GW and Leathes, Stanley. *The Cambridge Modern History, Volume VI*. Cambridge: Cambridge University Press, 1909.

Ward, Adolphus William. *The Electress Sophia and Hanoverian Succession*. London: Longmans, Green and Co, 1909.

Watkins, John. *Memoirs of Her Most Excellent Majesty Sophia-Charlotte, Queen of Great Britain*. London: Henry Colburn, 1819.

Wells, HG. *The Outline of History*. New York: Barnes & Noble, 1920.

Wilkins, WH. *Caroline, the Illustrious, Vol II*. London: Longmans, Green and Co, 1901.

Wilkins, WH. *The Love of an Uncrowned Queen*. London: Hutchinson & Co, 1900.

Wilkins, WH. *A Queen of Tears*. London: Longmans, Green & Co, 1904.

Williams, Robert Folkestone. *Memoirs of Sophia Dorothea, Consort of George I, Vol I*. London: Henry Colburn, 1845.

Williams, Robert Folkestone. *Memoirs of Sophia Dorothea, Consort of George I, Vol II*. London: Henry Colburn, 1845.

Williams, Thomas. *Memoirs of Her Late Majesty Queen Charlotte*. London: W Simpkin and R Marshall, 1819.

Williams, Thomas. *Memoirs of His Late Majesty George III*. London: W Simpkin and R Marshall, 1820.

Woodfine, Philip. *Britannia's Glories: The Walpole Ministry and the 1739 War with Spain*. Woodbridge: The Boydell Press, 1998.

Worsley, Lucy. *Courtiers: The Secret History of the Georgian Court*. London: Faber and Faber, 2011.

Young, Arthur (ed.). *Annals of Agriculture and Other Useful Arts, Vol I*. Bury St Edmunds: J Rackham, 1790.

Newspapers Cited

All newspaper clippings are reproduced © The British Library Board; in addition to those cited, innumerable newspapers were consulted.

Bath Chronicle (Bath, England), Thursday, July 30, 1789; issue 1451.

Caledonian Mercury (Edinburgh, Scotland), Thursday, December 9, 1819; issue 15331.

Caledonian Mercury (Edinburgh, Scotland), Saturday, July 8, 1820; issue 15421.

Caledonian Mercury (Edinburgh, Scotland), Thursday, November 16, 1820; issue 15477.

Daily Advertiser (London, England), Monday, May 5, 1783; issue 17249.

Daily Courant (London, England), Saturday, February 8, 1718; issue 5087.

Daily Gazetteer (London Edition) (London, England), Tuesday, November 22, 1737; issue 752.

Daily Post (London, England), Wednesday, November 6, 1728; issue 2848.

Evening Advertiser (London, England), March 15, 1757 – March 17, 1757; issue 472.

Gazetteer and New Daily Advertiser (London, England), Tuesday, September 29, 1767; issue 12034.

General Advertiser and Morning Intelligencer (London, England), Tuesday, May 12, 1778; issue 476.

General Evening Post (London, England), April 5, 1740 – April 8, 1740; issue 1020.

George Faulkner the Dublin Journal (Dublin, Ireland), March 21, 1747 – March 24, 1747; issue 2089.

Hampshire Telegraph and Sussex Chronicle etc (Portsmouth, England), Monday, November 5, 1810; issue 578.

Jackson's Oxford Journal (Oxford, England), Saturday, May 4, 1816; issue 3289.

London Chronicle (London, England), August 20, 1782 – August 22, 1782; issue 4014.

London Evening Post (London, England), Tuesday, November 12, 1734; issue 1090.

London Evening Post (London, England), May 23, 1738 – May 25, 1738; issue 1642.

London Evening Post (London, England), January 27, 1757 – January 29, 1757; issue 4560.

London Gazette (London, England), November 2, 1714 – November 6, 1714; issue 5274.

London Gazette (London, England), September 22, 1761 – September 26, 1761; issue 10142.

London Gazette (London, England), May 16, 1775 – May 20, 1775; issue 11562.

London Packet or New Lloyd's Evening Post (London, England), April 6, 1795 – April 8, 1795; issue 4001.

Middlesex Journal or Chronicle of Liberty (London, England), February 15, 1772 – February 18, 1772; issue 450.

Morning Chronicle (London, England), Friday, May 16, 1800; issue 9667.

Morning Chronicle and London Advertiser (London, England), Tuesday, May 10, 1774; issue 1548.

Morning Chronicle and London Advertiser (London, England), Saturday, June 4, 1774; issue 1570.

Morning Post and Daily Advertiser (London, England), Thursday, August 12, 1779; issue 2130.

North Wales Chronicle (Bangor, Wales), Thursday, July 1, 1830; issue 144.

Old Whig or The Consistent Protestant (London, England), Thursday, July 24, 1735; issue 20.

Oracle and Public Advertiser (London, England), Friday, January 8, 1796; issue 19 211.

Oracle and Public Advertiser (London, England), Wednesday, June 7, 1797; issue 19 642.

Post Man and the Historical Account (London, England), July 18, 1717 – July 20, 1717; issue 15120.

Public Advertiser (London, England), Monday, September 6, 1762; issue 8687.

Public Advertiser (London, England), Friday, May 12, 1786; issue 16216.

Sun (London, England), Wednesday, November 5, 1794; issue 657.

The Ipswich Journal (Ipswich, England), Saturday, August 11, 1821; issue 4346.

The Morning Chronicle (London, England), Friday, January 24, 1806; issue 11447.

The Morning Chronicle (London, England), Wednesday, February 6, 1811; issue 13025, .

The Morning Chronicle (London, England), Friday, November 7, 1817; issue 15138.

The Morning Chronicle (London, England), Thursday, August 3, 1820; issue 15996.

The Morning Chronicle (London, England), Saturday, November 11, 1820; issue 16082.

The Morning Post (London, England), Tuesday, June 24, 1806; issue 12029.

The Morning Post (London, England), Friday, June 01, 1810; issue 12275.

The Morning Post (London, England), Friday, November 20, 1818; issue 14925.

The Morning Post (London, England), Friday, January 31, 1820; issue 15299.

The Morning Post (London, England), Saturday, November 11, 1820; issue 15493.

The Morning Post (London, England), Thursday, July 19, 1821; issue 15707.

Weekly Journal or British Gazetteer (London, England), Thursday, January 7, 1720.

Weekly Journal or British Gazetteer (London, England), Saturday, January 22, 1726; issue 39.

Weekly Packet (London, England), August 10, 1717 – August 17, 1717; issue 267.

Whereas It Hath Pleased Almighty God to Call to His Mercy Our Late Sovereign Lord King George (London, England), Wednesday, June 14, 1727.

Whitehall Evening Post or London Intelligencer (London, England), October 23, 1760 – October 25, 1760; issue 2279.

Whitehall Evening Post (1770) (London, England), January 21, 1790 – January 23, 1790; issue 6467.

Whitehall June 23 1743 This Morning Mr Parker (London, England), Thursday, June 23, 1743.

Websites Consulted

19th Century UK Periodicals (http://gale.cengage.co.uk/product-highlights/history/19th- (century-uk-periodicals-parts-1-and-2.aspx)

British and Irish Women's Letters and Diaries (www.bwl2.alexanderstreet.com)

British History Online (http://www.british-history.ac.uk)

British Newspapers 1600–1950 (http://gdc.gale.com/products/19th-century-british-library-newspapers-part-i-and-part-ii/)

Hansard (http://hansard.millbanksystems.com/index.html)

Historical Texts (http://historicaltexts.jisc.ac.uk)

House of Commons Parliamentary Papers (http://parlipapers.chadwyck.co.uk/marketing/index.jsp)

JSTOR (www.jstor.org)

The National Archives (http://www.nationalarchives.gov.uk)

Oxford Dictionary of National Biography (http://www.oxforddnb.com)

The Proceedings of the Old Bailey (http://www.oldbaileyonline.org)

The Times Digital Archive (http://gale.cengage.co.uk/times-digital-archive/times-digital-archive-17852006.aspx)

Index